# Guestworkers in Germany

# Foreword by
# Irving Louis Horowitz

The Praeger Special Studies program, through a selective worldwide distribution network, makes available to the academic, government, and business communities significant and timely research in U.S. and international economic, social, and political issues.

# Guestworkers in Germany

## The Prospects for Pluralism

Ray C. Rist

**PRAEGER PUBLISHERS**
**Praeger Special Studies**

New York • London • Sydney • Toronto

Library of Congress Cataloging in Publication Data

Rist, Ray C.
  Guestworkers in Germany.

  Bibliography: p.
  Includes index.
  1. Alien labor--Germany, West. 2. Germany, West--
Foreign population. 3. Children of alien laborers--
Education--Germany, West. I. Title.
HD 8458.A2R58   331.6'2'0943        78-6282
ISBN 0-03-040766-4

**PRAEGER SPECIAL STUDIES**
383 Madison Avenue, New York, N.Y., 10017, U.S.A.

Published in the United States of America in 1978
by Praeger Publishers,
A Division of Holt, Rinehart and Winston, CBS, Inc.

89 038 987654321

© **1978 by Praeger Publishers**

**All rights reserved**

**Printed in the United States of America**

For Ulrich Littmann, Barbara Ischinger, Karl Roeloffs, Myron Baskin, and all the others who have made and continue to make the German-American Fulbright Program what it is—a remarkable example of international cooperation and friendship.

# FOREWORD

## Irving Louis Horowitz

*Guestworkers in Germany* is a major sociological effort, pure and simple. It combines many of the best elements in contemporary social science writing and, at the risk of hyperbole, might well become a recognized classic in its own time. This foreword is intended neither to render the reader faint with damn praise nor to hide behind reservations of those who accept such a task with mixed feelings, hence damning the book with faint praise. This work by my former student and now esteemed colleague, Ray C. Rist, has the supreme merit of breaking categories by ignoring them. *Guestworkers in Germany* is at once an empirical survey of the so called *Gastarbeiter* in Germany from less developed parts of Europe, a socialization study in the generational transition from foreign to native status, a work in the sociology of education with special attention to the pedagogy of poverty—how children from poor countries and lower classes speaking in strange tongues adapt to their new environments, and a work on social stratification covering subjects ranging from wage differentials to the civil and legal rights of newcomers. Above all, this is a study in international development, specifically the use of work and workers to build up surpluses that translate into higher levels of national productivity, but without any corresponding redistribution of equity in such expanded wealth.

For the most part, Professor Rist confines his study of guestworkers in Germany to the postwar period beginning in 1945. This is quite understandable, since the accelerated character of the new immigrants does begin with the postwar reconstruction period, the years of the *Wirtschaftswunder*. Certainly the crucial point Rist makes—that during the past quarter century European migration has changed its character from the movement of populations to the movement of manpower—entitles him to begin his analysis at that point. Nonetheless, the author is not oblivious to the terrible paradox of German history prior to 1945, a paradox encompassing perhaps a full century preceding the seizure of power by the National Socialist regime. On the one hand, there are the enduring racial foundations of both the nationalist and Nazi ideologies in both their Bismarkian and Hitlerian forms. *Volksgemein-schaft* (folk-unitedness) was the essential cement of a national war policy and a vast rearmament program that swept Europe in one great tidal wave from the lowlands to the Ukraine. On the other hand, there are the *ausländische Arbeiterklasse* (foreign working class), the human cadres of *Unterschichtungen*, or lower strata, who made possible the maintenance of high productivity on the home front while the *Übermenschen*, or supermen, went about their tasks of empire building and national destruction.

Writing in the *Deutsche Allgemeine Zeitung* on June 17, 1943, before he soured on the alien workers as Professor Rist indicates, Gauleiter Sauckel spoke in high praise of the same sorts of people from Southern and Eastern Europe who currently supply Germany with its guestworkers. The parallels in rhetoric between 1943 and 1978 are too painful to enumerate:

> Today many millions of men and women from all European nations are working for the German economy. ... In praise of these foreign workers I must admit that they are all striving successfully to emulate the example of German men and women workers and that they perform satisfactory, in part even very good work. A mighty fate has brought to Germany millions of people who had for many years been led astray and deceived in a manner hostile to Germany. The irrevocable truth is now being revealed to them. They are therefore making a valuable contribution with their work to the victory of a better world, and in this way rendering themselves and their own nations the greatest service.

The obvious hubris involved in such abstract songs of praise for foreign workers, echoing Nazi masters Röhm Ley and Paul Joseph Goebbels, disguised the actual situation: interruptions, disruptions, and sabotage committed by foreign workers and animosities engendered by the involuntary cross-fertilization of domestic and foreign workers.

This is by no means to equate the situation now confronting German labor with conditions that existed 35 years ago. For all of their fits and starts, the German people are led by a democratic regime; furthermore, the foreign workers, now two generations deep, view themselves as having a far greater leverage (both within Germany and in their countries of origin) than at any time in the past. The contest of national, ethnic, and class rivalries, despite the myopia of German officialdom, is far more complex than it was in the Empire or Nazi period. It is to Professor Rist's credit that each fundamental aspect of that relationship is explored, including the relative strengths of foreign workers and the relative weaknesses of the domestic German bourgeoisie that cannot function at top efficiency without them. *Guestworkers in Germany* is not simply a Manichaean story of ruler and ruled, or of masters and slaves. More pointedly, it is an analysis of labor shortage and surplus, of the economic strengths of Northern and weaknesses of Southern Europe. Still, one remains haunted by the historical background of the present story: the continuation of demographic and economic trends that withstand the test of time and destiny and overcome even catastrophic military defeat. What makes the study particularly engaging is that the guestworker phenomenon, like the German economy as a whole, has had the residual capacity to survive the ashes of war, and even to expand.

Whatever the background variables, the existence of guestworkers as a representative and large slice of the population in many Northern European nations and not just Germany, and as an inordinately large portion of many sectors of its industrial heartland, represents a unique challenge to sociological analysis. Professor Rist is up to the challenge. He appreciates the extent to which new cultural influxes make possible a political pluralism that marks a departure from older patterns of political ideology and even of social demography. The rich mosaic of Indians in England, Turks in Germany, Algerians in France, and Italians in Switzerland may inadvertently prove to be a democratizing agency. Reality has an odd way of triumphing over theory. The manifest purpose of the guestworkers is to solve economic problems of labor shortfalls in Northern Europe. But the latent response is a transformation of many of these societies into much more pleasant and pluralistic places. Old neighborhoods might become new ghettos, but they also represent new forms of human association, new styles of eating, new languages, musics, and arts. Here too, Professor Rist provides us with a model of scholarship, appreciating nuances in this relationship between domestic employers and foreign workers.

By the end of his book there emerge somewhat different premises than the originating assumptions that led him to study the guestworkers. Professor Rist's own odyssey is clearly etched in this work; his earlier efforts examining the urban black working class, problems of school integration in the United States, educational inequalities in the school system, and finally, patterns of social deviance all come together in this work. The volume does not treat the position of guestworkers in German society as some kind of exceptional situation, but only as a different focus for examining the same kinds of problems that confront industrial societies everywhere. We are reminded that the United States has no monopoly on benign neglect, nor are problems of race relations without their structural equivalents in the ethnic relations found in West Germany. Professor Rist, however, manages to avoid the obvious or the banal. His flinty style overcomes what might easily appear to be an overwhelming desire to take sides and offer an endless series of moral judgments, yet he introduces his own basic humanism in a very subtle fashion by simply noting, for example, that it is not remotely part of the German pedagogic framework to introduce the idea of affirmative action, and as a result it provides no special programs that would assure young people whose lives have been maimed by discrimination in public education or other public institutions participation in the larger society. This is done with a deft touch rather than a heavy hand.

*Guestworkers in Germany* is written with a careful focusing technique. Chapters move naturally and easily from a general economic description through the specific impact of immigrant labor on advanced economies, and then into an analysis of Germany and its migrant labor proper. Examination of the legislative condition and political rights of guestworkers in relation to the native born are carefully examined. Rist exhibits a clear understanding that these workers are not simply satisfying German needs but those of Turkey, Italy, and Spain as well. Guestworkers help offset trade imbalances by their considerable remittance of funds and also relieve pressures of employment in relatively backward economies of Southern Europe. This cycle of development and backwardness allows Professor Rist to conclude his work with problems of policy and education, as well as the specific dilemmas involved in second-generation immigrants for whom

Germany is home, for whom the old country may be as remote as it was for migrants from Europe to America earlier in the century.

Among the more noteworthy aspects of Professor Rist's work is the unusual fusion of history and anlaysis. He reminds us that the cross-section being examined is also part of a longitudinal network. Hence, the problem of guestworkers is viewed against the background of European twentieth-century history and not simply as a problem in social service or social welfare. There is a fine use of secondary data: OECD data, information supplied by the Bonn government in census tracts, as well as work culled out by earlier research of this subject. Too often research abroad is done *de novo*, without full recognition of antecedent information available. As a result, instead of utilizing the best of available information, we often receive summaries of standardized questionnaires designed from afar and without sensitivity to existing information. In a country like Germany, sound data is not only available but has a level of accuracy probably difficult to replicate or to exceed by foreign researchers.

Probably the most important aspect of Professor Rist's work, however, and that which deserves emulation by us all, is his ability to treat a problem in a foreign nation as a naturalistic event and not as an exotic happening. The issues he raises concerning economic benefits versus social costs of foreign and migrant labor are not unique to Germany but characteristic of many countries in the advanced sector. Placing the German situation in the context of a larger problematic allows him to establish a paradigm in the analysis of the subject, which in turn permits him to range far and wide among legal, political, housing, and educational elements. We thus see the consequences of different policies or absence thereof for the development of national consciousness. Professor Rist offers no single solution to the problem of foreign workers. Their existence is not simply a problem but represents a solution to other kinds of problems in economic life as well as to the transformation from a monistic unilingual society to a pluralistic and multilingual one.

The story of foreign workers in Germany is not simply one of raw anguish for newcomers and boundless riches for the host country. It is also a story of continuities and discontinuities in German society, the *de facto* emergence of pluralism in the midst of a stubborn *de jure* maintenance of cultural monism. It is a story as old as that of cultural migration itself but at the same time one that carries a special urgency at a point in time when the physical displacement of people is far simpler, and the circumstances more traumatic, than at any other time in previous history. The balanced awareness of this dialectic gives life and meaning to the volume.

# PREFACE

It is apparent to even the most casual of observers. Whether one meets the Algerian waiter in Paris, the Italian streetcar conductor in Zürich, the Turkish bellhop in Berlin, or the Yugoslav laborer in Stockholm, they are but individual confirmations of the fact that Western Europe has become a vast area of immigration. These new immigrants have come by the millions. There are at present in the countries of the European North approximately 15 million foreign workers and their families. Even beyond the sheer magnitude of this wave of peoples from the European South is the realization that almost all of them have come in the last decade. In comparison, the United States experienced over a period of three decades (1940-70) a migration from south to north of approximately nine million black persons.

The most immediate consequence of this immense infusion of people from so many varying ethnic, religious, and cultural backgrounds into the northern countries is that these countries have now become mosaics. Where they were once relatively homogeneous and their citizens easily identifiable, they have now become heterogeneous and pluralistic. It is but one example of the magnitude of this transformation, in absolute numerical terms as well as in its cultural manifestations, to note that Berlin is now the city with the third largest Turkish population in the world. Further, there is every indication that this movement of persons is as permanent as life can be among new immigrants. There is no reason to doubt that the ramifications of their presence will grow: for example, one of every two births in the city of Frankfurt, West Germany, is now to a foreign worker family.

It is the intent of this book to focus upon the situation of the guestworkers and their families in the Federal Republic of Germany. Of particular concern will be the social conditions in which they live and the social policies and programs instigated by the German government in response. There are more than 4 million guestworkers and their families in the Federal Republic, or approximately 8 percent of the national population. The guestworkers now comprise between 12 and 13 percent of the entire labor force. Even that most classic of German cars, the Volkswagen, is frequently made by Turkish and Yugoslav workers. The percentage of guestworkers on some of the assembly lines runs as high as 85 percent.

Succinctly, it is the basic thesis of this book that Germany has become a multicultural society with an ever-growing number of persons who claim social and cultural identity traits from their mother country as well as from Germany, their country of immigration. What have emerged are people who are Turkish-German, Yugoslav-German, Greek-German, and the like. The response of Germany has been to further the economic integration of the workers, but to sustain social and cultural separation. Such response, however, is ultimately untenable and sure to contribute to heightened social conflict and greater social problems within Germany.

That one finds economic integration coinciding with social and cultural marginality among the foreign workers is entirely logical and predictable if one accepts the rationale frequently espoused in Germany that these people are not immigrants but, rather, "guests." They have come to work in Germany for a period of time and will eventually return to the mother country. Since, so the view goes, they are not immigrants and have no intention of spending their lives in Germany, it is not appropriate to consider measures to foster social and cultural integration. On the contrary, it is more important to ensure that the workers and their families are able to maintain their ties and contacts to the mother country—the country of their eventual destination.

It must be acknowledged that this view does have some credibility, especially among those workers who have left their families in the mother country while they themselves have come to work in Germany. These workers may indeed consider themselves guests, and many do plan to return home. But for those hundreds of thousands of workers who have come to Germany with their families, who are now sending their children to German schools, and who are making, even when unemployed, five times the average standard of living in Turkey, the incentives to stay are great. As in other instances of international immigration, this first generation may not take on many traits of German culture or learn much of German society. Their identities are grounded in the socialization and experiences of the mother country.

Where the issue of forging a new identity does come to the fore is with the second generation—those who either were born in the mother country but came to Germany at a young age, or were themselves born in Germany. It is for this group, growing up as they are with a hyphenated identity, that the question of their status vis-a-vis Germany becomes particularly acute. For this generation, Germany is the only country they know. It is their mother country. Rural Anatolia is but an abstraction. The question is whether German society will accept this second generation and grant them equal opportunity, or continue to view them as being in the same category as their parents—outsiders who are economically necessary but who must remain on the social and cultural margins of the society.

Germany then, both at the level of governmental policy and in the lives of individual citizens, must recognize and respond to the transformation of its society and the new group of immigrants in its midst. After all, it was the active and vigorous effort on the part of the German government and German industry to recruit these workers that generated their presence in the country. (At the height of the active search for new workers [1968-72], Germany had between 500 and 600 labor recruiting offices scattered throughout the countries of the European South). To accept the pluralization of German society appears to be the only realistic solution. To assume that Germany is only for the Germans and that the new immigrants will return home is to distort present realities. German identity cannot be seen as something that has its origins in a vague and immutable tribal past. Those who live in the society, who contribute to its well-being and prosperity, who raise their children to live in the country, and who themselves wish to participate, should be granted acceptance.

To build and firmly establish the legitimacy of a multicultural society stands as perhaps the preeminent challenge to Germany today. To ignore the millions of persons who at present live in the society, but who are not of it, is to risk the perpetuation of marginality and lack of commitment. It is also to risk creating conditions that will tear at the fabric of the society. The history of the United States in this regard should be instructive.

It appears that Germany cannot long continue to have it both ways—both the economic benefits accruing to the society from the presence of the foreign workers, and the maintenance of a discriminatory society that relegates the immigrants and their children to inferior status and occupational positions. If Germany is not planning to expel the more than two million immigrant workers and ask German workers to take these positions, then it becomes both a political and moral imperative that these two million workers are recognized as indispensable to the continued well-being of the country. They should be granted the rights and privileges commensurate with their contribution to the growth and development of postwar Germany.

This present study is the result of a year's stay (1976–77) in the Federal Republic of Germany under the sponsorship of the German-American Fulbright Program. As indicated in the dedication, the Fulbright Program represents an outstanding example of international cooperation and friendship. The willingness of the sponsors to support this research effort, the findings of which are in several instances critical of current practices and policies, is also an indication of the integrity and commitment of the program.

There are two brief asides that must be made about this volume. The first concerns the translation of German material into English. I have tried to stay close to the original meanings while at the same time wording the material so as to be understandable to an English-speaking audience, most specifically that of the United States. Thus terms such as *Hauptschule* and *Gymnasium*, for example, are translated as vocational secondary school and academic secondary school, respectively. I realize my German colleagues may cringe at such a translation, but I do believe it clarifies for an American reader the relative status and orientation of differing educational programs. The second of the asides has to do with the terminology of guestworker, foreign worker, immigrant worker, immigrant, and migrant worker. All of these terms are used in this book to discuss the same group of persons—those who have come from the countries of the European South to take up employment in the countries of the European North. I use the terms interchangeably, though I attempt to draw distinctions in the analysis as to the implications from the governmental and cultural point of view of defining someone as an immigrant versus guestworker. I apologize in advance for whatever slight confusion this might cause in the early pages of the study, but hope that the literary benefit of a diversity of terms is worthwhile.

# ACKNOWLEDGMENTS

There are countless persons whose assistance and generosity with both their time and materials made this research possible. It was my extreme good fortune that as I conducted this study in a country and language different from my own that these good people were there to lend assistance. In Bonn, special thanks must go to Karl Roeloffs, Erhardt Schulte, and Joachim Dumrese, all from the Federal Ministry for Education and Science. Likewise, Wolfgang Bondenbender and Ernst Kreuzaler from the Federal Ministry for Labor and Social Affairs provided indispensable data. Among those academic researchers upon whom I leaned for assistance, Hermann Mueller of the University of Frankfurt, Hans-Joachim Hoffmann-Nowotny of the University of Zürich, Gebhardt Schweigler of the Deutsche Gesellshaft für Auswärtige Politik, Czarine Wilpert of the Wissenschaftszentrum in Berlin and Rinus Penninx of the University of the Hague all helped in ways far beyond what might be expected under the norms of academic reciprocity.

The bulk of this book was written during the seven months I was affiliated with the Max Planck Institute for Educational Research in Berlin. The months there have been among the most intellectually stimulating and challenging of my professional career. It is the closest I have come to finding that utopian blend of outstanding scholarship, friendship, and resources. Special recognition and thanks must go to Hellmut Becker, Dietrich Goldschmidt, Peter Siewert, Knut Nevermann, and especially Lothar Krappmann. The absence of one of these persons would have resulted in a weaker study.

Finally, and by no means less important, are those persons who by their acts of friendship and generosity helped to make our time in Germany memorable. I think this important to mention, for in conducting cross-cultural research I asked my family to leave home and to follow along after my interests. I seriously question how much research I could have accomplished were my family unhappy. For that reason the following persons are of special importance to us. They collectively made our time all the more enjoyable. Thus, Ulrich Hoffmann, Christina Karzunky, Karen and Cornelius Sommer, Rolf and Elfriede Hogel, Georg and Barbara Hasenkamp, Gebhardt and Corrine Schweigler, Dagmar Fyner, and Marion Hartwig have our warm thanks. For Roger and Wendy Chickering, fellow Fulbright sojourners in Berlin, what can be said but that without our many Sunday afternoons in museums and *Konditoreien*, our experiences in Berlin would have been considerably diminished.

It is my hope that some day and in some way it will be possible to reciprocate to these persons for all their countless acts of friendship and assistance. In the meantime, I trust that they will be pleased with this book. Each of them should know that without their contribution, it would not have come to fruition.

# CONTENTS

|  | Page |
|---|---|
| FOREWORD<br>Irving Louis Horowitz | vii |
| PREFACE | xi |
| ACKNOWLEDGMENTS | xv |
| LIST OF TABLES | xix |
| LIST OF ACRONYMS | xxii |

### PART I: THE NEW IMMIGRANTS

Chapter

1 GUESTWORKERS AND POST-WORLD WAR II EUROPEAN MIGRATIONS ... 3

    The Aftermath of World War II in Europe ... 4
    The Transformation of European Migration ... 6
    Migration and the European South ... 7
    Migration: Some Theoretical Concerns ... 14
    The EEC and Migration Policies ... 22

2 MANPOWER MIGRATIONS: ORIGINS AND IMPACTS ... 28

    Migration: Impact upon the Host Country ... 31
    Migration: Impact upon the Sending Countries ... 37
    Migration and the Return Home ... 47
    North-South Migration: Patterns and Prospects ... 52

3 GERMANY: A LAND OF IMMIGRATION ... 57

    A Historical Background ... 57
    The Postwar Period ... 60
    The Expansion Period ... 61

| Chapter | | Page |
|---|---|---|
| | The Current Profile | 63 |
| | Foreigner Policy | 74 |
| 4 | THE TURKISH CONNECTION | 89 |
| | The Turkish Association with the EEC | 98 |
| | Postscript | 104 |

### PART II: SOCIAL POLICIES AND SOCIAL CONDITIONS

| | | |
|---|---|---|
| 5 | ECONOMIC CONDITIONS AND LABOR POLICIES | 109 |
| | Foreign Labor and German Economic Conditions | 111 |
| | Foreign Labor and German Social Conditions | 114 |
| | Foreign Labor and the German Employment Market | 116 |
| | Guestworkers and the Trade Unions | 120 |
| 6 | CIVIL AND POLITICAL RIGHTS | 133 |
| | Constitutional Provisions | 134 |
| | The Alien Act | 135 |
| | Political Rights | 141 |
| 7 | HOUSING: TOWARD INTEGRATION OR SEGREGATION? | 149 |
| | Federal Housing Policies | 151 |
| | State Housing Policies | 155 |
| | Housing Conditions | 158 |

### PART III: THE EDUCATION OF THE GUESTWORKER CHILD

| | | |
|---|---|---|
| 8 | GERMAN EDUCATION AND THE GUESTWORKER CHILD: POLICIES AND PROGRAMS | 179 |
| | German Education: Traditionalism and Selectivity | 181 |
| | Educational Policies for Guestworker Children | 187 |
| | Equality of Educational Opportunity | 196 |
| | Equality of Educational Opportunity and the Guestworker Child | 201 |
| | Postscript | 204 |

| Chapter | | Page |
|---|---|---|
| 9 | AN EDUCATIONAL ALTERNATIVE: THE BAVARIAN APPROACH | 206 |
| | Perceptions and Policies | 207 |
| | The Educational Program | 208 |
| | The Bavarian Approach: A Critique | 212 |
| | Options for Failure | 218 |
| | Postscript | 222 |
| 10 | AN EDUCATIONAL ALTERNATIVE: THE BERLIN APPROACH | 223 |
| | Policies and Programs | 226 |
| | Integration and National Identity | 230 |
| | School Drop-outs | 231 |
| | The Berlin Approach: A Critique | 234 |
| | On the Will to Integrate | 242 |
| POSTSCRIPT: THE PROSPECTS FOR PLURALISM | | 245 |
| REFERENCES | | 247 |
| INDEX | | 259 |
| ABOUT THE AUTHOR | | 264 |

# LIST OF TABLES

| Table | | Page |
|---|---|---|
| 1.1 | Total and Foreign Population in Absolute and Relative Numbers in European Immigration Countries | 8 |
| 1.2 | Trends of Immigration in Europe, 1961-74 | 12 |
| 1.3 | European South Workers' Emigration Flows to European North Destinations | 15 |
| 1.4 | Italian Population in Selected Countries of the EEC | 26 |
| 2.1 | Return of Workers to Countries of the European South, 1972-75 | 33 |
| 2.2 | Transfers of Funds by Emigrants to Home Countries of the European South | 43 |
| 2.3 | Relation of Emigrants' Remittances to Balance-of-Trade Payment in Selected Countries of the European South, 1969-74 | 45 |
| 2.4 | Type of Employment in Turkey and in Germany | 50 |
| 3.1 | The Immigrant Worker Population in the Federal Republic of Germany, 1960-76 | 62 |
| 3.2 | Work Permits Issued in the Federal Republic of Germany, 1969-75 | 64 |
| 3.3 | Immigrant Workers in the Federal Republic of Germany, by Nationality, 1973-75 | 66 |
| 3.4 | Foreigners in the Federal Republic of Germany, by Nationality, September 1974 and September 1975 | 67 |
| 3.5 | Distribution of Foreign Population in the Federal Republic of Germany, by Länder, September 1974 and September 1975 | 68 |
| 3.6 | Distribution and Rate of Employment for Immigrant Workers in District Labor Offices, Federal Republic of Germany, January 1973 to September 1975 | 69 |

| Table | | Page |
|---|---|---|
| 3.7 | Distribution and Rate of Employment for Immigrant Workers, by Branches of Economic Activity, January 1973 to September 1975 | 70 |
| 3.8 | Comparative Rates of Unemployment for Immigrant Workers and the German Labor Force, March 1974 to December 1976 | 72 |
| 3.9 | Distribution of Family Allowance Payments, by Nationality, January 1-June 30, 1976 | 86 |
| 3.10 | Family Allowance, Tax Rates, and Net Disposable Income for EEC and Native German Workers Compared with Non-EEC Workers in the Federal Republic of Germany | 87 |
| 4.1 | Turkish Workers Sent Abroad through the Employment Service, by Year and Country of Destination | 92 |
| 4.2 | Emigrant Turkish Workers Sent Abroad through the Employment Service, by Year, Country of Destination, and Nature of Contract | 94 |
| 4.3 | Turkish Workers Sent Abroad through the Employment Service, by Year, Country of Destination, and Sex | 96 |
| 4.4 | Per Capita National Income of the EEC, Turkey, and Greece, 1974 | 102 |
| 4.5 | Sectoral Contribution to 1974 Gross Domestic Product in Countries of the EEC and Turkey | 103 |
| 4.6 | Distribution of the Working Population in EEC Member States and Turkey | 104 |
| 5.1 | Socioeconomic Status of Guestworkers in Germany, by Nationality and Sex, 1968 and 1972 | 122 |
| 7.1 | Location of Spouses of Foreign Workers, by Family Size | 162 |
| 7.2 | Housing of Foreign Workers, by Type of Dwelling and Nationality | 163 |
| 7.3 | Occupancy of Apartments, by Number of Rooms and Number of Persons | 165 |

| Table | | Page |
|---|---|---|
| 7.4 | Fixtures and Furniture in Foreign Workers' Apartments | 165 |
| 7.5 | Rental Costs for Apartments: National Data Compared with Those for Foreign Workers, Frankfurt, 1972 | 166 |
| 7.6 | Location of Living Accommodations in Frankfurt Preferred by Foreign Workers | 167 |
| 7.7 | Provision of Amenities in Current Residences of Foreign Workers in Berlin, 1974 | 171 |
| 7.8 | Distribution of West Berlin's Population, January 1974 | 172 |
| 7.9 | Degree of Concentration of Turkish and Yugoslav Foreign Workers in West Berlin's Districts | 173 |
| 10.1 | Foreign Worker Population of West Berlin, by Nationality, 1960-75 | 224 |
| 10.2 | Foreign Students in West Berlin, by Type of School, 1968-76 | 225 |
| 10.3 | Drop-outs among German and Foreign Pupils, West Berlin Secondary Vocational Schools, 1974-75 | 232 |

## LIST OF ACRONYMS

| | |
|---|---|
| BMBW | Bundesministerium für Bildung und Wissenschaft |
| CDU | Christian Democratic Union |
| DM | Deutsch Marks |
| EEC | European Economic Community |
| FRG | Federal Republic of Germany |
| GDR | German Democratic Republic |
| ICMC | International Catholic Migration Commission |
| IILS | International Institute for Labor Studies |
| IRC | International Red Cross |
| KMK | Kultusminister Konferenz<br>(Standing Conference of Ministers of Education and Culture) |
| OECD | Organization for Economic Cooperation and Development |
| OEEC | Organization for European Economic Cooperation |
| SOPEMI | Système d'Observation Permanente des Migrations |
| UNRRA | United Nations Relief and Rehabilitation Administration |

# PART I
## THE NEW IMMIGRANTS

# 1

# GUESTWORKERS AND POST-WORLD WAR II EUROPEAN MIGRATIONS

Over the past quarter century, European migration has changed its character from one of the movement of populations to the movement of manpower. The tradition established by millions of Europeans who moved to new, sparsely settled countries throughout the world has been broken. No longer do overseas migrations constitute the main stream of movement in Europe. The magnetism of the economic opportunities and political freedoms available in the West European industrial democracies has served to keep Europeans at home. Moreover, workers from less developed countries have been attracted by the seemingly insatiable demand for labor in the booming economies of Western Europe.

The extent of economic opportunities has been of sufficient magnitude that not only has European emigration been halted, but Europe has been transformed into an area of immigration. Western Europe has now become home, if only tenuously, to somewhere between 14 and 15 million migrants. The scope of this movement makes it one of the largest of its kind in history. Moreover, if one could count those who after some time have returned to their home countries or who now work in Europe on a seasonal basis, one could say that there have been even several million more migrants. Nor do such figures account for the countless millions of people who have migrated as the result of wars or the political realignments following wars. The German-Polish border realignments in 1945 would alone add as many as 15 to 18 million more persons to those who have experienced migration (Francis, 1976).

In conjunction with the changed direction of European migrations is the difficulty in trying to describe them. The traditional terminology (emigrant/immigrant; country of emigration/country of immigration; emigration policy/immigration policy) can no longer be used to accurately describe migrations in Europe since World War II. As Hoffmann-Nowotny has observed (1976, p. 2),

It is the very paradox of European migrations today that millions of people are living in foreign countries but are not designated as immigrants; neither do these countries see themselves as immigration countries. And vice versa, very few of the countries that send millions of their citizens to work abroad consider themselves as emigration countries in the narrow sense of the term. The concept of immigrant is paraphrased and terms such as "foreign worker," "guest worker," "foreign employee," or "migrant worker" are used.

A consequence of this collective denial implied by Hoffmann-Nowotny is that since neither the emigration nor immigration countries consider themselves as such, no well-defined or codified immigration or emigration policies have been developed, not even in those countries which have been receiving migrant workers for almost 30 years. The status of the migrants themselves remains provisionary in the host countries, and apparently permanently so—a fact as paradoxical and absurd as it is ultimately inhumane. This situation of permanent provisionality will be a central pivot of the analysis to be developed in this book: that European migrations after World War II are characterized by the fact that while there are millions of emigrants (or immigrants), no country will admit to being an emigration—let alone an immigration—country. Later chapters will examine in detail the consequences of permanent provisionality for the more than 4 million migrants in the Federal Republic of Germany, the country that is the central focus of this study.

First, and by way of background, a statistical description is necessary, focusing on the various aspects of European migration since World War II; and following that, this chapter will undertake an analysis of the guestworkers in Europe and the various forces that have generated their migration. As will be evident time and again, these latest arrivals are not viewed as immigrants by the host countries, but, nevertheless, they are immigrants, and thus an already difficult situation is made even worse by the fact that policies do not conform to facts. The consequence is a set of social conditions undesired but surely predictable.

## THE AFTERMATH OF WORLD WAR II IN EUROPE

Since 1945, migratory movements on an unprecedented scale have taken place throughout the world, with Europe on center stage. In the early years of the postwar period, millions were driven from their homes and the population structures of entire nations radically altered. Diplomacy and political upheavals involving redrawing of national boundaries, transfers of governmental authority, and changes of regime have forced large populations into exile and caused mass population movements that dwarf the major population movement in the United States during the postwar period—that of southern black people moving north.

One among many consequences of the war was that there occurred dramatic changes in the demographic patterns, a factor that affected the pattern of migration for the following quarter century. First and foremost, war casualties cut deeply into the younger working age groups. Though it is difficult to pinpoint precise percentages in various groups, the total figures suggest the immensity of the loss of life. In Western Europe the number has been placed at approximately 7.8 million persons, in Eastern Europe at 5.6 million, and for the Soviet Union, a conservative figure of 17 million (Borrie, 1970). These severe casualties alone would have drastically reduced any population surpluses that might have been available for emigration as was the case in the prewar period and earlier.*

Second, the war brought about major population transfers as the result of the use of forced labor during the war (one source citing an estimated 7.5 million; Castles and Kosack 1973, p. 23) and the political reorganization of national boundaries in its aftermath. While millions of persons uprooted by the war were eventually able to return to their homelands with the assistance of such organizations as the United Nations Relief and Rehabilitation Administration and the International Red Cross, many millions more were never able to return or chose not to. As an example of the immensity of such situations, one might look to West Germany which between 1945 and 1961 took in about 10 million persons expelled from the former German eastern territories and an additional 3.5 million refugees from the German Democratic Republic.

The third aspect of the demographic changes in Europe as a result of the war was the change in birth and natural increase rates compared with prewar years. In the traditionally low fertility areas of northwestern Europe there was a sharp rise in birth rates (the baby boom), while the rates in many of the southern and eastern European countries declined over this period. The result was a promise for Western Europe of a larger number of persons in the working population by the mid 1960s, but no relief for the immediate deficits created by war casualties or the low birth rates preceding the war during the 1930s. Conversely, southern and eastern Europe, having experienced high birth rates during the 1920s and 1930s, rather rapidly filled their work forces in the postwar years, but the falling birth rates portended later declines. As Borrie (1970, p. 93) summarizes the situation,

> The general pattern within Europe immediately after the Second World War was, therefore, one of relatively slow increases in the work forces of many of the countries of central and northern Europe

---

*The historians and economists who have studied nineteenth- and early twentieth-century European migrations place the figure for the whole period from 1846 to 1939 at more than 60 million persons (Thomas 1973). In some instances the outcome was far more than simply the migration of surplus populations. Ireland, for example, in the space of 100 years lost 50 percent of its population, falling from eight to four million persons.

and of relatively rapid increases in the south and east. This demographic profile, therefore, appeared to confirm pre-war judgement that the most likely source of emigration would remain the south and east. In central and northern Europe, the prospect of mass emigration was on the whole feared rather than welcomed.

The relative success of the efforts at resettlement of countless millions of persons highlights a significant difference between prewar and postwar migration patterns. Migration was no longer a laissez faire process but, on the contrary, it attracted the attention of governments, international organizations, and countless smaller private groups. In the postwar period, the recruitment and allocation of workers, the establishment and supervision of working conditions, the maintenance of housing, and the provision of educational and social welfare services were all seen as appropriate governmental efforts aimed at integrating these refugee groups. In subsequent years there has been a clear shift away from many of the social welfare programs originally instituted for war refugees and toward a more concerted effort to regulate migration as strictly a factor of manpower. Manpower migrations are now considered critical to those equations governing economic growth and development. It was with this transformation, both in migration policies and in the economic conditions of Western Europe, that a new form of migration began to emerge—a migration not of families and whole populations, but of solitary workers; a migration not of permanence, but of assumed short duration; a migration not of conviction, but of expediency.

## THE TRANSFORMATION OF EUROPEAN MIGRATION

The traditional role of Europe as a source of settlers in North and South America, Australia, Southern Africa, and other countries of the former British Empire was dramatically and systematically changed in the decade that followed the establishment of the European Economic Community (EEC). With the creation of this community through the Treaty of Rome in 1957 came a series of policies seeking to enhance and encourage European unification. One aspect of this policy orientation was the development of explicit legal and institutional arrangements designed to encourage intra-European movement of labor. Northwestern Europe quickly became a magnet for immigrants from the less developed regions of the EEC, most notably southern Italy. These intra-EEC migrations more than replaced the loss due to emigration from northwestern Europe to other hemispheres. And as far as countries like Italy were concerned, the opportunities for short intracontinental migration represented an important counterattraction to overseas movement.

Though emigration and immigration countries do not like being designated as such and do not call their immigrants or emigrants by those names, the terms will be used here, both for reasons of parsimony and for accurate reflection of the underlying assumptions of the following analysis. The countries designated in this study as immigration countries are the Federal Republic of Germany, Switzerland, Belgium, Sweden, the Netherlands, and France. Great Britain, though experiencing significant migration, both emigration and immigration, has been marginal in intra-European migrations.* In addition, the exclusion in this study of Denmark, Norway, Austria, Liechtenstein, and Luxembourg as countries of immigration is not because they have not become such, but because the numbers are so small that they are, in effect, statistically irrelevant for Western Europe as a whole. (The total immigrant population of these five countries combined approximates 2.5 percent of all immigrants in Western Europe.) It should also be noted that this analysis excludes the Eastern European countries, if they even can be called countries of immigration. Though it is well known that Poland has sent workers to the German Democratic Republic, at least in part to replenish the large gaps left by the fleeing of East German workers to the West, there is no reliable information about the duration or size of this work force. However, there is no doubt but that were the borders within Eastern Europe, let alone the ones between Eastern and Western Europe, opened to free passage, strong migratory movements would set in.

The data presented in Table 1.1 provide aggregate figures on the various components of the population in each of the six countries designated as immigration countries. The lack of absolute symmetry in comparing data from different countries results from the fact that each country collects census and immigration data according to a national rather than an international timetable.

Though the relative growth in the number of immigrants will shortly be discussed in more detail, Table 1.2 should provide in summary form a sense of the trends and magnitude of the immigrations over the past 15 years.

## MIGRATION AND THE EUROPEAN SOUTH

The large-scale manpower emigration from the Mediterranean basin to the countries of northwestern Europe, so critical to the sustaining of the post-World War II economies of these industrialized states, began in the 1950s and accelerated all through the 1960s. As a consequence of the vast concentrations of international capital in the countries of the European North, additional manpower was needed to facilitate continued economic growth. The emigration of workers from the Mediterranean countries has thus been inextricably linked with the prosperity experienced by the Western European countries for the past two decades. Placing this migration within the general context of the political-economic relations between emigration countries on the one hand and the immigra-

---

*By way of giving some indication of the flux in migration, the United Kingdom had the status of an emigrating country from 1950 to 1959, of an immigrating country from 1960 to 1965, and again of an emigrating country in the last decade. (OECD 1976a.)

## TABLE 1.1

### Total and Foreign Population in Absolute and Relative Numbers in European Immigration Countries

| Year | Total Population | Aliens |
|---|---|---|
| Switzerland | | |
| 1941 | | |
| Absolute | 4,265,703 | 223,554 |
| Percent | 100 | 5.24 |
| 1950 | | |
| Absolute | 4,714,992 | 285,446 |
| Percent | 100 | 6.05 |
| 1960 | | |
| Absolute | 5,429,061 | 569,935 |
| Percent | 100 | 10.50 |
| 1965 | | |
| Absolute | 5,945,500 | 810,243 |
| Percent | 100 | 13.47 |
| 1968 | | |
| Absolute | 6,147,000 | 933,142 |
| Percent | 100 | 15.21 |
| 1970 | | |
| Absolute | 6,269,783 | 982,887 |
| Percent | 100 | 15.68 |
| 1974 | | |
| Absolute | 6,442,800 | 1,064,526 |
| Percent | 100 | 16.52 |
| 1976 | | |
| Absolute | 6,310,000 | 958,599 |
| Percent | 100 | 15.19 |
| Belgium | | |
| 1947 | | |
| Absolute | 8,388,526 | 367,619 |
| Percent | 100 | 4.38 |
| 1954 | | |
| Absolute | 8,840,704 | 379,528 |
| Percent | 100 | 4.29 |

(Table 1.1 continued)

| Year | Total Population | Aliens |
|---|---|---|

Belgium (continued)

1961
  Absolute     9,189,741     453,486
  Percent           100          4.93
1965
  Absolute     9,499,234     636,749
  Percent           100          6.70
1970
  Absolute     9,650,944     696,282
  Percent           100          7.21
1973
  Absolute     9,756,590     775,185
  Percent           100          7.94

France

1946
  Absolute    40,125,000   1,743,619
  Percent           100          4.35
1954
  Absolute    43,228,000   1,766,100
  Percent           100          4.09
1958
  Absolute    45,015,000   1,621,075
  Percent           100          3.60
1960
  Absolute    45,904,000   1,633,410
  Percent           100          3.56
1965
  Absolute    48,954,000   2,683,490
  Percent           100          5.48
1970
  Absolute    51,012,000   3,393,457
  Percent           100          6.65
1972
  Absolute    51,921,000   3,775,804
  Percent           100          7.21
1974
  Absolute    53,614,441   4,128,312
  Percent           100          7.70

(continued)

(Table 1.1 continued)

| Year | Total Population | Aliens |
|---|---|---|
| Federal Republic of Germany | | |
| 1951 | | |
| Absolute | 50,241,400 | 485,763 |
| Percent | 100 | 0.99 |
| 1955 | | |
| Absolute | 52,383,000 | 484,819 |
| Percent | 100 | 0.92 |
| 1961 | | |
| Absolute | 56,175,000 | 686,160 |
| Percent | 100 | 1.22 |
| 1968 | | |
| Absolute | 60,184,000 | 2,318,100 |
| Percent | 100 | 3.96 |
| 1970 | | |
| Absolute | 60,651,000 | 2,976,500 |
| Percent | 100 | 4.90 |
| 1972 | | |
| Absolute | 61,672,000 | 3,438,700 |
| Percent | 100 | 5.58 |
| 1974 | | |
| Absolute | 62,054,000 | 4,127,400 |
| Percent | 100 | 6.65 |
| 1975 | | |
| Absolute | 61,991,500 | 4,089,000 |
| Percent | 100 | 6.59 |
| Sweden | | |
| 1945 | | |
| Absolute | 6,673,749 | 35,111 |
| Percent | 100 | 0.53 |
| 1950 | | |
| Absolute | 7,041,829 | 123,720 |
| Percent | 100 | 1.76 |
| 1954 | | |
| Absolute | 7,234,664 | 111,111 |
| Percent | 100 | 1.54 |

(Table 1.1 continued)

| Year | Total Population | Aliens |
|---|---|---|
| Sweden (continued) | | |
| 1960 | | |
| Absolute | 7,497,967 | 190,621 |
| Percent | 100 | 2.54 |
| 1968 | | |
| Absolute | 7,931,659 | 320,580 |
| Percent | 100 | 4.04 |
| 1970 | | |
| Absolute | 8,081,229 | 411,280 |
| Percent | 100 | 5.09 |
| 1974 | | |
| Absolute | 8,176,691 | 401,158 |
| Percent | 100 | 4.91 |
| Netherlands | | |
| 1947 | | |
| Absolute | 9,715,890 | 113,871 |
| Percent | 100 | 1.17 |
| 1956 | | |
| Absolute | 10,957,040 | 106,480 |
| Percent | 100 | 0.98 |
| 1960 | | |
| Absolute | 11,556,008 | 107,018 |
| Percent | 100 | 0.93 |
| 1964 | | |
| Absolute | 12,212,269 | 134,792 |
| Percent | 100 | 1.12 |
| 1968 | | |
| Absolute | 12,798,346 | 181,376 |
| Percent | 100 | 1.43 |
| 1973 | | |
| Absolute | 13,491,020 | 282,361 |
| Percent | 100 | 2.11 |

Source: H. J. Hoffman-Nowotny, "European Migrations after the Second World War." Paper presented to the Conference on Migration, New Harmony, Indiana, April 14, 1976.

TABLE 1.2

Trends of Immigration in Europe, 1961-74
(net migration in thousands)

| Countries | Annual Average 1961-66 | 1967 | 1969 | 1971 | 1974 |
|---|---|---|---|---|---|
| Belgium | +26 | +18 | +7 | +24 | +78 (1973) |
| France | +229 | +135 | +151 | +177 | +64 |
| Germany (FR) | +284 | -177 | +572 | +430 | +46 |
| Netherlands | +14 | -13 | +20 | +32 | +15 |
| Sweden | +20 | +10 | +44 | +7 | +11 |
| Switzerland | +52 | +31 | +24 | +10 | -65 (1975) |

Source: Organization for Economic Cooperation and Development, SOPEMI Continuous Reporting System on Migration (Paris: OECD, 1975).

tion countries of Western Europe on the other, Nikolinakos (1975a) defines it as one aspect of the north-south problem of Europe. It is those countries that have provided the labor for the development of the North without participating in development themselves that Nikolinakos terms the European South.*

Three groups of countries comprise the European South. The first are those countries of southern Europe proper, namely, Portugal, Spain, Greece, and the lower regions of the Italian peninsula. To the second group belong those countries with a history of European colonialism and subservience—Algeria, Morocco, Tunisia, Syria, Lebanon, Jordan, Egypt, and Libya. The final group consists of those countries with a high surplus of unskilled labor or skilled labor not yet utilized within their own economic systems. Two countries—Turkey and Yugoslavia—have determined to build their own economies and to utilize migration as a component of modernization and development through the anticipated benefits believed to accrue through the eventual return of their workers trained and skilled in industrial Europe.

Nikolinakos contends that the European South must be understood in the context of the needs of European capitalism, both politically and economically.

---

*As can be noted, Sweden was listed among the immigration countries, though a close examination of the various groups comprising the immigrants there reveals, that only 18 percent come from the European South. The reason for including Sweden is that it had in 1974 a total of 401,158 immigrants, of whom 183,181 (46 percent) were from Finland. Thus Finland must also be considered a country of emigration, though outside the conceptual framework elaborated upon here.

Further, the present migrations of manpower are merely the latest manifestation of the North-South relationship that dates back several hundred years. This is evident in an examination of the economic and strategic interests of Great Britain in its various colonies in the area—Cyprus, Iraq, Jordan, Egypt, Malta, and Gibraltar. The same can be said for France with Algeria, Morocco, Tunisia, Syria, and Lebanon. All of these countries were very closely bound in economic, political, and geographical terms to the colonial powers. They comprised, in short, the satellites of the various European metropolitan states.

In the period of most concern here, that of the post-World War II era, there have been modifications in the traditional colonial relations between the North and the South, though the basic relational patterns have remained. (The exceptions to this would be the countries of Libya, Egypt, Iraq, Syria, and Algeria which have actively sought to break the traditional economic, political, and cultural links.) One modification of clear importance is that the internal distinctions within the North have given way to the emergence of a closely knit and unified European economic system. This is particularly so with the establishment of the EEC and its subsequent enlargement in 1971 to nine members. The intensification of economic and political interests among these countries has created a broadly based cohesion and integration.

The EEC as a unit has thus acted to insure that the countries of the South remain closely bound to the economic interests of the North. This has been done through a variety of agreements whereby the countries of the South are granted associate status.* For some the carrot is made even more enticing through the suggestion of eventual full membership in EEC, as is presently the case with Portugal, Spain, Greece, and Turkey, all of which are in negotiations for membership. Nikolinakos suggests (1975a, p. 9) that there are five fundamental elements that constitute the economic meaning of the European South for the North: the need of northern capital to have lucrative locations to invest; the need of the North for markets for its finished goods; the need for manpower to sustain production; the need for oil as an energy source; and political and military needs including NATO, protection of sea lanes for oil, monitoring of Soviet military activities, and so on.

With gradual industrialization and modernization, several of the countries geographically adjacent to the North, most notably Greece, Italy, and Spain, are moving into a transition phase out of a strictly southern country role and toward a position more like that of the North. The intensified movement of European capital into these countries and the gradual increase in wages will result in a growing tendency to view them as integrated into the European economic arena. They are slowly becoming absorbed into the economic system as constituent parts.

---

*The EEC has even gone so far afield as to establish associate relations with former French and Dutch colonies in the Caribbean (cf. Andic 1970).

The result of this annexation of countries in transition is that the more strictly southern functions must be developed in other countries and expanded elsewhere when possible. Thus the role of the hinterland—and that is essentially what the southern countries have played—is being picked up by such countries as Turkey and Yugoslavia, as well as several of the North African states.* Nikolinakos elaborates upon this relationship (1975a, p. 20):

> It is necessary for the expansion of capitalist production that there exist a hinterland, which serves as a supplier of raw materials, as a source of the reserve army, as a market for industrial products, and finally, as a location for industry when the profit margins in the metropolis have been reached.

An effort to sketch the dimensions and magnitude of the emigration from the countries of the European South meets several obstacles. First, not all countries have the same level of sophistication in the monitoring of the movements of their peoples. Second, migrants from Italy, as a member of the EEC, do not need work permits or visas to enter any of the other eight EEC countries, as all share an agreement for free movement within their collective boundaries. Third, the number of illegal immigrants (emigrants) is unknown but thought to be growing as a result of the ban on further legal immigration of guestworkers by the six major receiving countries. Fourth, there is the problem of *frontaliers*, those who live in one country but who daily commute to work in another. Thus, for example, the number of persons who live in Spain or Belgium but who work in France is unknown. Finally, there is the question of how to tabulate seasonal workers. Germany, for example, does include such workers in its statistical reporting while Switzerland does not.

In spite of the problems and shortcomings listed above, Table 1.3 attempts to provide some indication of what is known regarding emigration from the European South to the industrial countries of Western Europe.

## MIGRATION: SOME THEORETICAL CONCERNS

In an effort to elaborate upon the previous comments regarding the causes of immigration and emigration, it is well to note that there are at least two distinctive theoretical frameworks employed for such causal analysis. The first grows out of the literature on modernization and development which emphasizes

---

*It is important to note that the role of hinterland is not necessarily international in character. The same situation prevails in Italy where the southern section serves as the hinterland for the industrialized north. It is for this reason that Nikolinakos (1975) speaks of the "marginal character" of the Italian south.

TABLE 1.3

European South Workers' Emigration Flows to European North Destinations
(net migration in thousands)

| Country | 1961-67 | 1968 | 1969 | 1970 | 1971 | 1972 | 1973 | 1974 | 1975 |
|---|---|---|---|---|---|---|---|---|---|
| Turkey | +203 | +43 | +104 | +129 | +88 | +85 | +137 | +20 | +4 |
| Greece | +37 | — | +67 | +68 | +43 | +29 | +15 | +11 | +10 |
| Yugoslavia | — | — | — | +125 | +81 | +57 | +100 | +20 | +15 |
| Italy | +71 | +130 | +57 | +69 | +167 | +141 | +123 | +112 | +88 |
| Spain | +133 | +53 | +39 | +16 | — | — | +96 | +51 | +21 |
| Portugal | +61 | +49 | +110 | +143 | +119 | +94 | +97 | +44 | +22 |
| Morocco | — | — | — | — | — | +35 | +30 | +31 | +10 |
| Algeria* | — | — | — | — | — | +22 | — | — | — |
| Tunisia | +12 | +3 | +7 | +13 | +14 | +10 | +12 | +9 | — |

*Algeria suspended all labor-based emigration in September, 1973.

Note: The data supplied here, incomplete as they are, are only for emigrating workers, and do not include the emigration of family members not in the work force. Thus, in almost every instance, the figures are considerably below those of total emigration.

Source: Organization for Economic Cooperation and Development, SOPEMI Continuous Reporting System on Migration (Paris: OECD, 1975, 1976).

that modern migrations usually follow the developmental gaps between different social systems (cf. Lutz 1961; Hoffmann-Nowotny 1970, 1973; Thomas 1961; and Rose 1969). In this view, migration is seen as a natural phenomenon and one to be encouraged for the stimulation of growth and modernization in the home country. It becomes a means of leveling and diminishing discrepancies at the macro level between regions, between nation states, or even within a single nation, as has happened in Italy, the United States, and the Soviet Union.

In the context of Western Europe, this view of migration has found wide acceptance and support. With the emigration of workers from the less developed countries into the industrial states of Europe, it has been assumed that the worker will improve his vocational skills, acquire modern standards of living, and thus become an innovative change agent who will contribute, upon his return to the home country, to the modernization of that economy and society. This concept found its manifestation in the development of what is known as the rotation principle. This principle implies that the workers should rotate between the emigrant and immigrant countries on a scheduled basis, staying in the immigrant country for a stipulated period, assumed to be no more than three to five years. The short-run benefit of such rotation for the emigration countries would be that social tensions arising from the inability of the home country to provide meaningful employment would be exported. In the long run, benefits would accrue through the adaptation of the emigrants to their host countries, their acquisition of modern values and outlooks, and thus their aspiration to the same development in their home countries.

An important dimension of this view of modernization as it relates to migration patterns is that such patterns are not seen as serving exclusively economic functions, but socialization functions as well. The goal is that the emigrant will return imbued with a value orientation aimed toward the pursuit of national development. This view recognizes that modernization is not reducible simply to economic terms, but that is must have its roots in the values and aspirations of the people to change their social condition and their orientation to the rest of the world.

In the context of migrations in Europe, what has been desired has been the integration, on an international level, of developmental values. The aim has been an enlargement of the relevant political and economic arena and the establishment of a consensus as to the appropriate approach to issues arising within that arena. The establishment of rights guaranteeing free movement of workers within the EEC is but one manifestation of linking migration with the economic and political socialization of the migrating workers.

It must be noted, however, that the developmental process is not simply one way, that is, from the more to the less developed countries. The very fact that modernization is encouraged brings into the international arena those problems that were previously only national in character. What the EEC must now confront are the claims of the disposessed and underprivileged, both within and on the fringes of its own boundaries. The quest of these groups for participation in and enjoyment of the goods and activities represented by the modern sector is one that cannot be resolved within the national borders of any one member of the EEC. Having encouraged in the underdeveloped countries the adoption of values congruent with their own, the developed countries cannot now refuse to recognize the validity of the claims for assistance and direction. By responding in a positive manner the developed countries assist in the modernization process, thus reducing the developmental gap between the two groups of countries. The end product is one essentially beneficial to all concerned.

An alternative theoretical orientation for the study of migrations in Europe is one that emphasizes a center-periphery relationship between the developed and underdeveloped countries. Migration is viewed as a force that exacerbates the impoverishment and depletion of resources in the labor-sending countries, rather than a mechanism promoting modernization and development (cf. Galtung 1971; Myrdal 1963; and Schiller 1970). It should be readily apparent that the analysis offered by Nikolinakos on the European North-South relationship is one example of this broader perspective of center-periphery relations. Asymmetrical interactions, as Galtung has noted, characterize the relations between nations which have developed as the result of a certain form of the division of labor. Center nations gradually require higher levels of skills and education from their indigenous work forces, whereas periphery nations continue to supply raw materials, markets for manufactured goods, and a surplus labor force that is easily exportable.

Within this theoretical perspective, migratory labor leads to an increase in extant inequality rather than its decrease. Present discrepancies become even more pronounced. The cycle of dependency deepens. An outcome of this set of relations is that even when one of the developing countries manages to sustain a relatively high level of growth in its gross national product, it is not sufficient in and of itself to disrupt this disequalized pattern of exchange. While Turkey has been averaging an annual increase in its GNP of nearly 7 percent since 1968 (cf. Varlier and Ilkin 1975, p. 403), this growth has not been transformed into a set of structural relations that would decrease the need for migration. As a result, the average 7 percent growth in GNP is matched by a growth in employment opportunities of only somewhere between 0.2 and 1 percent per year. Endemic unemployment (and underemployment) coupled with the desire for the benefits of modernization sustains a commitment to a migratory flux. But as has been emphasized by Nikolinakos' study of North-South relations, labor exportation by itself can provide no remedy for underdevelopment. Rather, it contributes in substantial ways to its perpetuation.

When one turns from an assessment of macroeconomic and political forces that propel migration to the individual level, other considerations must be noted. If one is in an underprivileged position and wishes to change that condition, there are theoretically two possible means of doing so. The first is to seek individual improvement through the improvement of one's entire group—for instance, by regional or national development. Here individual mobility becomes a by-product of group mobility. The alternative is to seek an improvement only in one's personal situation, as within the present analysis, through emigration from a less to a more highly developed region or country (cf. Ronzani 1975, p. 138).

If the former approach to individual mobility represents adherence to a political-ideological model of improvement, the latter represents a more personalistic or psychological view of one's place in the social system. After a detailed study of Dutch emigrants to overseas countries, Frijda (1961) offered a three-factor theory of emigration:

> Firstly, a background of dissatisfaction, predominantly but not solely of an economic nature; secondly, a special stimulus to leave the community, either through the pull of ties with emigrants or through the push arising from an orientation that differs from that of the community, and a lesser degree of adhesion to that community and the people who comprise it; and thirdly, a more specific motive is sometimes present in the shape of longings which already contain the germ of "somewhere else."

With only slight modifications, such an anlaysis would seem to fit the current migrants to the European North as well. And taken together, what such a framework suggests is that the economic factor, present in all three dimensions of Frijda's analysis, can become the primary if not exclusive motivation behind the choice to migrate.

The emigration from the European South gives credence to the view that literally millions of persons are no longer content to wait for the success of collective mobility in their home countries. Rather, they have opted for personal migration (with the blessings of their governments which hope that such migrations will become a shortcut to achieving the collective mobility that is ultimately desired). Taking the two theoretical perspectives outlined earlier, one can come to nearly opposite conclusions as to the merits of this massive effort at personal betterment. If, indeed, this migration does come about as the result of a strong desire for development and if those who emigrate do choose to return, then the consequent benefits will be worth the inconveniences and hardships suffered in the interim. But, as the contrary view would hold, if this emigration essentially seals the fate of the sending countries to remain in a dependent position to the host countries, then any personal benefits will be far outweighed by the long-term negative consequences for the country and its citizens. What occurs from this perspective is the establishment and ritualization of an international *lumpenproletariate*, an industrial reserve army available to the highly developed countries at their beckon and created by the perpetuation of the asymmetrical relations between the developed and underdeveloped countries. Applying a phrase from Myrdal (1963), the European South finds itself trapped in a relation of "cumulative and circular causation," from which there are no exits, only greater dependencies and discrepancies.

It would appear, then, that the center-periphery analysis, and its elaboration by Nikolinakos as the European North-South relationship, is a more accurate reflection of current conditions in Europe. The evidence that will be presented in the chapters to follow seems nearly incontrovertible: the European South has not closed the developmental gaps existing between itself and the North; rather, the inequalities have remained and become even more firmly entrenched in the patterns of relations between these two groups of countries. Nearly two decades of migration have only exacerbated a condition that many had hoped would be abated.

Within a short period of time following the war, manpower migration within Europe began to assume such proportions that the countries concerned were very quickly persuaded to modify, if not abandon, the strict framework of bilateral relations and begin instead to approach the issue on a multinational and multilateral basis. With the support given to these developments by the newly emergent European intergovernmental organizations, many governments developed rather similar attitudes and viewpoints on the migration situation. As has been noted in a report from OECD (1975a, p. 7),

> In the post-war climate of European reconstruction, there was a certain measure of agreement between ethical and legal principles and the practical interests of the international community, that manpower shortages which were holding up the repairs to the productive apparatus should be alleviated by improving the use of human resources and transferring these from "surplus" countries to "deficit" countries.

This viewpoint found clear and concrete expression in 1948 with the establishment of the Organization for European Economic Cooperation (OEEC), the forerunner of the OECD. The OEEC was the first intergovernmental organization in Europe to be given a specific mandate to undertake work in this area. According to Article 8 of the Convention of 16 April, 1948 (establishing OEEC):

> The contracting parties will make the fullest and most effective use of their available manpower. They will endeavor to provide full employment for their own people and they may have recourse to manpower available in the territory of any other Contracting Party. In the latter case, they will, in mutual agreement, take the necessary measures to facilitate the movement of workers and to ensure their establishment in conditions satisfactory from the economic and social point of view. Generally, the Contracting Parties will cooperate in the progressive reduction of obstacles to the free movement of persons.

In the years to follow, the OEEC and then the OECD developed a series of codes that were to serve as normative guidelines for the policies of the member countries with regard to manpower migration.* These frequently coincided with attempts on the part of the organization to develop standards for the liberalization of trade and tariffs. The first of these legal instruments was adopted in October 1953, and was entitled "Governing the Employment of Nationals of Member Countries." The second, "Recommendations of the Council Concerning the Introduction and Employment of Foreign Manpower" was passed in 1961. In the Recommendations were stated a number of provisions that were to have increasing significance as the wave of migrations began to grow. They appear to have influenced the guidelines eventually developed by the newly formed EEC in the late 1960s.

The important points raised in the Recommendations (OECD 1975a) were the extension of the residence and work permits in terms of time, occupation, and location; the granting of status to the wife and children comparable to that of the worker himself; the granting of necessary labor and travel documents free of charge; the elimination of other expenditures and taxes related to the worker's employment or his family's travel; and the forming of guidelines for the operation of an international clearance scheme for job vacancies and applications.

It is well to note that such policy guidelines and recommendations were not made in a void. There had developed a rather elaborate and detailed doctrine regarding manpower migrations in Europe. Various views on development and modernization were espoused, economic forecasts were prepared to ascertain the projected manpower needs of the industrial countries, and there was the incessant and seemingly insatiable demand for workers to man the factories, build the buildings, sweep the streets, wait on tables, and carry out all the other myriad occupational tasks available to both skilled and unskilled workers in advanced societies. The political and economic realities demanded that governments address themselves to the manpower problem, be those governments in emigration or immigration countries. It is of interest, beyond the substance of the assumptions regarding migration itself, that there was such general agreement on the validity and merit of these policy views that they encompassed countries as diverse as Germany and Turkey or Yugoslavia and Switzerland.

---

*The term normative is used here advisedly as the OECD does not have the power to require adoption of its recommendations by its various member countries. Rather, these recommendations are presented to the various members (numbering 24 in 1977) for their consideration. The degree to which member nations respond is noted in the annual report of the OECD. Given the diversity—political, geographical, economic, and cultural—among the members, such recommendations of necessity have tended more to suggest alternatives than to address specific circumstances. Such recommendations have also been the basis for bilateral agreements among nations both within and outside the OECD. The Swedish-Yugoslavian agreement of 1966 and the Swiss-Spanish agreement of 1961 are but two early examples of bilateral agreements in the area of manpower and migration, both based upon the 1961 OECD recommendations noted in the text above.

By the beginning of the 1960s, the basic assumptions underlying manpower migration in Europe could be stated quite explicitly. They have been summarized as follows (OECD 1975a, pp. 9-11):

1. By allowing manpower to move from countries where it is in surplus to countries where it is in deficit, migration entails general benefits for both groups of countries.
2. At the individual level, migration enables a migrant worker to obtain a job at a fair wage and the possibility to improve his work skills and chance of social promotion (especially if he returns to his own country).
3. Compared with these advantages, the collective and personal disadvantages are regarded as of minor importance; in any event, activities in the fields of adaptation, training, housing, and more broadly, social welfare should help to reduce if not eliminate them altogether.
4. Freedom to emigrate should therefore be recognized and normalized as a natural right and the formalities for entering and residing in the country of immigration should be simplified and relaxed.
5. With regard to employment, the worker should be free to accept offers from abroad provided this freedom does not jeopardise the interest of the (national or foreign) workers already on the immigration country's own market.
6. After a specified period of employment (which should not exceed 4 or 5 years and should be gradually reduced), it should be possible to integrate the foreign worker into the national employment market and, to this end, restrictions on the choice of employer, occupation, and place of work should be gradually removed.
7. The creation of zones of free manpower movement or, better still, of real common employment markets is a desirable target.
8. Public services should be instructed to provide applicants for emigration with detailed information and to supervise the international clearance of job vacancies and applications for both individual and collective recruitment. These same services or others (which should in any case be free) should be instructed to apply measures to facilitate the departure and reception of migrants. International coordination of these activities should be established through a strong liaison structure, together with in-service training and exchange of officials.
9. Migrant workers should without exception (within the firm as well as outside) enjoy the same contracts, terms and benefits as well as the same protection as national workers, including such assistance as is provided by the guidance, training and employment services. The same applies to membership of the trade unions and participation in their activities. In addition, special measures should be taken to ensure that the foreign worker is not in any position of inferiority.
10. The benefits of social security should be maintained independently of the worker's movements, and periods of insurance or employment should be aggregated.

11. The transfer of earnings and savings to the country of origin should be guaranteed.

12. Families should be encouraged to reunite and the status of their members should be identical with that enjoyed by the head of the family.

13. The exchange of young workers may improve their chances of general and occupational education. It should therefore be facilitated in the context of bilateral or multilateral programs.

Though it is readily apparent in hindsight that these basic assumptions underlying the encouraged growth of immigrant labor during the 1960s constituted an unrealistic view of migration and the costs and benefits entailed, the shortcomings only slowly came into view. At first it was as if it were possible to plan an effort at social change, international in its scope as was this, with all benefits and no costs. But there were costs, and they began to mount, not only for the receiving countries, but for the sending ones as well. Even so, the doctrine outlined above stayed intact, for with the boom years of the 1960s, the magnitude of the costs was obscured and those that were evident were minimized or at least tolerated by both sets of countries as the pecuniary benefits continued to accrue on all sides. The simple economic equation of matching jobs and workers inside an international labor market appeared valid and was working for millions of people, even if not as well as had been anticipated.

## THE EEC AND MIGRATION POLICIES

It was a full decade after the Treaty of Rome before the EEC was able to effect the full freedom of movement of labor within its boundaries. This full freedom was the culmination of a three-stage plan, based on Articles 48 and 49 of the Treaty of Rome which stipulated that full freedom of labor mobility was to be achieved by the end of 1969. The EEC, in fact, was able to conclude such agreements a year and a half early with the final documents signed on July 1, 1968. The treaty looked forward to the "abolition of any discrimination based on nationality between workers of the Member States as regards employment, remuneration, and other working conditions" and stated that the several individual rights granted to the workers of the member states should be subject to limitations only where justified by reason of "public order, public safety, and public health."

In examining more closely the various provisions and regulations contained in the agreements regarding the free movement of labor between member states, it is evident that the doctrine of mutual benefits of labor migration was clearly adhered to and implemented. The status of an EEC worker was given clear and unequivocal existence through the ratification of Community Law, binding on all member countries.* The Preamble to Regulation 1612/68 of the EEC states:

> Freedom of movement constitutes a basic right for workers and their families. Mobility of the labor force within the Community must be one of the means by which the worker is guaranteed the possibility of improving his living conditions and securing his social advancement, while helping to satisfy the economic requirements of the Member States.

The first stage of moving toward this freedom of movement was inaugurated by EEC Council Regulation 15 issued August 16, 1961,† which contains five major provisions: labor permits are to be given automatically to member-state nationals for occupations in which there is a labor shortage; the domestic labor administration can restrict employment opportunities to its own nationals for only three weeks, after which it must make the openings available to other member-state nationals regardless of preexisting restrictive numbers or quotas; foreign workers who are specifically requested by an employer will in certain cases be granted a work permit without reference to the domestic labor market; member-state nationals are to be given preference over other foreign workers in filling jobs; and member-state nationals are granted the right to renew their labor permits for the same occupation after one year of employment, for any other occupation for which they are qualified after three years, and for any kind of paid work after four years of regular employment.

The second stage of the EEC movement toward open and free migration began in 1964 with the issuance of Regulation 38. Here member countries were able to restrict the priorities accorded the domestic labor force to only select labor surplus occupations and regions. The civil rights of the migrant workers were extended through granting them the same privileges as member-state local workers. Workers were also given the right to vote in factory elections after three years of employment by the same firm. They were allowed to bring in dependents in addition to spouse and minor children if the worker could produce proof of satisfactory accommodations. There was also instituted at this time an EEC-

---

*European Economic Community: Regulation 1612/68, Title III, Article 10 and Regulation 1251/70, Articles 2 and 3. It is also important to note that the concept of "worker" is defined not in terms of international law or in terms of municipal law of the various member states, but has acquired a distinct meaning according to Community Law. It refers to all blue-collar and white-collar workers other than those employed in the public service. The self-employed do not fall under the provisions for freedom of movement of workers, but rather come under separate Treaty of Rome provisions (cf. Böhning 1972, pp. 15–16).

†Summary provided by Rose (1969).

wide clearing house to facilitate offers of and applications for employment within the member-states.

With the ratification of the final stage of the agreements governing the movement of workers, full internal freedom of movement was achieved. From July 1, 1968, onward, a worker from any EEC member state has been able to accept employment in any other member country without the necessity of obtaining a work permit or arranging employment in advance of entering the host country. If the worker cannot locate work within a three-month period, he may be required to leave, but is entitled to return again. Residence permits must be accorded as a right by the receiving country to Community workers upon their obtaining employment, subject to certain formalities (for example, the necessity of police registration or *Anmeldung* in Germany). All Community workers have the same legal and trade union rights with respect to their employment, and the worker's dependents (defined as spouse, children under the age of 21 or otherwise dependent upon the worker, and other dependents in a direct line of descent) have the right to take up residency with him, whatever their nationality. Both the worker and his family are entitled to full social security rights, and the contributions paid while working within the host country are to be credited to him when the decision is made to return home. The worker has the option to remain with his family permanently within the borders of the host country, subject to certain liberal conditions, if he reaches pensionable age or must cease employment as a result of a permanent incapacity to work. The members of the family also have the right to remain in the host country after the death of the worker, again within certain generously worded limitations.

In the effort to implement these provisions, the EEC has concentrated upon the development of guidelines both to identify and then remove obstacles in the way of its pursuit of a cross-national common policy with respect to migration. The obstacles have generally been those of regulations and legislative mandates in the member countries which have sought to place restrictions upon and limit the opportunities afforded foreign labor. While these obstacles have gradually diminished, they are in reality only half the issue. To move from the elimination of negative sanctions to the promotion of positive steps toward the integration of these workers within the Community has been an exceedingly difficult transition. In fact, it appears to have been tacitly set aside with the severe economic recession suffered in Europe as a result of the oil embargo and the subsequent quadrupling of oil prices in 1973. Unification and cooperation on this matter appear to have been much more feasible while economies were strong and workers were needed in large numbers regardless of their national origins. This is in stark contrast to the present situation where unemployment in the member countries numbers in the millions (Germany alone in early 1977 had nearly one million unemployed) and the balance-of-trade deficit is in the billions. (The balance-of-trade deficit in 1976 for the nine-member EEC was $6 billion and would have been $25 billion if West Germany were excluded.)

With a time span now of nearly two decades since the EEC first made efforts to insure the full and free movement of workers, it is possible to give some assessment as to the actual impact of such policies. Succinctly, it appears that such policies have had only limited impact upon the actual movement of workers, for the Community as a whole has been consistently short of manpower and unable to fulfill its needs from within its own boundaries (cf. Yannopoulos 1975, p. 81). For this reason, the EEC has had to move far beyond its member states in pursuit of labor. The regulations, therefore, have not hindered movement, but there simply have not been enough workers free to move. This view is confirmed in the British White Paper of July 1971:

> The movement of labor within an enlarged Community [Denmark, Ireland, and Norway were scheduled to join the EEC at the same time as Great Britain] will probably continue to be dominated by economic and social factors rather than by regulations, and the position in practice is likely to be similar to that which now prevails.

The only country that represents an exception to this analysis of extensive EEC labor shortages is Italy. It is here that labor surpluses have existed since the beginning of the EEC (and before) and it is Italy that has made the most extensive use of the freedom of movement provisions for the exportation of its surplus workers. During the six years 1961-66 in which the EEC regulations for the freedom of movement were in their first and second stages of implementation, an average of 270,600 first work permits were issued each year to workers of the member states moving from one country to another. Of this figure, more than 80 percent were granted to Italian workers. Table 1.4 provides information on the movement of Italian workers since the initiation of full internal freedom of movement in 1968. Also included are the data on the largest countries of destination within the EEC.

In addition to the agreements within the EEC regarding the movement of workers, there exists in Europe a large and intricate network of migration accords worked out between the industrial countries on the one hand and the labor-exporting countries on the other. Such agreements include the countries of the EEC, and other labor-importing countries as well—for example, Switzerland and Sweden. What one observes in the study of such agreements is that while the very first dealt almost exclusively with the questions of recruitment procedures, job placements, visa requirements, and duration of contract, they were gradually modified throughout the 1960s to include many of the same concerns expressed by the EEC member governments for their own workers. The revised agreements had stipulations covering such areas as working conditions and opportunities for the changing of employment, the provision of educational and vocational training, and assistance for the re-integration of the worker into his home country. The OECD report of 1975 provides brief summaries of two such agreements, one being bilateral (between Germany and Turkey) and the second between the

## TABLE 1.4

### Italian Population in Selected Countries of the EEC

|  | Belgium | France | Germany (FR) | Netherlands | Total |
|---|---|---|---|---|---|
| **1968** | | | | | |
| Absolute | 233,490 | 632,080 | 514,600 | 14,236 | 1,394,046 |
| Percent[a] | 33.57 | 22.37 | 21.61 | 7.84 | |
| **1970** | | | | | |
| Absolute | 249,490 | 592,737 | 553,600 | n.a.[b] | 1,395,827 |
| Percent | 35.83 | 17.46 | 18.59 | n.a. | |
| **1972** | | | | | |
| Absolute | 256,603 | 573,817 | 589,800 | n.a. | 1,420,220 |
| Percent | 34.26 | 15.19 | 17.15 | n.a. | |
| **1974** | | | | | |
| Absolute | 259,800 | 564,660 | 629,600 | 19,269 | 1,473,329 |
| Percent | 33.51 | 13.96 | 15.25 | 6.82 (1973) | |

[a] of all aliens.
[b] data not available.

Note: If one were to add to these figures the number of Italians in Switzerland, the figures would be considerably higher. In 1974, for example, there were 554,925 Italians living in Switzerland, 52.10 percent of all foreigners in that country. The Swiss figures are provided, though Switzerland is not a member of the EEC, to suggest more accurately the magnitude of Italian emigration within continental Europe.

Source: H.J. Hoffmann-Nowotny, "European Migrations after the Second World War." Paper presented to the Conference on Migration, New Harmony, Indiana, April 14, 1976.

---

Netherlands and the several countries which have sizable emigration populations within its boundaries. The Dutch agreements are described as follows (OECD 1975a, p. 31):

> The Government intends to facilitate a fairer division of labour by helping to create relatively labour-intensive industries in the less-developed countries. Finance will be given to special projects prepared in the countries concerned. In addition, training courses will be organized for migrants who wish to return home. These courses will be given both in the Netherlands and in the countries of origin, but in both cases the syllabuses will depend upon the special require-

ments of the latter. For the future, funds might be transferred to credit institutions in the less-developed countries which could thus finance the productive ventures of former migrants having regard to their experience and training.

With the movement of the EEC in particular and the European North in general outside of its own boundaries in the pursuit of manpower, the repercussions of the large-scale importation of labor began to be manifest. While the boom years of the 1960s and early 1970s hid much of the social debt that was accumulating, it could not be ignored for long. The belief that labor could be exported and imported on a rotational basis to come to the countries of the North, take up the tasks gladly left behind by the national workers, and then leave with a minimum of impact upon the fabric of either the emigration or immigration countries, was naive. There have been social costs and they have been considerable.

At one level, one can survey the broad consequences of the migration of tens of thousands of Turks, Yugoslavs, Spaniards, or North Africans to the industrial countries; they find clashes of cultures, housing ghettos, growing racism. Second generation immigration youth wander in a cultural limbo, and thousands of children enter school systems that are neither prepared nor anxious to undertake the efforts necessary to create a milieu in which all can flourish. At another level, that of the solitary individual, the tragedy is of a more personal sort. The workers of the South were brought to the North as if they were an abstraction or an image. Behind the term guestworker was a belief that such workers were like replaceable parts. Like cogs in a machine, for every part that broke down there was a seemingly endless supply of replacements.

Behind the abstraction, however, lay, of course, a human being who was more than simply the sum total of his working hours per week. Beyond the role of worker were other roles that each migrant filled, and each role had its own implications for the host societies. The worker was father, husband, friend, countryman, neighbor, consumer, believer, and carrier of language, to name but a few. Midst it all remained the unresolved ambiguity that encompassed his existence—whether in fact he was a "guest" or, more likely, an unwanted but tolerated intruder.

# 2
# MANPOWER MIGRATIONS: ORIGINS AND IMPACTS

Until very recently, it was widely agreed that the European migration of labor made it possible to respond to shortages or surpluses in manpower needs in a way that benefited both the emigration and immigration countries. Situations, however, are not always as one might hope. Slowly and steadily the evidence began to mount that in fact the migration of labor to the countries of the European North solidified the dependency status of the countries in the European South. As one of the three major requirements of production, and probably the most critical, labor became the key component in the differentiation between the dominance of the industrial countries as a world power and the continual lag of those labor-exporting countries to the south (cf. OECD 1975a, p. 12). One brief but vivid example is that in 1975, 55 percent of all skilled workers from Yugoslavia were working outside their own country to fuel the economies of other countries. In such circumstances, the ability of Yugoslavia to plan and execute the development activities necessary for its own growth is severely affected.

The growing schism between the countries of the North and South has quite naturally entailed increasingly sharp political, economic, and social reactions. Among the countries of the South, Algeria ceased all labor-based emigration after the fall of 1973; Spain and Turkey began to link the continuation of U.S. and NATO military installations on their soil to concessions for freer entry of their workers into the EEC; and Greece had to begin the importation of workers from North Africa to meet its own manpower requirements. In the North, the Swiss held a national referendum (the so-called "Schwarzenbach Initiative") on whether to expel all migrant workers from the country; Rotterdam experienced an anti-Turkish riot in 1972; two bombs exploded at a Turkish bank and a Turkish consulate office in Zürich in May 1976; race riots broke out in Marseilles in 1973 that left six Algerians dead. From all sides has come the evidence that to treat the consequences of migration with benign neglect is to court even further schism and more intransigent difficulties.

In summarizing the manner in which the demand for foreign labor arose and the consequences it had upon the center countries in particular, the following points have been made (OECD 1975a, pp. 12-13):

1. Constant general demand (in which the international components played a very important role) has nourished continuous economic growth.

2. Full employment of the national labor force has been maintained or achieved. It has naturally affected the demand for consumer and capital goods, helping to feed growth.

3. Over-employment phenomena have been observed almost everywhere. Manpower has become a scarcity, being increasingly attracted to better paid or more satisfying jobs. This has helped to raise the already high demand for training and education, which has had the effect of reducing the total supply of labor still more.

4. Other constraints having joined the preceding (demographic constraints, difficulty of fully utilizing the theoretical manpower potential, technical constraints, rigid structures and behavior), the use of foreign manpower which was originally only for jobs in building or agriculture (usually seasonal), for some skilled jobs or else for jobs regarded as typically dependent on the short-term economic situation, has spread to other branches of industry as well as to certain services. Immigrants have finally taken unskilled or semi-skilled jobs where their presence has, incidentally, had the effect of putting a brake on the rise in certain categories of nominal wages, thus contributing even from this standpoint toward the faster departure of national labor to better paid jobs.

5. Thanks to immigration, the countries of industrial Europe are practically in the same situation as countries with an almost unlimited labor supply, but, as distinct from the latter, they also have capital, the basic and productive structures and "know-how," and the required technical and skilled workers. This has stimulated the expansion of investment and has made it possible to avoid any immediate exhaustive review of the social structure of employment and production. To a varying but often considerable extent, immigration has slowed down the transfer of productive capital abroad and has probably contributed towards the inflow of international capital.

6. As this cycle has continued, immigration has become structural. With the demand for labor adjusting to the nature of the supply which could satisfy it, the employment market in most industrialized countries in Western Europe split up into two parts: One is represented by the national labor force (whose employment opportunities not only increased but their chances of obtaining a better job) and the other consists largely of foreigners (whose employment opportunities have also increased). By their very nature, these two components of the market have usually proved complementary and not competitive.

7. Immigration (which has grown—in spite of the turnover—by including an increasing number of the members of migrant workers' families) has been reflected in an additional demand for consumer goods and infrastructure and this has led to further manpower requirements. At the same time, the continuation of productive investment has been reflected, as we have just shown, in a further increase in the demand for labor and for labor of a certain type. This is when we can speak of immigration as being self-feeding (of the increasing autonomy of immigration in relation to the size of previous flows, its rate of renewal, the types of employment where it penetrates tends to perpetuate and to multiply); i.e., a cumulative and fairly complex process which could be halted or limited by outside intervention.

Turning from the demand to the supply side of the equation, it is important to acknowledge that in Western Europe, the market situation has benefited the industrial, immigration countries: they, the demanders, have been in a position of clear dominance over the supplying countries. The result is that the flow of manpower, its structure and frequency, have been guided by the needs of the labor-importing countries. It is worth noting, moreover, that such conditions have little similarity with the waves of trans-Atlantic migrations that occurred throughout the nineteenth and early twentieth centuries. If the early migrants were pushed out of Europe by famine, war, and persecution, the latter-day migrants are being pulled by higher wages, the desire to participate in an industrial economy, and the opportunities for broader vocational, educational, and personal experiences.

The differences in wage earnings between the countries of the North and the South are dramatic. In the late 1960s, when the movement of manpower into the industrial countries was running in the several hundreds of thousands each year, the average earnings of a worker in Germany were 318 percent higher than in Portugal and nearly 400 percent higher than in Yugoslavia. The impact of such inducements is felt not only by those who are unemployed or underemployed in the home countries, but by those who have stable employment as well. To have the option to increase one's earnings by as much as four times could pull at almost any worker. This differential in wage earnings seems to explain the migration of Finnish workers into Sweden or the frontier workers of Belgium into France (cf. Nikolinakos 1976, p. 21).

Alongside these aspirations for the improvement of one's personal condition, there is the factor alluded to in the previous chapter—that of the spread of modernization and developmental values into the periphery countries. The powerful appeal of these values leads not only to social and cultural emulation in the home country (for example, the desire for Western clothes, foods, and entertainment), but to the wish to move out of the rural past into the urban and technological present. It is perhaps hard to demonstrate such inducements in strictly economic terms, but it is evident they exist and exercise a powerful motivational effect, for there seems to be little other explanation for the hardships and sufferings peoples of the South are willing to endure in order to come and stay in the center countries. Such willingness, of course, does not excuse discrimination and exploitation on the part of the northern countries. The perseverence in the face of such obstacles only reconfirms the degree to which peoples of the South are seeking a new and different way of life for themselves. And the impact of such pursuit on both the northern and southern countries is not to be minimized.

## MIGRATION: IMPACT UPON THE HOST COUNTRY

The period of the massive and encouraged immigrations that characterized the European North-South relationship during the 1960s and early 1970s has gone. During the expansion phase of the European boom period, experts were predicting that the numbers of guestworkers in Europe would continue to rise at a steady pace, perhaps by as many as 500,000 per year through 1980. The Institut National d'Etude Démographiques in Paris provided an estimate that the number of foreign workers in Europe would total 22 million by 1980, a figure that suggested a doubling of the number of workers between 1970 and 1980.

The economic crunch of 1973 suddenly put an end to all such speculations. Almost without exception, the industrial countries of northern Europe introduced stringent restrictions on the further numbers of immigrant workers to be allowed entrance.* (Such controls, of course, could not be placed on any fellow member of the EEC, according to Article 48 of the Treaty of Rome. During the oil crisis and the subsequent recession, no country of the EEC tried either to break or rescind that article.) The industrial countries also implemented regulations to protect the jobs and employment opportunities of their own nationals. In the months following the first political decisions to suspend migration flows into the industrial countries, there were a variety of additional efforts to extend and reinforce such barriers. The result was not an absolute extinguishing of all immigration, but the reduction to such an extent that one might speak of the aftermath as more like a trickle in comparison to the preceeding flood. For example, the number of workers leaving Turkey for Europe dropped from

---

*There is some debate among scholars as to the actual impact of the economic crisis upon the decision of a number of countries of the North to impose bans on further immigration of foreign workers. Hoffmann-Nowotny (1976), OECD (1975a), and Nikolinakos (1975b) all make mention of their belief that the bans were going to be imposed in any event and that the oil crisis simply became a convenient pretext for doing so. Further, Nikolinakos in particular argues that the reasons were not even economic, but political. He suggests that the conditions in the host countries, the gathering resentment against foreign workers, and the concerns about political stability all pushed governments of the North to pursue immigration bans. In the official pronouncements of the governments, however, only economic reasons for the ban have been offered (Federal Republic of Germany 1975).

137,000 in 1973 to 1,600 in 1975. In France, the number of permanent workers admitted dropped from 132,055 in 1973 to 25,591 in 1975.

Neither emigration nor immigration has therefore ceased to be a reality. The European South is still providing workers for the North, but in smaller numbers and occassionally not equal to the number of workers departing for the home countries. The result is a decline in the absolute numbers of workers, though the immigrant populations have remained relatively stable, given the number of both births and family reunions taking place. As to the size and origins of these migration flows between 1973 and 1975, the OECD (1976a, p. 5) has noted:

> In all, the seven principal European emigration countries "exported" slightly under 140,000 workers in 1975, whereas the flow in 1973 had amounted to over 500,000. Moreover, it should be noted that 40 percent of the present flow consists of Italians, who move freely inside the Common Market area, as against only 17 percent in 1973: without the Italians, the flow falls from 424,000 to 81,000 between 1973 and 1975.

Whereas prior to the immigration bans, the discussions among the northern countries were based on the anticipated rise in the numbers of workers coming from the South, the postcrisis/recession view became one of assuming large numbers of migrants would be returning to their homelands, taking their unemployment with them and thus opening up work places for the national labor force (cf. Lohrmann 1975, p. 119). Neither aspect of this anticipated outcome appears to have materialized.

In examining the figures on the numbers of workers returning home, there is evidence of a slight upswing, but the evidence is mixed. With Yugoslavia, for example, the number of returnees actually decreased by 20 percent between 1974 and 1975. The data on the number of returnees to select countries of the European South are contained in Table 2.1.

Two explanations are generally offered for the absence of a large return migration during the economic slowdown of the industrial countries. The first is that the workers decided to stay in Europe for fear that if they did return home, the imposition of stringent immigration bans would foreclose any opportunity they might have to return at a later date and again take work. This view is borne out by that fact that in the post-immigration ban period, large numbers of workers began to send for and reunite with their families in Europe. In France, the numbers of women and children entering the country for purposes of joining the husband or father totaled 203,000 for the three years 1973-75 inclusive. Such figures do not count the members of families of nationals from within the EEC. It would not be unrealistic to assume that nearly one-third of a million persons entered France during that thirty-six-month period for reasons of reunion.

TABLE 2.1

Return of Workers to Countries of the
European South, 1972-75

|  | 1972 | 1973 | 1974 | 1975 |
|---|---|---|---|---|
| Yugoslavia | n.a.* | n.a. | 80,000 | 65,000 |
| Italy | 138,246 | 125,168 | 116,708 | 119,229 |
| Spain | 80,000 | 73,900 | 88,000 | 110,200 |
| Greece | 27,552 | 22,285 | 24,476 | 34,214 |

*data not available.
Source: Organization for Economic Cooperation and Development, SOPEMI Continuous Reporting System on Migration (Paris: OECD, 1976).

The second anticipated impetus for the mass exodus of foreign workers from Europe was based on the view that they would suffer extremely high rates of unemployment during the recession, and that the longer the recession, the more tenuous their economic position in Europe would become. This would be due both to the marginal nature of their employment and the press of nationals for whatever jobs might be available to alleviate their own unemployment. Such a view was not unfounded, based on the experiences of the migrant workers in Europe during the 1966-67 recession (Kudat and Sertel 1974). But nothing of the sort occurred. The unemployment rates for the immigrant workers were generally of the same magnitude as were those for the national work force. In Germany, the overall unemployment figure for 1975 was 4.5 percent, and for the guestworkers, 5.4 percent. In France, the 1975 figures for the nation as a whole and for the migrant workers in particular were 5.0 and 7.5 percent, respectively. Not only do such figures indicate that in Germany 94.6 percent of all migrant workers were employed, but that in comparison, they would have had no reason to assume they were being especially singled out to bear the brunt of the recession. The adage of "last hired, first fired" did not hold true.

What also must be noted with regard to the numbers of workers who stayed in Europe in spite of the economic difficulties is that the unemployed workers were provided with a variety of unemployment payments and services that cushioned the severity of their unemployment, whether they were or were not nationals from EEC countries. Thus vocational training, unemployment benefits, housing allowances, family children's allowances, and medical care were all available. The sum total of such benefits might easily exceed the option for earned income in the home country.

Beyond the specific rationales offered for anticipating a large out-migration of the workers, there was exposed an underlying assumption that, prior to the recession, was never seriously questioned. It was that the workers who came from the South were, in the final analysis, superfluous to the basic economic structures of the various industrial societies. That is, it was nice to have them so as to be able to sustain the rapid growth, but if it became necessary to tighten up the economy, the migrant workers would rather easily be set aside. They were viewed as an industrial army in reserve, able to be called upon in times of need and then dismissed just as easily (cf. Kudat and Özkan 1976, pp. 8-10). But the special characteristics of the foreign unemployment in the European North necessarily draw attention to the fact that these workers did not constitute merely an industrial reserve, but were integral to the functioning of the society. The recession did not lead to large-scale unemployment or expulsion of the migrant workers. They were in reality little or no more affected by the economic downturn than were the national workers. The new immigrant workers had become structurally integrated into the labor markets of the northern countries.

An important question to be raised then, and one to be explored from several perspectives in the chapters to come, is whether it will be possible for the northern European countries, having created an integrated labor market with the immigrant workers, to maintain a separatist (perhaps segregationist) social system. It appears this is what the industrial countries have envisioned, though not on a scale with the apparatus of social control to maintain it as one finds elsewhere. Returning to earlier comments on the center-periphery relationship of the European North-South, the exchange that the North appears to have offered the South has been one of allowing a sizable number of the citizens from the South to come and participate in the economic sector of the North, but not in the cultural, political, or social sectors. Migrants from the periphery countries are to remain on the periphery in the center countries, save for the manner in which they offer their labor.

It is within this context of recognizing a duality of approaches taken by the center countries toward the periphery countries that resorting to a mechanistic application of the principle of equality (as stated by the EEC or otherwise) with the migrant workers vis-a-vis the national workers becomes manifestly inadequate. There are myriad contingencies affecting the lives of the migrant workers that are absent in the lives of the national workers. To attempt to apply uniform and universalistic criteria to situations and conditions of inequality will only perpetuate that division. As has been noted in a recent report of the OECD (1975a, p. 19):

> It is pointless, for example, to state that foreigners can enjoy the same advantages as nationals with regard to working conditions, housing, vocational training or societal security when the conditions of their employment, their length of residence, the restrictions affecting them and the fact of not knowing the language or of having qualifications that are not recognized prevents them from fulfilling the necessary criteria to benefit from these advantages.

What is necessary, suggests the report, is the modification and expansion of social and labor legislation to "restore the balance between economic positions that are too different." This is to be done through a broad program of social action aimed at preventing the "foreigners from being isolated, forming ghettos and finally living on the margin of a society which disregards or perhaps even despises them" (OECD 1975a, p. 19).

The irony of this proposal is that at the very time of its writing, the processes described there were already well under way and entrenched in the host countries. In June of 1973 nearly 40,000 persons were living on the outskirts of Paris in shanty huts made of cardboard and old car doors. There are others across France, in Lyons and Marseilles, and in Naterre. The total estimate of immigrants living in these French shanty towns is at least one million. In the Ruhr region of Germany, the migrant workers in 1970 were allotted the oldest housing; 84 percent had no baths in their flats, 68 percent had no lavatory of their own and 10 percent did not even have one in the house, 8 percent lived in lofts, 6 percent in cellars, 4 percent in barracks, and 2 percent in sheds. Sixteen percent of the families lived in one room and as many as 39 percent lived in two rooms. This was while the Germans in the area averaged 0.79 persons per room. Despite this accumulation of deprivation, the immigrant population of the Ruhr region was paying on the average one-third more rent than were the nationals (Power 1975).

Data such as the above would suggest that it is important to consider the contributions of the migrant workers as multidimensional rather than simply the single factor of supplying labor. And even the consideration of what labor is supplied and what jobs are performed that nationals would choose not to do is important. Every economy has the "dirty work" jobs that have to be carried out—jobs that are dangerous, dirty, temporary, dead-end, undignified, and menial. The large labor pool provided by the presence of the migrant workers generates a willing—or rather, unable to be unwilling—contingent of workers to perform the tasks at generally low wages (cf. Schiller and Diefenbach 1975, p. 120). These tasks must be done, and the presence of the migrant workers to do them frees the national work force to take higher paying and "cleaner" employment that tends not to be dangerous, dirty, or temporary. In short, the presence of the migrant workers provides an underclass for the host society that of itself generates social and economic mobility for the national labor force. Hoffmann-Nowotny (1976, p. 10) refers to this creation of a new societal stratum beneath the existing social structure of the immigrant country as a process of *Unterschichtung*. He notes:

> This stratum is ethnically different, its members have no political rights and, with regard to stratum characteristics, they do not conform to the general development level of the immigration country. This means first that the social distances existing in the society increase and second that a highly developed society has again to deal with problems specific to different, i.e., lower levels of development, problems which were believed to have been resolved long ago.

A variety of other contributions can be noted which are made by the migrants for the benefit of the host society. First, the migrants make use of goods and materials otherwise no longer useful because of their perceived undesirability on the part of the national population. Thus, as is evident from the housing data from the Ruhr, to live in cellars, sheds, or barracks prolongs the usefulness and, thus, the economic benefits from accommodations otherwise empty. The same can be said for the migrants' use of deteriorating automobiles and buildings in the central cities. Second, the migrants subsidize many activities that benefit the nationals, be it in providing domestics, or more generally working for lower wages that maintain lower prices, thus freeing a larger proportion of the incomes of the nations than would be possible if wages were paid to local labor to perform the tasks. Finally, the presence of the migrant workers generates a number of additional jobs for the national population in several occupations and professions, both legal and illegal. Teachers, social workers, immigration personnel, transportation workers, and those who provide entertainment services (bars, restaurants, theaters, and so forth) all find additional employment as a result of the presence of the migrant workers. So also do those who are involved in or on the border of illegal activities, that is, transportation of illegal migrants, prostitution, gambling, and providing services to new arrivals for fees, for such services as the location of housing, employment, or schooling for the children.

Several attempts have been made to apply economic cost-benefit analysis to the presence of the migrant workers in Europe. For Germany, the first such studies came with respect to the "value" lost to the German Democratic Republic (GDR) and gained by the Federal Republic of Germany (FRG) with the net migration from the GDR to the FRG of more than 3 million people. Blitz (1976) reviews this series of studies, all of which point to major gains by the FRG. One study suggests that the FRG gained more than 22.5 billion Deutsch Marks (DM) (in 1962 prices) through prior investments by the GDR in this population with respect to education and subsistence. Another estimate places the figure for all refugees from the GDR from the end of World War II until the time of the erection of the Wall in 1961 at a total value of DM 28.5 billion (again in 1962 prices). Taking into account not only the prior investments by the GDR in that population group, but also the gains to the FRG resulting from higher productivity, better utilization of capital, and greater opportunities for the use of occupational qualifications, the estimates of benefits to the FRG then rise to more than DM 36 billion in 1962 prices. At 1976 prices, the figure would be approximately DM 55 billion. Kindleberger (1967, p. 28) observed:

> The expellees and refugees constituted one of the finest sources of additional labor in all Europe. They were skilled in much higher proportions than the unemployed, peasants, and foreign workers. To the extent that the Peoples Republic was antagonistic to middle class people, the proportion of professional and managerial person-

nel among these classes was probably higher than those of West Germany. They were much more assimilable than the foreign workers.

With respect to a longer time frame and one that includes the rapid influx of migrants from the European South, Blitz's (1976) own assessment is that the economic benefits to Germany have been nothing less than extraordinary. Having developed a model to account for prior investments by the home countries in education and subsistence, the cumulative net annual investment created by the pool of freed resources not having had to be spent on the migrants in the host country, as well as the costs of immigration borne by the FRG, he is able to compute a figure suggesting the net benefit of immigration to West Germany. Relying on 1962 as the benchmark for the worth of the DM, he provides the following computations of what has accrued to the FRG on a yearly basis:

| Year | DM |
| --- | --- |
| 1961 | 6,380,470,000 |
| 1963 | 4,667,100,000 |
| 1965 | 7,759,230,000 |
| 1967 | 13,381,280,000 |
| 1969 | 15,498,630,000 |
| 1971 | 13,225,680,000 |
| 1973 | 8,316,710,000 |

It is with figures such as these in mind that one begins to have a sense of the economic impact of the massive postwar migrations into the countries of northern Europe. Further, hidden behind these figures are the implications for the host societies in terms of general development, growth in the well-being of the members of the society, the increasing strength and status of their currencies on international money markets, the influencing of policies of international organizations due to the higher subsidies offered by the center countries, and countless other examples. In the next section, attention will be focused upon the impacts of migration for a very different set of countries—those who have exported their labor. These are the countries of the South, the periphery region where benefits are scarce, problems plentiful, and few solutions in sight.

## MIGRATION: IMPACT UPON THE SENDING COUNTRIES

Through the 1960s and early 1970s the assumption was widespread that the largely government-promoted exodus of workers from the countries of the Mediterranean basin was beneficial, and totally so, for the emigration countries. It was believed by officials in these less developed areas of the European South that migration had many advantages and few costs. As Böhning (1975a) has indicated, there were essentially three basic components that justified the support of manpower migration by the sending countries. The first of these was that migration could help reduce internal unemployment and underemployment problems by removing some of the stress of the acute imbalance between the working population and the available employment opportunities. Emigration meant countries could export their unemployment to the industrial countries who desperately sought additional manpower.

A second basis for the support of emigration was that with the large remittances sent home by the migrant workers, it was expected that emigration countries would be the recipients of a significant foreign exchange income which would be valuable both for equalizing the balance-of-trade deficits accruing to the countries of the South and for making capital available for internal productive investment. It was this latter activity, productive investment in the national economy, that the South thought would make possible the beginnings of their own development and, over time, make sufficient employment opportunities available to their own people, thus negating the need for migration.

The final aspect of the benefits thought to be inherent in supporting the emigration of labor was that the workers abroad would be receiving valuable industrial training, thus raising their qualifications, expertise, and working capacity. The acquirement of industrial sector skills along with the assimilation of values inherent in the developed countries were thought to be of critical importance for the emigration countries. This was to be one-half of the combination necessary for development to take place: skilled workers were to be matched with the newly created employment opportunities generated through productive investment.

Viewed in this context, emigration was thought to be a transitional process necessary for the developing countries as they worked to modernize their societies. Migration would be increasingly unnecessary as the local economy grew stronger and able to absorb available workers. Furthermore, the creation of an industrial sector in the emigration countries would mean that their workers would no longer have to go abroad to learn the necessary industrial skills. The need for migration was thought to be in direct correlation to the developmental gap. As the gap was closed, the need of further emigration would be correspondingly reduced. What follows in this section is a brief assessment of the above-listed three factors of Böhning and an analysis of their relative contributions to the development of the emigration countries.

## Migration and Labor Force Employment

For the countries of the European South, most of which have had serious structural deficiencies in their labor markets resulting in high levels of both unemployment and underemployment, migration was thought to be beneficial mainly through diminishing the surpluses in the labor force. Outward migrations, by reducing employment pressure, would help to lessen labor tensions, maintain social cohesion, and encourage the possibilities of economic growth. However, as

Mendez and Moro (1976, p. 8) note in their assessment of a variety of studies on this matter, migration has not even in the short term solved the problem of safeguarding a labor market eroded by concealed unemployment and underemployment. It is their assessment that "this enormous drain that the current international movements of manpower have meant on the total human resources available in the emigration countries has had and still has clearly adverse consequences in the progress towards achieving the objectives of a balanced and harmonious economic and social development."

To assume that emigration is beneficial to the sending countries through relief of pressure on the remaining population of available workers presupposes one important condition: that the characteristics of the remaining workers are conducive to the development process and that these workers are able to participate effectively in these efforts. But such an assumption is open to serious question. Emigration is a selective and negative process which hinders rather than assists the development prospects. It is selective as to age (it is the young men and adults who leave), as to sex (most emigrants are men), and as to working capacity (the most competent, strong and ambitious). The emigration flows of the past decade or more have generated geographic and demographic imbalances within the emigration countries, both in the rural and urban areas. The adverse effects upon regional development become acute when large segments of the manpower force leave the area. As Kayser has noted (1971, p. 37),

> Emigration is in no way a simple answer to local overpressure. It does not create more favorable conditions for development, nor does it contribute to interregional homogeneity. On the contrary, as a product and consequence of capitalist growth, it supports and creates support for the law of inequality.

In the rural areas, which contribute in large measure to the migratory flows, emigration has a number of adverse effects. One of prime concern is that some rural population centers are undergoing a profound change in their demographic makeup, even to the extent of becoming uninhabited. The basic structures of rural areas change as the population decline results in a direct loss of potentially available manpower. The effect of this is a reduction in land utilization, which might result as well in a condition of lower food production and ultimately a decrease in exports with consequent repercussions on the balance of payments (cf. Böhning 1975a). And the cycle is completed as the governments encourage yet more emigration in hopes of redressing the deficit in the balance of trade through increased remittances sent home from the new workers abroad.

This loss of rural manpower also results in mechanization and the subsequent consolidation of small farms by large agricultural enterprises. They in turn offer few employment opportunities for those agricultural workers who do remain or for those of rural backgrounds who might wish to return there after their time abroad. These processes accentuate the general slide toward greater rural impoverishment and regional imbalance of the emigration countries, thus further fueling the forces of emigration for potential workers.* One additional aspect of this emigration that hinders the potential for development among the countries of the South is noted by Abadan-Unat et al. (1976, p. 3):

> Mediterranean lands are for the most part characterized by dispersed settlements: scattered villages can only be provided with an infrastructure at excessive costs and in isolation are hardly viable economic entities. The demographic erosion attendant on international migration hinders the emergence of rural growth centers and lessens the likelihood of their development, even when roads, electrical power and availability of resources have been assured.

In the urban areas, the emigration of semiskilled, skilled, and specialist workers has also had a serious impact upon the development potential of the emigration countries. Large holes are left in the urban labor markets with the departures of these groups of workers, gaps that are difficult to fill with those who remain. The replacement costs are high in lost productivity, job training periods, wage pressures, and the inflated costs of producing a particular item.

---

*Though it is perhaps jumping ahead a bit in this analysis, it is worth noting that Power (1975, pp. 35-36) sees the reversal of this trend through an emphasis upon the development of the rural sector of the sending countries as central to any resolution of their current plight. He has written:

> Once we begin to dismantle the engine of economic development we find at least three other major related faults. There is the problem of unemployment and underemployment. In some Third World countries unemployment rates run as high as 40 percent. There is the problem of income distribution. All the indications are that when there has been rapid economic growth and urbanization, the new wealth instead of easing the social condition has worsened it—increasing the disparities between men, indeed in some countries even making the poor poorer. And towering above all these problems is the food crisis—the result of years of neglect of the rural sector coupled with the mushrooming growth of population.
> 
> The real tragedy behind these interlocking faults is the missed opportunity. The fact is that if emphasis were given to developing the countryside—not the countryside of the landowner, the estate, the latifundia, but that of the small independent farmer—these problems could be dealt with simultaneously. Already we know about agricultural techniques to get the smallholder to raise his productivity so that by 1985 his yields would be increasing at 5 percent per year. But this depends on certain bottlenecks being removed: archaic land tenure arrangements, lack of credit, poor research and extension services, unproductive agricultural techniques, shortage of fertilizer and water supply and an underdeveloped rural-industrial sector.

Emigration thus involves special costs of some magnitude for those who do not emigrate, for it is they who bear the burden for the support of public services, increased costs for the purchasing of local products, the dampening of options for local development, and lost opportunities for gaining international competitiveness and the generation of additional employment. In fact, the emigration of skilled workers from the industrial sector "strikes the country of departure at the very heart of its development efforts, and one of the fundamental problems that it causes is the shortage of skilled workers and the abundance of unskilled workers " (Böhning 1975a, p. 265).

In assessing the relation of migration and labor force employment in the emigration countries, the conclusion is clear. The situation for the sending countries has not evolved as they anticipated it would. Most basically, it is because this vision of the role of emigration in enhancing the development of the European South floundered on the hard rock of reality—*that labor as an export product could not alleviate nor remedy underdevelopment. What the exportation of labor resulted in was the solidification of a set of asymmetrical relations between the emigration and immigration countries.* With the receiving countries in a clear position of dominance and thus able to control the ebb and flow of migrations, the emigration countries have been in no position to forecast their own internal development needs because the decisions that predetermine these needs are made elsewhere. A five-year development plan begun in any of the European South countries in 1972, and predicated upon the assumption of a steady stream of workers leaving the country for the North and a stream of workers likewise returning from the industrial countries with new skills and experiences, would have had to be scuttled within the first 12 months. What has emerged since 1973 has been both the generation of a tremendous backlog of persons wishing to emigrate to the North, but finding no opportunity to do so with the existing immigration bans, and the simultaneous decision on the part of those already in the North to remain for a longer period of time. Some indication of the magnitude of the backlog that has been building is to note that for a period of 12 months beyond the 1973 immigration ban, Germany continued to receive applications at its recruiting offices in Turkey for those interested in emigration. At the end of this period, a total of nearly 1.4 million Turks had requested immigration visas to go to work in Germany (Bodenbender 1976, p. 12).

There is a final comment to be made with regard to the role of migration and labor force employment in the home countries. It is that even when there are opportunities within the emigration countries for industrial and technological employment (for example, in Yugoslavia and Finland), these opportunities are not sufficient to check a considerable exodus to nearby countries (for example, Sweden and Germany) where there exist employment markets that offer higher wages and more desirable working conditions (cf. Allefresde 1972). In what has essentially become an international competition for manpower, the countries of the South face an exceedingly difficult situation both to hold their present work force and to attract back those currently working in more developed economies. The end result is the continual aggravation of the imbalances between the North and the South.

## Migration and Remittances

In the debates over the various costs and benefits to the emigration countries of exporting large numbers of their workers to other countries, there appears to be one point on which most analysts agree: that the remittances of the migrant worker have been a positive asset to the emigration countries. The effects were expected to be positive in several ways. First, these payments would provide the much needed and unencumbered capital for productive investment in the national economy. Second, such funds would have a positive effect upon the balance-of-trade payments, offsetting the deficits accumulated through the importing of millions of dollars of finished products from the countries of the North (cf. Paine 1974, pp. 114-18). Third, the remittances would allow for the individual worker to upgrade his standard of living upon his return home through a variety of investments and purchases of goods, housing, autos, and appliances. Finally, the transfer of funds provided a means by which to supplement the earnings and resources of what were frequently the poorer sections of the society, those from the rural areas. With the lack of an adequate social security system in many of the countries of the South, the provision of these remittances became the margin between sufficiency and insufficiency for countless tens of thousands of families. There is little wonder, given these assumptions, that the countries of emigration have thought remittances to be of unquestionable importance and have sought ways to sustain and encourage yet additional transfer of these funds.*

Table 2.2 provides some indication of the magnitude of the remittances moving from the European North to the South. Some caution should be exercised in interpreting the data, for they do not account for all forms of remittances—only those transferred by banks or savings institutions, or through postal money orders. There is no way of knowing, for example, how much money was simply mailed home in the form of endorsed checks, or brought back with the worker on home visits or at the time of final remigration. Thus the data pre-

---

*One manifestation of the importance attached to these remittances by the emigration countries was made evident to the author during his visit (December 1976) to the Turkish Embassy in Bonn, Germany. In the center of the large reception room on the main floor there was a table stacked with literally hundreds of the forms workers would use at their banks in Germany to have funds transferred to Turkey. There was no other material whatsoever in the entire room, not so much as a travel poster or picture of the prime minister, simply the remittance forms.

TABLE 2.2

Transfers of Funds by Emigrants to
Home Countries of the European South
(in millions of U.S. dollars)

|  | 1970 | 1971 | 1972 | 1973 | 1974 | 1975 |
|---|---|---|---|---|---|---|
| Turkey | 273 | 471 | 740 | 1,183 | 1,426 | 1,300 |
| Greece | 243 | 458 | 567 | 735 | 645 | 734 |
| Yugoslavia | 440 | 650 | 790 | 1,398 | 1,621 | 1,695 |
| Italy | – | – | – | 844 | 753 | 979 |
| Spain | 467 | 548 | 599 | 1,185 | 1,070 | 969 |
| Portugal | 324 | 456 | 596 | 1,025 | 1,100 | 690 |
| Morocco | – | – | 152 | 243 | 372 | 516 |
| Total | 1,797 | 2,583 | 3,444 | 6,613 | 6,987 | 6,983 |

Note: Abadan-Unat et al. (1976, p. 380) make the following comment with regard to the slight decline in remittances to Turkey in 1975: "The drop is perhaps to be attributed to unemployment abroad for some Turkish workers and concern for the near future among them and many others. There is no doubt that the reunion of increasing numbers of Turkish families abroad, encouraged by integration policies in host countries, will in the long run further reduce quantities of foreign exchange remitted to Turkey from Europe."

Source: Organization for Economic Cooperation and Development, The OECD and International Migration (Paris: OECD, 1975); Organization for Economic Cooperation and Development, SOPEMI Continuous Reporting System on Migration (Paris: OECD, 1975, 1976).

sented here should be viewed as a conservative estimate of the total funds transferred by the migrant workers.

Within the limitations of the available data, it is possible to assess the impact of the remittances upon the balance of trade payments for the emigration countries.* The findings would bear out the contention that remittances

---

*Though much is made of the benefits to the emigration countries through the remittance of savings by their workers who are abroad, it is important to note that these same savings also provide large benefits to the host countries as well. There is some evidence that

serve as a near equalizer to the deficits accumulated in other sectors of these societies. Nikolinakos (1975b, p. 15) suggests from his analysis that the impact of remittances upon the trade balance in the European South is the "only positive effect of emigration." Table 2.3 provides for selected countries of the South some data on the relation of remittances to the balance of payments. Again, caution is necessary in interpreting these data, for they provide at best a conservative estimate of the impact of remittances upon the economy of the home countries.

A somewhat different assessment than that offered by Nikolinakos regarding the impact of remittances upon the balance of trade payments is offered by Böhning (1975a, p. 266). He acknowledges that the flow of foreign currency has eased trade deficits in some countries, that it has boosted consumption, but it has hardly had an impact upon the need for productive investment. When the transfer of money ceases, the countries will have gained little. He notes:

> Mechanically adding remittances to the trade deficit makes even less sense than mechanically subtracting emigrants from the unemployed, quite apart from the possibly inflationary repercussions of such an inflow of disposable income. On the individual level remittances are used in the first instance to cater for daily needs or to pay off old debts. A continuing inflow subsequently goes for consumer goods sometimes of quite a fancy kind and often of foreign origin. None of this expenditure is more than marginally productive. In macro-economic terms, the foreign currency tends to be used wherever there is no strict control of imports, to pay for imports of foreign consumer goods, sometimes by the non-migrant population, and by recipients of remittances. This tendency leaves little if any room for domestic productive investment.

The consequence is that little money is added to the industrial sector. Rather, the money flow, as Böhning suggests, has tended to gravitate toward the building or tertiary sector of the economy.

As with other aspects of the emigration/immigration relation, concern has begun to be expressed over the adverse effects of these remittances on the emigration countries. It has been suggested that these funds are seldom used in con-

---

more immigrant workers keep their savings in the banks of the host countries than in the banks of their home countries. Kudat et al. (1974, p. 119) report that a larger percentage of workers had their savings in German banks than in either Turkish or Yugoslav banks. While 37.6 and 41.9 percent of the Turkish and Yugoslav workers had savings in home banks, 41.0 and 58.7 percent, respectively, had savings in German institutions. This fact contributes to the further intensification of the power of European capital and its ability to enhance the very processes that remittances home were to counteract through plans of national development.

TABLE 2.3

Relation of Emigrants' Remittances to Balance-of-Trade Payment in Selected Countries of the European South, 1969-74
(in millions of U.S. dollars)

|  | 1969 | 1970 | 1971 | 1972 | 1973 | 1974 |
|---|---|---|---|---|---|---|
| Portugal |  |  |  |  |  |  |
| a. Balance of trade, import/export | -214 | -390 | -492 | -414 | -564 | — |
| b. Emigrants' remittances | +266 | +324 | +456 | +596 | +740 | +1,100 |
| c. Compensation rate* | 124.29 | 83.0 | 92.6 | 143.9 | 131.2 | — |
| Turkey |  |  |  |  |  |  |
| a. Balance of trade, import/export | -264 | -359 | -494 | -678 | -796 | -2,245 |
| b. Emigrants' remittances | +141 | +273 | +471 | +740 | +1,183 | +1,426 |
| c. Compensation rate | 53.2 | 76.0 | 95.4 | 109.2 | 153.8 | 63.5 |
| Spain |  |  |  |  |  |  |
| a. Balance of trade, import/export | -926 | -580 | +88 | -295 | -856 | — |
| b. Emigrants' remittances | +400 | +467 | +548 | +599 | +913 | +1,070 |
| c. Compensation rate | 43.2 | 80.5 | 622.7 | 203.0 | 106.6 | — |
| Greece |  |  |  |  |  |  |
| a. Balance of trade, import/export | -636 | -763 | -833 | -949 | -1,919 | — |
| b. Emigrants' remittances | +277 | +243 | +458 | +567 | +735 | +645 |
| c. Compensation rate | 43.5 | 31.8 | 54.9 | 59.7 | 38.3 | — |

*b as percent of a.

Sources: Organization for Economic Cooperation and Development, The OECD and International Migration (Paris: OECD, 1975); N. Abadan-Unat et al., Migration and Development (Ankara: Ajans-Turk Press, 1976), p. 102.

vertible deposit accounts as a means of investing in savings (OECD 1976a); that they may "cause serious upsets in the development of the system and even permanent inflationary tensions" (OECD 1975a, p. 28); or that they may, in the analysis of a study prepared for the Intergovernmental Committee of European Migration (Mendez and Moro 1976, p. 11)

> cause structural distortion whether these migrant investments are non-productive—investment in housing, domestic equipment, the purchase of land without proper plans for exploiting it—or whether they are productive and are used in adequately financed or less profitable sectors such as small service activities—for example, small transport or taxi companies, modest hotels or shops.

In an effort to overcome these present shortcomings in the use of remittances, a series of objectives has been suggested to utilize more effectively this vast source of capital. The efforts have included attracting yet additional funds from the emigrants through such schemes as offering high rates of interest and/or high flexibility in the utilization of the funds (cf. Schiller 1975); through the channeling of savings into productive investments by means of both direct and indirect measures (Mendez and Moro 1976); through the channeling of the emigrants' savings into activities capable of increasing employment opportunities for the emigrants upon their return to their home countries (OECD 1974); and finally, utilizing this capital essentially as "seed money" to attract foreign investments into the emigration countries, thus generating new employment opportunities both for those who did migrate as well as for those who did not (Marshall 1974). What is inherent in all these proposals is that the use of remittances must be incorporated within a coherent development plan and always accompanied by adequate programming and technical assistance (cf. Bonhedji 1974, p. 57). The fact that these conditions do not exist in the South suggests that the effective management of the remittances is likely to lag and that with each passing moment, the countries of the South lose both precious time and resources in their efforts to develop and begin to partake of the industrial feast.

In an effort to assess the current situation with regard to the role and impact of remittances and to suggest what means are necessary for their more effective utilization within the countries of the South, the OECD (1975a, pp. 28-29) has provided the following summary:

> 1. The measures adopted by the emigration countries have been aimed principally at increasing the flow of savings, hence the rather secondary nature of the efforts made to guide the utilization of these savings.
> 2. These efforts have included encouragement for house purchasing as well as for farming, crafts, and trade, but only Yugoslavia and Turkey have endeavored in different ways to promote direct investment of these savings in business of any size.

3. The consequences of this action on the creation of jobs have therefore been quite marginal, and in some cases distortions have occurred or increased.
4. These measures should therefore be reviewed in order:
   a) to ensure that the creation of new businesses by former migrants fits in with a strategy of rational development of the small enterprise;
   b) to support co-operative ventures that are recognized as valid;
   c) to prevent house purchasing from becoming speculation or from proliferating in areas which have no future;
   d) to enable migrants to invest their savings in industrial enterprises whose expansion can contribute towards the country's development;
   e) to amend the banking, tax, and customs legislation to this end and the technical methods of granting loans and finance;
   f) to provide migrants and groups of migrants who wish to invest their savings in businesses recognized as useful for employment purposes with assistance in the administrative, tax, technical, professional and other fields;
   g) to ask immigration countries to contribute towards these efforts, particularly with regard to i) vocational training, ii) the management of small enterprises and co-operatives, and iii) the creation by migrants of funds to finance ventures in their home country.

## MIGRATION AND THE RETURN HOME

In assessing the impact of the emigration/immigration relation of the European North and South, it has generally been claimed that the benefits to the emigration countries would accrue in two stages. The first is that described above and includes reducing unemployment in the home country, providing a setting for the learning of industrial skills and values, and accumulating savings in the home country through the use of remittances. It has been noted that all three parts to this benefit package are open to question and there are serious reservations as to whether they in fact do constitute benefits to the emigration country.

The second stage of the rewards of emigration for the home countries was to begin with the return of the workers (cf. Council of Europe 1975). It has been posited that the returning migrant worker would make an individual contribution to the economic and social development of his country of origin by being a catalyst to the support of modernization. Such a view is based on the belief that social and economic development can be directly influenced by individual behaviors (cf. Pekin 1975). This assumption is not supported by available evidence. To the contrary, the process of modernization and development is one in which practically every action in political, economic, and social terms is guided and directed by a very small sector of modern political elites, be they in business, government, or the military. It is, in fact, the latter group which in many countries of the European South plays the key role in defining, directing, and executing the policies of modernization (cf. Horowitz 1972).

But even if the contrary evidence were put aside and it were assumed that there is a possibility for the cumulative influencing by individuals of the modernization process in the emigration countries, there is the immediate problem of recognizing that only a small portion of all returning migrants are in a position to contribute to the implementation of the desired standards and values in the cultural, organizational, and professional sectors in their countries of origin. The typology of returnees developed by Cerase (1974) should elucidate this analysis. He characterizes the reasons for returning as follows:

> 1. *Return of Failure*: This is the category of worker, mainly rural, working in an inferior and tenuous position abroad, who returns to his home country essentially as he left. He was not economically integrated into the host country and experienced few or no opportunities for learning or up-grading his employment credentials.
> 2. *Return of Conservatism*: This is the group of workers who have made some success of the migration, but who have maintained their traditional standards and rules of conduct. They frequently choose to return due to their perception of an erosion in the values they thought important in their children or spouse. Their goal was primarily to make some stipulated sum of money and return to establish a small business, usually in the service sector.
> 3. *Return of Retirement*: If an emigrant had reached retirement age or had reached an age where he found further efforts at the adaptation to the host country more difficult than the perceived benefits, he is likely to return to be among friends and enjoy in his home country what pension or savings he might have accrued.
> 4. *Return of Innovation*: This is the group most sought after by the home country for when they do return, they are that group of workers who during their time abroad up-graded their employment skills, acquired new attitudes with regard to employment and modernization, and returned with the intention of using their new qualifications to find a better place for themselves in their home country.

In assessing the characteristics of those who do return home, what is immediately evident is that the factors of selectivity operate here just as they did among those who first emigrated. The evidence from an extensive survey of returnees in Turkey (Abadan-Unat et al. 1976) suggests that those emigrants who had achieved positions of skilled, semiskilled, or specialist worker were those who tended to stay for the longer periods in the host countries. It was that group at the other end of the continuum (group 1 in Cerase's typology) who were most willing to return home and who did so more quickly and after a shorter length of stay in the North. Such selectivity in the intentions of the

Turkish workers has also been confirmed in a study in Berlin by Kudat et al. (1974). A factor that further differentiated the groups as to their desire to stay in the host countries was that those workers who had been successful in securing relatively stable and profitable employment were also those who were most active in bringing their families from the home country to be reunited in the host country (Kudat and Özkan 1976).

There are several other aspects of this assumed relation of individual return and societal development that deserve mention. The first is that since the emigration countries, locked in the center-periphery relation noted earlier, could not affect their own development in such a way as to reduce the distance separating them from the industrialized countries of the North, they have been unable to provide the employment opportunities that would encourage the remigration of their workers who have been successful abroad. What this implies for successful workers is that to return home would be to subject themselves to employment risks they had overcome in the first place by leaving the home country. As an OECD report of 1975 described the situation, "The majority of migrants returned to a society and productive structures over which they had practically no influence and in which they could only be re-integrated on similar terms to those they had experienced before their departure" (OECD 1975a, p. 23). Such conditions mitigate against the home countries in their efforts to lure back the innovative workers, the only group who truly would be of benefit in the development process.

A second point is that the expectations of the emigration countries regarding skills their workers would be able to acquire in the immigration appear to have been quite unrealistic. A number of studies have confirmed that the emigrant workers end up with the unskilled and undesired positions within the economy of the host countries (Kudat and Özkan 1976; OECD 1975a; Mendez and Moro 1976; and Bundesanstalt für Arbeit 1972). As but one example of the creation of a homogeneous emigrant work force largely concentrated in the lower echelon positions within the host society, consider Table 2.4 taken from Kudat and Özkan (1976, p. 25). It indicates that the degree of the compression of the emigrant work force upon its arrival in Germany is only slightly modified even after an average length of stay of more than four years. The study was conducted among a sample of Turkish workers who had lived in Berlin as their last residence before returning home.

Taken in the context of the previous comments about the selectivity of returnees to the home country, data such as these suggest that the countries of the South will experience severe difficulties in being able to move toward the modernization of their countries, should they rely too heavily on the belief in the critical role of their workers abroad who have achieved skilled status. What is apparent, on the contrary, is that not only do skilled workers constitute only 30 percent of the total of all workers, but it is exactly this group that is least likely to return to the home country. Thus a relatively small population is made even smaller by the attraction of the options and standard of living in the north-

TABLE 2.4

Type of Employment in Turkey and in Germany

| Qualification | In Turkey Number of Workers | Percent | First Job in Germany Number of Workers | Percent | Last Job in Germany Number of Workers | Percent |
|---|---|---|---|---|---|---|
| Unemployed | 527 | 33.7 | – | – | 12 | 0.8 |
| Unskilled | 229 | 14.6 | 1258 | 80.4 | 1093 | 69.8 |
| Skilled | 216 | 13.8 | 246 | 15.7 | 364 | 23.3 |
| Foreman | 252 | 16.1 | 36 | 2.3 | 67 | 4.3 |
| Clerical | 158 | 10.1 | 12 | 0.8 | 29 | 1.9 |
| Housewife | – | – | – | – | – | – |
| Farmer | 145 | 9.3 | – | – | – | – |
| Own shop | 33 | 2.1 | – | – | – | – |
| Other | 5 | 0.3 | – | – | – | – |
| No data | – | – | 13 | 0.8 | – | – |
| Total | 1,565 | 100.0 | 1,565 | 100.0 | 1,565 | 100.0 |

Source: A. Kudat and Y. Özkan, Internal and External Migration Effects on the Experience of Foreign Workers in Europe (Berlin: Wissenschaftszentrum, 1976), p. 25.

ern countries. And it is almost as if the cycle of dependency is completed when one notes that Kudat and Özkan (1976, p. 139) posit that for the countries of the South to move toward the development they aspire to have, they will have to use scare capital to *import* the necessary skilled workers, since they cannot count on the return of their own countrymen who have achieved such skills while abroad!

Another inference from Table 2.4 that should be noted is that, with the process of employment homogenization that occurs while in the immigrant countries, the workers have little or no opportunity to practice their original skills and thus tend to lose them. Upon their return, they have neither retained the skills with which they departed for the North, nor have they gained new credentials sufficient to find them employment in a sector different from what they previously occupied. A response to this marginality, and one that is counterproductive to the goals of modernization, is the frequent retreat into a small, personalized one-man operation of running a taxi, restaurant, farm, or store (cf. Böhning 1975b, p. 35). And what such operations result in is not only the creation of oversupply in an initially small service sector, but the draining off of valuable savings and remittances for an activity with no growth potential and no means of enhancing productive investment.

Linking back to comments made earlier in this chapter, it is evident from this table that support is given to the contention that a sizable portion of the migration from the European South is derived from the extremely high levels of unemployment that exist there. In this particular sample, fully one-third of the migrants were unemployed at the time of their departure for Germany. Data such as these have been behind the contention that migration is of benefit to the emigration countries, both at the level of macro-economics and in terms of personal betterment. Not only are the countries of the South able to export their unemployment to the North, but for each of the individuals concerned, those who were unemployed, emigrated, and found work thus improved their lot. But as has been noted, such benefits have their costs as well. The understandings of European migration that existed only a short decade ago have been drastically altered.

The inferences drawn from Table 2.4 cannot be left without a word of caution. There are several matters on which Kudat and Özkan are quiet and thus interpretations are guarded. First, they do not say how long the last job was held by the returnees, nor how many other jobs were held in the interim. Thus it is difficult to have a clear picture of the employment activities of the sample. Second, it must be kept in mind, noting earlier comments on the propensity of certain segments of the migrant labor force to return more readily and quickly than others, that this sample is most likely skewed toward the "returnees of failure." This should not then be taken as a representative sample of the extent of mobility among the migrant workers, for the very group experiencing the most mobility is that group least likely to be included in a returnee sample.

Finally, in the absence of comparative data (which are admittedly difficult to obtain) it is not possible to know whether the characteristics of those migrants who return from Berlin are different in any fundamental way from those who return from other parts of Germany. The sample is of such magnitude that one might assume sufficient latitude in the tapping of those with different experiences and backgrounds, but one is not certain of having done so. Keeping these reservations regarding the data in mind, the general outlines remain the same: that a significant percentage of those who do emigrate with the hopes of experiencing greater occupational and employment options are disappointed and return with much the same skills as when they left, if they are fortunate.

## NORTH-SOUTH MIGRATION: PATTERNS AND PROSPECTS

In the period since the European North initiated policies aimed at the deliberate halting of migratory flows from the European South, the pattern of previous migrations has been severely ruptured. Immigration flows to the industrial countries of Europe, halted by the bans of 1973 and 1974, have very nearly dried up. More precisely, they have stabilized at a very low level in comparison to prior periods. With this occurrence, the focus of attention in the North with regard to manpower migration has shifted away from a concern with flows and toward the twin issues of the nature of the supply of workers in the various countries and the reshaping of their respective migration policies. As the OECD (1976a, pp. 5-6) has noted:

> All in all, the number of foreign workers in Europe did not fall appreciably in 1975; from one end of the year to the other, it appears to have declined from 6.5 million to about 6.3 million (before the recession, in 1973, the SOPEMI estimate put this number at 7.5 million). But does the variation not now depend on domestic resources (the natural growth of foreign manpower) as much as, or still more than, on external flows? In point of fact, the reduction in the number of immigrant workers is appreciable only in Switzerland and Germany and, even there, the *restructuring* of the foreign population seems to be more significant than its reduction: irregular variations depending upon nationality, contrasting trends according to sex and age, and even a slight tendency to concentrate in the tertiary sector.
>
> In all countries there is still a ban on the recruitment of foreign manpower, apart from the free movement areas and a few individual derogations, and there is every reason to believe that this will continue for the next few years. But the inability of the public authorities and the enterprises to go on using immigration as a means of influencing the labor market made some important changes necessary: development of the labor force now depends essentially on the mobilization of domestic reserves rather than recourse abroad.

One might add that there are several other important changes that have been made necessary as a result of the ban on further immigration of migrant workers. First, the manner in which European countries have approached the concepts of surplus and shortage regarding manpower, and the achievement of their balance through a marketing of migration flows, has become more and more questionable. The pre-immigration ban view of labor as an expendable and expandable industrial reserve army seems open to serious challenge, which leads to point two: the original requirements of a transient labor force brought in to meet a particular economic need have turned into an overall necessity of the economic systems in the North. Migration has exposed structural deficiencies in the economies of the North and forestalled systemic efforts at dealing with them by moving in and filling that vacuum. Thus the migrants have become a key component of the current economic arrangements and have themselves become a structural phenomenon that could be dislodged only at the peril of the entire economic apparatus now in place. It is for this reason that the host countries have begun to speak of the necessity of dealing with the integration of the workers and their families.

Third, the recourse in the European North for future needs so far as foreign manpower is concerned is likely to be effected less through additional recruitments abroad than through the utilization of the ever-increasing numbers of families that have come to join the workers. In particular, it will be the second-generation immigrants, the sons and daughters of the workers now in the North who will fill a significant number of the employment opportunities open to foreign labor. But the lurking danger in such an arrangement is that with the integration into the host cultures, these sons and daughters will hold values more like those of the native work force so far as employment expectations are concerned and thus not to be content with the dirty, dreary, and dead-end jobs taken by their parents (cf. Schrader, Nikles, and Griese 1976). The contradictions between integration and discrimination will become even more apparent with this forthcoming generation if no positive steps are taken by government and employees to ensure the presence of occupational and educational options greater than those available at present.

Finally, it appears that the industrial countries are rapidly moving toward a basic decision that will govern their economic and manpower policies for the foreseeable future. The options appear to be either a continuing reliance on a sector of the manpower force that is set apart and constrained as to its role and ability to participate in the host country, or giving up this use of migrant labor and designing new employment structures that remodel the productive apparatus. Initially, the ban on further migration appeared to be precipitating this decision, but then the actions of the host countries to encourage the reuniting of families postponed the decision date. The presence of additional family members and the potential numbers of second-generation migrant workers will continue to expose the deficiencies in the economic structures of the northern countries, but it also will continue to postpone the reckoning with a restructuring that appears inevitable (OECD 1975a, p. 40).

If one places the changes brought about as a result of the recession and the ban on further recruitment in juxtaposition with the prospects for the medium-term economic growth in Europe, (OECD 1976b), it appears possible to formulate some basic assumptions as to the pattern of North-South migratory relations in the near future. These four assumptions have been stated as follows (OECD 1976a, pp. 9-10):

> 1) The target of "moderate but sustained expansion" seems to imply that the more industrialized countries of Western Europe will need to follow a policy leading only gradually to the restoration of full employment. In addition to its purely cyclical components, current unemployment (or, to be more precise, the under-utilization of human resources) comprises a number of structural elements which a moderate rate of growth (without excessive inflation) will not be able to absorb entirely. . . . With regard to the less industrialized countries, the OECD scenario suggests that they may suffer the more from the consequences of their partners' moderation of growth, since (a) the expansion of their own industry, even if it were to continue at the present pace, would not suffice to absorb the manpower still available (owing in particular to under-employment in agriculture and certain services), while (b) their own growth rate will in fact slow down because of serious balance of trade constraints, the imbalance being accentuated by the reduction or stoppage of emigration.
> 2) In view of the pressure exerted by this unemployment and a political environment now hostile to the resumption of large flows of foreign manpower, available labor supply at home will be able to be put to better use, with the recruitment of women, in particular, to meet growing needs in the tertiary sector.
> 3) On the other hand, the unemployment benefit schemes, the rise, albeit moderate, in the general standard of living and the cultural patterns disseminated through education and the mass media will together continue to dissuade available labor from taking jobs regarded as "inferior." The deliberate reduction of the sources of workers prepared to take these jobs might therefore create very real bottlenecks in the productive apparatus.
> 4) The new pattern of migratory relations is unequally differentiated. On the one hand, in spite of obvious variations in economic growth rates, the industrial countries are tending to align their migration policies: the convergence achieved since 1973, without deliberate concertation, in stopping the flow but retaining the stock of foreign workers is eloquent in this respect. In the "North" there is indeed a "block" of ex-immigration countries. On the other hand, in the "South", the group of emigration countries is becoming progressively differentiated. . . . The differences between them all are great

and would in principle make it necessary to modulate the prospective operation of the new pattern. However, the fact is that these countries have one thing in common, i.e., their vulnerability to a fall in the growth rate among their more industrialized partners.

If the four assumptions outlined here are accepted, the implications, then, for the pattern of North-South migratory relations are several. And though it is difficult to predict the precise dimensions of this new relationship, drawn against a background of European uncertainties and disequilibria, there are aspects that appear relatively certain. This is especially so, given the fact that uncontrolled immigration to the North has ceased for the foreseeable future. As an alternative to such a laissez faire approach toward manpower migration, the countries of the North have opted for a relationship of strenuously controlled migration (save for EEC agreements), whereby there is maintained a minimum constant flow, a significant part of which is due to the encouragement of family reunions in the host countries. The first point to be made then, is not that migration to the North has ceased, but that it has been drastically altered and reduced.

Second, the aim of the immigrant countries appears to be the creation of a stable migrant worker population committed to a long-term residency. It is thus in this sense that the countries of the North are speaking of integration of the migrant workers, an integration of expedience that will allow this sizable group to function at a minimum level of efficacy within the host country. It is not an integration aimed at the enhancement of either assimilation or pluralism, but rather a process to institutionalize marginality. As Nikolinakos (1975b, p. 7) has noted in this regard:

> I think that in any case you cannot speak of integration under present conditions, since the recipient societies have not made and perhaps cannot in the short run make decisions as to their growth targets. It is this very decision on which the employment of the foreigners depends. This is the cruel reality. These societies are willing to accept at times as many foreigners as is necessary for the achievement of their growth targets. This implies that just so much integration is allowed or accepted as will not endanger this fundamental condition. Basically, foreigners must remain displaceable serving as a reserve army in the process of capital accumulation. This is the real law governing the migration phenomenon as it appears under the condition of capitalist development in Western Europe.

What is implied by the above is that though the migration ban is in effect, the role of the foreigner on the labor market does not disappear. To the contrary, some number of them are absolutely essential to carry out the dirty-work tasks in the host society; thus the efforts on the part of governments to support integration and implement measures to enhance their retention. One finds an increasingly liberal approach to the present immigrants going hand in hand with a conservative approach toward further immigration.

Third, there is the fact that in spite of the ban, the total foreign population is increasing appreciably due to family reunions, its youth, its higher birth rates, and to its still considerable demographic vitality (OECD 1976a, p. 10). As to the matter of birth rates, it is this fact alone that transforms the negative population replacement rate of native Germans into a positive one for the population as a whole. Thus not only do the immigrants contribute substantially to population growth in the host societies, but they also will contribute for the foreseeable future to the labor market with a sizable number of new recruits—both youth and females looking for their first employment. But again, as noted earlier, if the host countries do not make efforts to expand opportunities, and anticipate instead that sizable segments of the migrant population will remain passive and in reserve, they may face a rude awakening when demands are made for greater options to participate in the society.

Though there is some recent evidence of a slackening of migratory pressure in both Italy and Greece as the employment opportunities there have expanded, the reality remains for most other labor-exporting countries of continued pressure due to both population increases and the lack of development within the employment sectors of the economies. In fact, it is becoming more and more apparent that the hike in oil prices has had a greater adverse effect upon the less developed than upon the more developed countries. Many of the countries of the Mediterranean basin have actually lost ground in their efforts to close the developmental lags between themselves and the countries of the North. The consequence of this situation is an intensification of the very forces that needed, at the least, to be neutralized in order for development to proceed. The countries of the South face high levels of unemployment, increasing populations, staggering import/export deficits, loans in the billions of dollars from international banks and monetary funds, and little infusion of new capital, save for the remittances sent by their workers abroad. Even this latter source may begin to diminish as workers spend longer periods of time in the host countries, become reunited with their families, and choose to invest more of their resources in making comfortable their stay abroad.

The forecast is not an optimistic one for either the immigrant workers in the countries of the North or for the countries of the South. Those who are in the North, will continue to exist as an Unterschichtung segment of the labor force, set apart from the national workers and used for a set of tasks refused by others. Furthermore, they will have little or no security while in the host countries, no means for political expression of their aspirations, and will be ignored as to what they desire in terms of a relation to the host society, and constantly reminded of the perversion inherent in terming them guestworkers. For the South, the present asymmetrical relation with the North shows every evidence of becoming even more so. The dependencies will deepen. Life on the periphery will continue to be exactly that. And the goals of development and modernization will slip further and further out of reach.

# 3

# GERMANY: A LAND OF IMMIGRATION

The Federal Republic of Germany, in spite of the official orthodoxies and public protestations, has become a land of immigration. The realities do not bear out the claim, reiterated time and again, that Germany is only a transient stop for guestworkers who, in due course, will leave and be replaced by another group, equally mobile and determined to return to their homelands. *Germany has become a culturally and ethnically pluralistic society*, in spite of the failure of the native population to legitimate this fact.

There are now literally hundreds of thousands of hyphenated Germans: for example, Turkish-Germans, Greek-Germans, Portuguese-Germans, Yugoslav-Germans, and Italian-Germans. These new immigrants have found a home in Germany and have no intention of returning to their villages in rural Anatolia or Croatia. The tragedy of this situation is that with Germany failing to come to grips with the implications inherent in the presence of its new members, millions of persons remain on the margins of the society, dispossessed and nearly invisible.

## A HISTORICAL BACKGROUND

Though the present movement of more than two million migrant workers and another two million of their dependents into Germany possesses characteristics distinct unto itself, it is not without historical antecedents. The importance of intra-European labor migration can be traced back to the beginnings of the industrial revolution. As Castles and Kosack (1973, p. 15) note:

> A basic precondition for industrialization in nineteenth-century Europe was the existence of labour reserves, almost always in rural areas. Evicted peasants and destitute artisans, who had lost their

livelihood through competition from the new capitalist methods of production, flooded into the new industrial towns and became part of the proletariat. Once local labour reserves were used up, labour migrants were induced to come from further afield. Often they crossed national frontiers in their search for employment. The social history of industrialization is that of mass movements from country to town; international migration is a special case within this general pattern.

In Germany, the industrial development began in the western regions of the country, the famed Ruhr area. The first immigrant workers were those from the more eastern provinces where the social structure was still semifeudal in character. At the heart of this area of industrial development lay a ready and cheap source of energy, the Ruhr coal mines. These mines began to expand at a very rapid rate to keep pace with the demands for energy from the surrounding industries. By 1913 and the beginning of World War I, it has been estimated by Stirn (1964, p. 27) that 164,100 of the 409,900 Ruhr miners were Poles. At the same time large numbers of additional migrant workers were being recruited from Italy for the growing industrial areas of southern Germany. In 1907, there was a total of 800,000 migrant workers in Germany, and they comprised 4.1 percent of the total labor force. A census in 1910 tabulated a total of 1,259,880 foreign residents, including their dependents.

The conditions under which such workers were recruited and employed were not much different from those experienced by some of the present generation of migrant workers. As Castles and Kosack (1973, pp. 19-20) describe the former conditions:

> This immigration was uncontrolled and unorganized. Foreign workers were frequently recruited by private agents out to make a quick profit. The workers could be exploited due to their weak legal positions and their ignorance of prevailing conditions. The accommodations provided by the mine-owners were overcrowded and primitive: a breeding place for crime, disease, and social problems. Such conditions led to mistrust and fear on the part of the local population. Further causes of conflict arose at the workplace itself. Foreigners had a high accident rate due to their frequent job changes, their inexperience in industry, and also because safety regulations in their own languages were usually lacking. They often worked harder and longer for the less money than Germans, undermining improvements gained by the trade unions.

Agitation against the foreign workers by the native populations began to take place and to have an impact on government policy. In 1907, there were several mass expulsions of Polish workers, and those not expelled were forced to leave the country for a stipulated period of time at the end of each year so they would not have met the requirements necessary for a permanent residency permit. In 1908 a law was passed decreeing the use of Polish in public illegal. The Polish workers retaliated by organizing "dumb assemblies" where everyone remained silent, but leaflets written in Polish were passed through the crowds (Stirn 1964, p. 35). The immigrant workers formed associations to both articulate and defend their economic and social interests. In reality, the labor demands of the industries in the region were such that it was not feasible to think of any absolute restriction on further immigration. Then, as now, migrant workers were needed to fuel economic growth.

The continued prosperity and development of the Ruhr region resulted in a situation in which many thousands of the Polish miners remained in the area and eventually did take up German citizenship. That many have remained in the area is evident by a quick examination of a local telephone book, or a look at the roster of a soccer club. This migration and subsequent integration represent the first significant instance, in the period since industrialization, of Germany serving as a land of immigration.

In the period between the first and second world wars, the rate of labor migration to the industrial sectors of Europe was considerably lower than it was prior to World War I. This was so for two main reasons: first, there were the servicemen to re-integrate into the economies, many of whom were finding it difficult to locate work. Second, there came the acute economic downturn of 1929. Work was simply not available, regardless of one's nationality.

The reversal of these trends in Germany came in 1933 with the ascent of the Nazis to control of the government. The consequence has been summarized by Castles and Kosack (1973, p. 23):

> In Germany, the growth of production brought about after 1933 by the change to a centrally directed war economy led to a renewed demand for labor. The reserves of unemployed Germans were absorbed within a few years and agreements on the recruitment of foreign labor were made with neighbouring countries. By May 1939, there were about 525,000 foreign workers in Germany. During the war there was a tremendous increase in the number of foreign workers as they were used to replace the 11 million German men withdrawn from the labor force for military service between May 1939 and September 1944. By the latter date, 7.5 million foreign workers were employed in the Reich. . . . Some of the foreign workers were recruited through agreements made with 'friendly and neutral' countries—i.e., Italy, Slovakia, Bulgaria, Hungary, Rumania, Croatia, and Spain. But more were recrutied by force in the occupied areas, both east and west, and 1.8 million were actually prisoners of war.

In his book entitled *Foreign Labor in Nazi Germany*, Homze (1967) provides detailed accounts of the treatment of the migrant workers. Nazi propaganda continually denigrated them as the *Untermenschen*, the subhumans. The head of the office supervising foreign labor in Germany, Sauckel, is quoted as having said, "All the men must be fed, sheltered and treated in such a way as to exploit them to the highest possible extent at the lowest conceivable degree of expenditure." While this isolation and exploitation of the workers was justified on the one hand as a necessary condition leading to the ultimate victory of national socialism, there were even more despotic motivations and these lay at the very center of Nazi ideology.

At a time when the German men were away at the front defending the fatherland, the more than seven million foreign workers who remained in Germany were perceived as a threat to the racial purity of the German nation. Efforts were considerable to maintain distance and preserve the glorified role of German womanhood.* Himmler ordered that German women caught associating with Polish workers were to be publicly humiliated and then sent to concentration camps. The men were frequently executed on the spot. The propaganda was continuous and intense. The emphasis upon the racial inferiority of the workers was reinforced time and again. And it did not abate in the slightest during the entire war, even at the end when it was readily evident that the foreign workers were a major reason the Nazis were able to continue to fight. It has been estimated that by 1944, "Every fourth German tank, lorry, field gun, every fourth piece of ammunition was made by the hands of a foreign worker." (Pfahlmann 1968, p. 232)

## THE POSTWAR PERIOD

At the war's end, Germany lay shattered. Its male work force had been decimated, its industrial facilities demolished, and its transportation system left nonexistent. It was widely predicted that it would be some time before there would be sufficient employment for those Germans who did survive the war, let alone the influx of 8-10 million refugees from the former German territories of Prussia, the Sudetenland, and others. Germany was predicted to become a land of emigration, for there would be no possible way in which the Western sector of the country could provide for the masses that were gathering there.

There was an exodus from Germany in the first years after the war as had been anticipated, but it was neither of the magnitude nor the duration that had been predicted (Rose 1969, p. 20). Efforts were begun by the Allies almost im-

---

*An implication of this continual barrage of propaganda has been noted by Castles and Kosack (1973, p. 25):

"The whole German population was regularly exposed to official propaganda against foreign workers. However much the German population has repressed its experiences under Hitler since the war, the attitudes and behavior developed then must still have some effect in shaping prejudices in modern Western Germany."

mediately after the cessation of hostilities to reconstruct the industrial capacity of Germany. This together with the currency reforms of 1948 prompted an economic recovery of such speed and depth that the labor surpluses were soon absorbed. About the same time began the flow of refugees from the Eastern sector of Germany. This steady stream of people continued throughout the fifties and up until the construction of the Berlin wall in 1961. It totaled more than 3.1 million persons. This group also was rapidly integrated into the economy and by the end of the 1950s and early 1960s, serious labor shortages were being experienced.

## THE EXPANSION PERIOD

As a response to these shortages, the German government concluded a number of agreements with countries in a position to export labor. The first of these was drawn up in 1955 with Italy and concerned the importation of laborers for the building and agricultural sectors. It proved so successful that it was expanded to other areas where labor was needed. By 1959, only about 10 percent of the workers recruited in Italy came to work in the agricultural areas. Nearly half were slated to work in the industrial plants springing up and expanding all through the country. Additional bilateral agreements were made throughout the 1960s: with Greece and Spain in 1960, Turkey in 1961, Portugal in 1964, and Yugoslavia in 1968.

The provisions in each accord were more or less comparable. The German government through its labor recruiting offices in the sending countries would make known available positions. The labor authorities in the recruitment countries would then be responsible for locating suitable candidates. The prospective candidate was given a medical examination by a German doctor attached to the Labor Ministry, and if this examination was passed, a search was conducted to learn if the worker had a criminal record, as well as to further assess the suitability of the worker for the position in question. If all was in order, a contract with the worker was signed, usually for an initial one-year period. Before departing for Germany, the worker was to be supplied with information on life in Germany and the specific details of his future employment. He was then transported to the location of his work, usually at the expense of the German government. During the peak year of migration, fleets of chartered jets shuttled back and forth between Germany and the countries of the South for the sole purpose of bringing more workers.

Table 3.1 provides an indication of the flow of foreign workers into Germany from the year 1960. It must be noted that these data include only an estimate of those workers who came into the country under EEC agreements after July 1, 1968. As these workers are free to come and go as they wish, it has been extremely difficult to ascertain their exact numbers. Several estimates have placed it, as of 1974, at approximately 560,000. It must also be noted that these data do not include dependents. (For the total figures, the reader is referred

## TABLE 3.1

### The Immigrant Worker Population in the Federal Republic of Germany, 1960-76

| Year | Employed Immigrant Workers at the End of September | Comparison with Previous Year (Absolute) | Comparison with Previous Year (Percent) | Percent of All Workers |
|---|---|---|---|---|
| 1960 | 329,356 | +162,527 | +97.4 | 1.5 |
| 1961 | 548,916 | +219,560 | +66.7 | 2.5 |
| 1962 | 711,549 | +162,543 | +29.6 | 3.2 |
| 1963 | 828,743 | +117,284 | +16.5 | 3.7 |
| 1964 | 985,616 | +156,873 | +18.9 | 4.4 |
| 1965 | 1,216,804 | +231,188 | +23.5 | 5.7 |
| 1966 | 1,313,491 | +96,687 | +7.9 | 6.1 |
| 1967 | 991,255 | -322,236 | -24.5 | 4.7 |
| 1968 | 1,089,873 | +98,618 | +9.9 | 5.2 |
| 1969 | 1,501,409 | +411,536 | +37.8 | 7.0 |
| 1970 | 1,948,951 | +447,542 | +29.8 | 9.0 |
| 1971 | 2,240,793 | +291,842 | +15.0 | 10.3 |
| 1972 | 2,352,392 | +222,599 | +5.0 | 10.8 |
| 1973 | 2,595,000 | +242,608 | +10.3 | 11.9 |
| 1974 | 2,350,000 | -245,000 | -9.4 | 11.2 |
| 1975 | 2,171,000 | -179,000 | -7.6 | 10.5 |
| 1976 | 1,932,600 | -238,400 | -10.9 | 9.7 |

Sources: H. Müller, Ausländische Arbeiter in unserer Gesellschaft (Munich: Kösel, 1975); Organization for Economic Cooperation and Development, SOPEMI Continuous Reporting System on Migration (Paris: OECD, 1976); and Federal Ministry for Labor and Social Affairs, Federal Republic of Germany, "Continuous Reporting System on Migration: A Report to the Organization for Economic Cooperation and Development," Bonn, 1976.

back to Table 1.1.) Finally, the data do not reflect the number of illegal immigrants in the country. Diamant (1970, p. 50) estimated that the number of illegal workers could be as high as 15 percent of the number legally in the country. If that estimate is approximately correct for more recent years as well, it would suggest for 1975 an additional 292,000 migrant workers in Germany.* Taking

---

*The *Annual Labor Report*, prepared by the U.S. Department of State, on labor and economic conditions in the Federal Republic of Germany places the number of illegal workers for 1975 at approximately 200,000 (U.S. Department of State 1976, p. 56).

that figure together with the figures for legal migrant workers provides a total of approximately 2.5 million guestworkers, or between 12 and 13 percent of the entire labor force in Germany in 1975.

There are several implications to be drawn from these data, given the limitations noted above. First, it is clear that the recession of 1967 did have a significant impact upon the employment opportunities of the migrant workers; but it is also evident that there was considerable resiliency and permanence in that same labor force, for nearly one million migrant workers retained employment at a time when a comparable number of German workers were unemployed.

Second, when one views these data in relation to those presented in Chapter 2 on the impact of the recession and subsequent immigration ban of 1973, it is plausible to assume that the immigrant workers were by this time structurally integrated to an even greater degree into the German economy. The evidence has several parts: the decline in numbers employed in absolute terms was less than in 1967, though the number of workers had doubled; some portion of the decline has to be attributable to the continuing pattern of some workers choosing each year to return to their home lands (and since 1973 not being replaced); and finally, the unemployment rate since the beginning of the 1973 recession has been almost identical to that of the native worker population. And though it is perhaps moving ahead of this analysis a bit too rapidly, it should be noted that by September 1976, the unemployment rate of 3.7 percent for the immigrant workers was actually below the national average of 4.2 percent (OECD 1976a, p. 32).

## THE CURRENT PROFILE

The decision to halt the immigration of foreign workers dates from November 23, 1973, and so it was not until 1974 that the ban began to have a noticeable impact in terms of drastically reducing the flow of new immigrants into the country. Concurrent with this effort was the establishment of policy guidelines protecting the working rights of the German nationals by restoring the rule of employment priority for German workers. This was accomplished by renewing employment permits for migrant workers only if no German national applied for the same position. In reality, these two policy guidelines have had little impact upon the conditions of the guestworkers in Germany. The reasons are that, as a rule, migrant workers are not in competition for the same employment opportunities as the local workers, and so far as data from the work permits would indicate, German nationals have little desire to experience the downward mobility inherent in taking on the jobs held by migrants. The data on work permits are found in Table 3.2.

Commenting on this period of the postban declaration as it influences the immigrant populations, OECD (1976a, pp. 12-13) noted:

TABLE 3.2

Work Permits Issued in the Federal Republic of Germany, 1969-75

| | | Applications Approved* | | | Applications Denied | |
|---|---|---|---|---|---|---|
| | Total | First Employment in the FRG | Renewed Contracts | Continuation of Employment | Number | Percent |
| 1969 | 1,285,305 | 301,101 | 445,197 | 490,157 | 5,467 | 0.4 |
| 1970 | 1,333,732 | 183,123 | 485,233 | 650,029 | 6,823 | 0.5 |
| 1971 | 1,654,825 | 143,723 | 611,995 | 884,876 | 5,863 | 0.4 |
| 1972 | 1,271,885 | 136,727 | 507,870 | 617,106 | 5,422 | 0.5 |
| 1973 | 1,094,688 | 121,436 | 443,791 | 517,456 | 8,654 | 0.8 |
| 1974 | 1,393,878 | 79,064 | 387,906 | 918,572 | 20,869 | 1.5 |
| 1975 | 1,477,080 | 21,906 | 382,541 | 1,139,675 | 43,685 | 3.0 |

*Includes frontier workers.

Source: Federal Ministry for Labor and Social Affairs, "Continuous Reporting System on Migration: A Report to the Organization for Economic Cooperation and Development," Bonn, 1976.

In 1975, for the first time in years, the foreign population of the Federal Republic of Germany went down. The decline was very slight, which is itself a sign of the stabilization that was aimed at in the November 1973 decision to halt recruitment, but it is nevertheless a noteworthy feature in the demographic history of Germany. In 1974, there were well over 4 million foreigners, an increase of 161,000 over 1973 (including 100,000 births of children to foreign parents). In 1975, the number fell by 38,000 to stabilize at 4,089,000. There was a much more pronounced reduction in the number of foreign workers, though natural movements and the admission of families offset the departure of some workers. At the end of September 1975, 2,039,000 foreign workers were employed in Germany, in addition to which there were 132,000 unemployed making 2,171,600 in all as against 2,610,700 (including 15,700 unemployed) at the end of September 1973, two years previously, i.e., a decrease of 439,100 or 16.8 percent.

However, this last figure does not mean that all the workers involved returned to their country of origin: on the contrary, a number of workers—especially women—have withdrawn from the labor market but are still resident on federal territory as latent reserves. According to the statistics for entries and departures at the frontiers, which cover the period from June 1974 to June 1975, the balance of foreign workers leaving the country only works out, in fact, at 178,000 people (349,000 departures and 171,000 entries).

What is of further importance, given this slight decline in the number of foreign workers within Germany, is that the decrease has been a highly selective process related to the nationality of the workers. While nearly one-third of all Italian and Spanish workers left the country, the number of Turkish workers remained virtually unchanged. In the middle were the groups from Yugoslavia, Portugal, and Greece, whose numbers declined between 15 and 20 percent. The data are presented in Table 3.3.

There are also data available that allow a closer examination of the nationality of all foreigners in Germany as of September 30, 1975. While such data do not provide inferences as to the permanence of such groups in Germany, they do bear out the earlier contention that Germany has become an ethnically and culturally pluralistic society where peoples from throughout the world have come to live. The data suggest that in the first two years after the imposing of the immigration ban, the foreign populations remained stable. And though the actual number of workers declined by 179,000 (cf. Table 3.2) between 1974 and 1975, the total population of foreigners in Germany declined by only 38,000. As mentioned previously, two factors appear to account most heavily for this small decline. First, even though some persons are no longer in the labor market, they have not necessarily left Germany. This may be particularly true for women, which bears on the second reason: there were more than 100,000 live births to foreign parents in Germany during the year 1975. The data on the quantities of different nationalities in Germany are contained in Table 3.4.

## TABLE 3.3

### Immigrant Workers in the Federal Republic of Germany, by Nationality, 1973-75

|  | 1973 | 1974 | 1975 |
|---|---|---|---|
| Turks |  |  |  |
| Absolute | 605,000 | 590,000 | 582,200 |
| Percent* | 23.0 | 25.1 | 27.0 |
| Yugoslavs |  |  |  |
| Absolute | 535,000 | 470,000 | 436,300 |
| Percent | 21.0 | 20.0 | 20.0 |
| Italians |  |  |  |
| Absolute | 450,000 | 370,000 | 318,000 |
| Percent | 17.0 | 15.7 | 15.0 |
| Greeks |  |  |  |
| Absolute | 250,000 | 225,000 | 212,000 |
| Percent | 10.0 | 9.7 | 10.0 |
| Spaniards |  |  |  |
| Absolute | 190,000 | 165,000 | 132,100 |
| Percent | 7.0 | 7.0 | 6.0 |
| Portuguese |  |  |  |
| Absolute | 85,000 | 85,000 | 70,000 |
| Percent | 3.0 | 3.6 | 3.0 |
| Others |  |  |  |
| Absolute | 495,000 | 445,000 | 421,000 |
| Percent | 19.0 | 18.9 | 19.0 |
| Total |  |  |  |
| Absolute | 2,610,000 | 2,350,000 | 2,171,600 |
| Percent | 100.0 | 100.0 | 100.0 |

*of all immigrant workers.

Sources: Organization for Economic Cooperation and Development, SOPEMI Continuous Reporting System on Migration (Paris: OECD, 1975, 1976).

As to the regional distribution of all foreigners in Germany during the years 1974 and 1975, two factors are apparent. First, the populations were stable (the largest change was an increase of 0.8 percent in North Rhine-Westphalia), and second, the populations are, as might be anticipated, concentrated in the industrial areas of the country. Four of the German states (*Länder*) accounted in 1975 for nearly 80 percent of all foreigners in Germany. The data on the size of the foreign populations in the eleven Länder are found in Table 3.5.

TABLE 3.4

Foreigners in the Federal Republic
of Germany, by Nationality,
September 1974 and September 1975

|  | September 1974 | | September 1975 | |
| --- | --- | --- | --- | --- |
|  | Absolute | Percent | Absolute | Percent |
| EEC countries: | | | | |
| Italy | 629,600 | 15.3 | 601,400 | 14.8 |
| Netherlands | 109,900 | 2.7 | 110,500 | 2.7 |
| France | 59,100 | 1.4 | 60,400 | 1.5 |
| Great Britain/ North Ireland | 52,200 | 1.3 | 55,500 | 1.4 |
| Belgium | 14,800 | 0.4 | 15,300 | 0.4 |
| Denmark | 9,400 | 0.2 | 10,000 | 0.2 |
| Luxembourg | 4,200 | 0.1 | 4,200 | 0.1 |
| Ireland | 2,300 | 0.1 | 2,500 | 0.1 |
| Subtotal, EEC | 881,400 | 21.5 | 859,800 | 21.1 |
| Turkey | 1,027,800 | 25.0 | 1,077,100 | 26.5 |
| Yugoslavia | 707,800 | 17.2 | 677,900 | 16.7 |
| Greece | 406,400 | 9.9 | 390,500 | 9.6 |
| Spain | 272,200 | 6.6 | 247,400 | 6.1 |
| Austria | 177,000 | 4.3 | 174,000 | 4.3 |
| Eastern European countries | 108,800 | 2.6 | 108,100 | 2.7 |
| Portugal | 121,500 | 2.9 | 118,500 | 2.9 |
| Switzerland | 26,200 | 0.6 | 27,000 | 0.7 |
| Sweden | 8,800 | 0.2 | 8,800 | 0.2 |
| Finland | 8,800 | 0.2 | 8,600 | 0.2 |
| Other European countries | 13,900 | 0.3 | 13,700 | 0.3 |
| Africa | 69,300 | 1.7 | 70,900 | 1.7 |
| America | 113,900 | 2.8 | 121,300 | 3.0 |
| Australia | 6,700 | 0.2 | 6,700 | 0.2 |
| Stateless persons | 30,700 | 0.7 | 30,700 | 0.8 |
| Unsettled nationality | 25,600 | 0.6 | 24,500 | 0.6 |
| Total | 4,127,400 | 100.0 | 4,089,600 | 100.0 |

Source: Federal Ministry for Labor and Social Affairs, Federal Republic of Germany, "Continuous Reporting System on Migration: A Report to the Organization for Economic Cooperation and Development," Bonn, 1976.

## TABLE 3.5

Distribution of Foreign Population in the
Federal Republic of Germany, by Lander
September 1974 and September 1975

|  | September 1974 Absolute | Percent | September 1975 Absolute | Percent |
|---|---|---|---|---|
| Schleswig-Holstein | 76,000 | 1.8 | 77,300 | 1.9 |
| Hamburg | 114,100 | 2.8 | 115,600 | 2.8 |
| Lower Saxony | 275,700 | 6.7 | 264,300 | 6.5 |
| Bremen | 39,900 | 1.0 | 42,000 | 1.0 |
| North Rhine-Westphalia | 1,200,400 | 29.1 | 1,244,500 | 29.9 |
| Hesse | 443,700 | 10.8 | 445,900 | 10.9 |
| Rhineland-Palatinate | 155,100 | 3.8 | 150,200 | 3.7 |
| Baden-Württemberg | 914,200 | 22.2 | 882,100 | 21.6 |
| Bavaria | 702,900 | 17.0 | 672,100 | 16.4 |
| Saarland | 43,600 | 1.1 | 42,800 | 1.1 |
| Berlin (West) | 161,800 | 3.9 | 172,800 | 4.2 |
| Total | 4,127,400 | 100.0 | 4,089,600 | 100.0 |

Source: Federal Ministry for Labor and Social Affairs, Federal Republic of Germany, "Continuous Reporting System on Migration: A Report to the Organization for Economic Cooperation and Development," Bonn, 1976.

In assessing the rates of employment among the foreign workers in Germany, the data base shifts slightly. In an effort to develop a more rational picture of the labor force in Germany, the regional areas are divided according to the principle of unifying urban and regional areas as opposed to simply taking the boundaries of the eleven Länder. Thus there are in Germany what are known as district labor offices which provide the statistical base for computations regarding labor and employment. (See Table 3.6.) There is a rough approximation to the boundaries of the Länder, though several notable exceptions do occur: the city-states of Hamburg and Bremen are included in the data for the Länder contiguous with and surrounding them, the Saarland is combined with its neighbor state (Rhineland-Palatinate), and Bavaria is split into two districts. An examination of the data on regional distribution and employment rates for 1973, 1974, and 1975 indicates that while there has been a general decline in employment in the wake of the recession, the decline was more marked in the highly industrial areas of the North Rhine-Westphalia, Baden-Württemberg, Hessen, and South Bavaira.

TABLE 3.6

Distribution and Rate of Employment for Immigrant Workers in District Labor Offices
Federal Republic of Germany, January 1973 to September 1975

|  | Distribution by District Labor Office ||| Rate of all Employment in District Labor Office |||
|---|---|---|---|---|---|---|
|  | 1973 | 1974 | 1975 | 1973 | 1974 | 1975 |
| Schleswig–Holstein/Hamburg | 4.3 | 4.4 | 4.6 | 6.6 | 6.7 | 6.5 |
| Lower Saxony/Bremen | 6.6 | 7.2 | 6.8 | 5.9 | 6.7 | 5.9 |
| North Rhine–Westphalia | 29.0 | 28.0 | 28.7 | 11.2 | 10.9 | 10.3 |
| Hessen | 11.7 | 11.2 | 11.1 | 13.6 | 13.0 | 12.1 |
| Rhineland–Palatinate/Saarland | 4.5 | 4.7 | 4.7 | 6.9 | 7.5 | 6.9 |
| Baden–Württemberg | 24.3 | 24.6 | 24.1 | 16.5 | 16.5 | 15.2 |
| Bavaria–North | 4.8 | 5.3 | 5.0 | 6.9 | 7.5 | 6.6 |
| Bavaria–South | 11.4 | 10.8 | 10.7 | 13.0 | 12.7 | 11.6 |
| Berlin (West) | 3.5 | 4.0 | 4.2 | 9.6 | 12.0 | 11.6 |

Source: Federal Ministry for Labor and Social Affairs, Federal Republic of Germany, "Continuous Reporting System on Migration: A Report to the Organization for Economic Cooperation and Development," Bonn, 1976.

TABLE 3.7

Distribution and Rate of Employment for Immigrant Workers, by Branches of Economic Activity, January 1973 to September 1975

(percent)

| Economic Activity | Distribution 1973 | Distribution 1974 | 1975 Absolute | 1975 Percent | Rate of Employment within Sectors of Economic Activity 1973 | 1974 | 1975 |
|---|---|---|---|---|---|---|---|
| Agriculture, livestock, and fishing | 0.8 | 1.0 | 21,000 | 1.0 | 6.8 | 10.7 | 10.1 |
| Energy, water, and mining | 1.4 | 1.4 | 33,400 | 1.6 | 6.2 | 6.8 | 7.5 |
| Manufacturing | 61.4 | 61.9 | 1,218,600 | 59.8 | 14.9 | 15.3 | 14.1 |
| Construction | 16.4 | 11.9 | 228,100 | 11.2 | 21.9 | 14.9 | 13.4 |
| Commerce | n.a.* | 5.3 | 114,700 | 5.6 | 5.6 | 4.2 | 4.1 |
| Transportation and communication | n.a. | 3.5 | 74,600 | 3.7 | n.a. | 7.7 | 7.5 |
| Banks and insurance | 18.4 | 0.6 | 12,200 | 0.6 | n.a. | 1.7 | 1.7 |
| Services | n.a. | 11.8 | 273,200 | 13.4 | n.a. | 9.1 | 9.1 |
| Private household | — | 0.5 | 11,600 | 0.6 | n.a. | 3.7 | 3.7 |
| State security and social | 1.6 | 2.1 | 49,200 | 2.4 | 2.1 | 3.7 | 3.7 |
| Total | 100.0 | 100.0 | 2,038,800 | 100.0 | 10.8 | 10.1 | 10.1 |

*data not available.

Source: Federal Ministry for Labor and Social Affairs, Federal Republic of Germany, "Continuous Reporting System on Migration: A Report to the Organization for Economic Cooperation and Development," Bonn, 1976, p. 12.

Just as the guestworkers are concentrated in certain geographical areas, so also are they concentrated in a few occupational fields. In 1973, just prior to the ban, more than 90 percent of all guestworkers were concentrated in three occupational areas: manufacturing, construction, and services. Two years later, in September 1975, the total in these three areas was 84.4 percent, which suggests that the dispersal of workers into other economic and employment sectors was moving at a very slow pace. Such data concur with those of Kudat and Özkan (1976) presented in Chapter 3 (cf. Table 3.1) which indicated that between their first and last employment in Germany, the number of Turkish workers who experienced either upward or horizontal occupational mobility was no more than 12 percent for the entire sample. (See Table 3.7.)

These data would indicate that in those economic sectors most sensitive to business cycles (manufacturing, construction, and transportation), the number of foreign workers declined, as did the number of German workers. On the other hand, there is evidence of an increase in the numbers of foreign workers moving into the service sector. This same increase holds true for German workers as well. There should be caution in assuming, however, that the movement for the foreign workers into the service sector is necessarily a move of upward mobility. In fact, it may well represent a downward slide away from the sectors of the economy where there are more opportunities for better pay and greater vocational options. To leave a factory for work in a hotel may or may not be considered an advancement.

A final set of data relevant to the current economic conditions of the guestworkers is that relating their unemployment rates to those of the entire work force. While the unemployment rate for the immigrant workers during the 1967-68 recession was more than double that of the work force as a whole (11.6 percent versus 5.2 percent, respectively), the same situation did not occur during the 1973 recession and its aftermath. The guestworkers did experience, during the first part of the recession, rates higher than those of the total work force. But the return home of some of the unemployed plus the fact that many immigrant workers were in positions not contested by German workers, even in a time of recession, meant that their unemployment rates remained comparable to those of the remaining workers in the country. This would offer additional confirmation that the stability and economic integration of the migrant work force grew between 1967 and 1973. And while many of the positions held by the guestworkers are those in the very lowest strata of the employment ladder, it by no means follows that in times of recession, those are the first jobs to be abolished (for example, garbage collection, street cleaning, road construction). The data on the comparative rates of unemployment for the guestworkers and the native work force are contained in Table 3.8.

In an effort to summarize the situation for the foreign workers in Germany at the end of 1975, the U.S. Department of State noted the following in its *Annual Labor Report* on the Federal Republic (U.S. Department of State 1976, p. 57):

TABLE 3.8

Comparative Rates of Unemployment for
Immigrant Workers and the German
Labor Force, March 1974 to
December 1976

|  | Immigrant Labor Force | German Labor Force |
|---|---|---|
| March 1974 | 1.7 | 2.5 |
| June 1974 | 1.8 | 2.0 |
| September 1974 | 2.9 | 2.4 |
| December 1974 | 5.4 | 4.2 |
| March 1975 | 7.4 | 4.9 |
| June 1975 | 6.5 | 4.4 |
| September 1975 | 5.5 | 4.4 |
| December 1975 | 6.3 | 5.3 |
| March 1976 | 6.1 | 5.2 |
| June 1976 | 4.1 | 4.0 |
| September | 3.7 | 4.2 |
| December 1976 | 4.6 | 4.8 |

Sources: Federal Ministry for Labor and Social Affairs, Federal Republic of Germany, "Continuous Reporting System on Migration: A Report to the Organization for Economic Cooperation and Development," Bonn, 1976. Federal Labor Office, 1976; U.S. Department of State, 1975 Annual Labor Report (Bonn, 1976) and Annual Labor Report, 1976, Federal Republic of Germany (Bonn, 1977).

Aware that their own birthrate is declining and would continue to do so, Germans became more conscious that the FRG would continue to need foreign workers indefinitely, unless they were willing to accept less economic growth. But 1975 did not bring the West Germans any closer to reaching a decision regarding the long range future of the foreign workers in the FRG.

However, many West German leaders are aware that severe social problems are in store if foreign workers remain in the FRG as second class citizens. 62 percent of the foreign worker population is between the ages of 21 and 45. There are now approximately 950,000 children and youth in the foreign worker communities. 50 percent of the children of foreign workers do not finish (secondary) school as compared to 26 percent of German children. Unless the next generation of foreigners are allowed to participate in German society with the hope of a way of life which approximates that of their

German neighbors, the relationship between foreign workers and their German neighbors will deteriorate.

Despite these gloomy prognoses, Germans are not yet ready to take the next step. With the assertion that "Germany is not an immigration country", most Germans are reluctant to send the foreigners home or to allow them to become citizens.

In the absence of a set of decisions regarding the long-range future of foreign workers in the FRG, what has emerged is a set of ad hoc policies and guidelines that are intended to forestall any final or more definitive policy pronouncements. The ambivalence as to the status to confer upon the guestworkers has resulted in the perpetuation of a set of temporary accommodations. Such conditions have left the foreign workers in an extremely tenuous and precarious position so far as not knowing what the future holds in store for them is concerned. Yet they have, in increasing numbers, been making the de facto decision to remain and raise their families in Germany. Even in the absence of knowing whether they will be allowed to stay and for how long, Zubrzycki (n.d., p. 39) cites data indicating that 15 percent of all guestworkers would choose to make Germany their permanent home. In the light of the anomic situation in which Germany policies place the guestworkers, this is a rather remarkable figure. And if one added to this group those who might also choose to stay were it in fact a realistic option, the figure would undoubtedly go much higher.

An alternative approach by which to ascertain the commitment of the foreign workers to remain in Germany is to examine their length of stay. While a series of surveys have all reported that the workers anticipate leaving Germany within three to five years of their arrival, what occurs is a continual series of postponements that prolongs the time abroad (cf. Kudat et al. 1974). This expressed intention of returning home in a short time, coupled with the extreme difficulties of realizing this desire, has been appropriately termed by Braun (1970) as *Heimkehrillusion* (illusion of returning). Hoffmann-Nowotny interprets this illusion as a reaction to the "foreigner policy" of Germany. He has noted (1976, p. 23):

> This illusion permits him to reduce his sense of uncertainty created by the "foreigner policy", about the duration of his stay because he can tell himself that he himself does not really care either about staying for good. As can be shown, this mechanism which sociologically may be interpreted as an adaption to an anomic situation, is not at all suited to do away with the actual uncertainty of the foreigner's situation.

In the Kudat et al. 1974 sample of more than 2200 migrant workers in West Berlin, the expressed intention was on the average to remain in Germany for no more than four years. This was at a time when more than 58 percent of the sample had already been in Germany for at least five years.* With the impact of the 1973 immigration halt, plus the year-by-year increase in the numbers of families coming to Germany to be reunited, one can anticipate that the duration of residence will grow even longer. As of September 1976, more than one-third of the immigrant labor force from non-EEC countries had been in Germany for eight years or longer (cf. Bodenbender 1976, p. 14).

In the light of such data it would be well to examine in more detail the substance of the policies that both define and confine the opportunities of the immigrant workers in Germany. Against the background of the lack of resolution of many important questions regarding the guestworkers in Germany, it is not surprising to find that the policies are frequently contradictory and irreconcilable. This is only to be anticipated, given that the basic economic and social/political forces in the society are not in agreement as to the role and status of the guestworkers while in Germany.

The economic necessity of the guestworkers is obvious, given current production and labor arrangements; but the simultaneous rejection of any political, cultural, and social integration of these same workers and their families creates a situation of inherent tension. It is a condition experienced in many other countries as well, where a host society finds itself in absolute need of the services and labor of migrants, but chooses not to grant recognition or acceptance. There is thus a continual need for the host country to provide sufficient incentives for the laborers to stay, but not to the extent that such incentives would threaten the political, social, or economic well-being of the national population. The current situation in West Germany is but another manifestation of a center country forced into a continual series of improvisations when confronted with a sizable periphery population in its midst.

## FOREIGNER POLICY

Traditionally, immigration was to serve one of two goals from the perspective of the receiving country. The immigrants would come either to increase the size and work force of an originally small population or to make use of empty spaces and other resources. Both such goals are absent in the new European immigration countries. These countries are characterized by high population density and their only true resource is accumulated capital not yet produc-

---

*A comparable set of data has been reported by Hoffmann-Nowotny. He reports (1976, p. 23) that in a sample of more than 500 guestworkers in Zürich, 41 percent expressed at the time of their arrival a desire to return to their homelands within five years. But by the time of his survey, more than two-thirds of the group had already been in Switzerland for more than 10 years. Only 29 percent thought they would be returning home within the next five years. Thus one can surmise that at least 50 percent of the workers from this initial sample will be living in Switzerland for 15 years.

tively used. Traditionally, immigration policies have been undertaken with a view to making the new immigrants permanent members of the host society.

The approach of the immigration countries of the European North has been quite the opposite. The policies of these countries, save for Sweden as a notable exception (cf. Goshko 1975), are, succinctly, directed toward preventing permanent residence as well as the gaining of citizenship. Hoffmann-Nowotny (1976, p. 12) accurately points out that "it is not possible to speak of an immigration policy in these countries. It is more adequate—and the term is also officially used—to designate the rules concerning the immigrants as a 'foreigner policy'." What follows now is an examination of several of the basic components underlying the foreigner policy of Germany as it relates to the emigration/immigration process. Other aspects of this policy will be examined in more detail in later chapters.

## Residence/Work Permits

It is the general rule in Germany that the granting of a work permit precedes the granting of a residence permit. The exception is that workers from the EEC countries are allowed to enter the country without having to ask for a work permit. If an immigrant from an EEC country receives a work contract anywhere in Germany, he has a legal claim to a residence permit valid for at least five years. However, those who desire to immigrate from non-EEC countries have no legal claim either to enter the country or to have a work permit. In fact, it is precisely the objective of the immigration ban of 1973 to prohibit further numbers of workers from coming into Germany and seeking such permits. Though the ban continues, the regulations covering the issuing of work permits remain in effect, if only because the ban is not absolute and each year some new permits are issued. The procedures governing the granting of work permits are stated as follows (Federal Ministry for Labor and Social Affairs 1976, pp. 15-16):

> Foreign workers—with the exception of workers from EEC member states must have a work permit before taking up and exercising an employment. For foreign workers who have yet been lawfully employed in the federal territory for a period of five years, work permits are granted in accordance with the situation and development of the labor market (priority of German workers and foreign workers assimilated to them in status). After an uninterrupted employment of five years, the foreign worker has acquired a legal entitlement to the grant of a work permit and is thus assimilated in status to his German colleagues. . . . For foreign workers who have not yet acquired this legal entitlement the grant of a work permit is governed by the following principles:
> —Applications for a work permit for a first employment are, as a rule, refused.

—Foreign workers who want to take up employment with another employer are granted the work permit only if there are no suitable national workers available for the job.*

—A work permit for the continuation of an existing employment relationship is, as a rule, granted even in cases where suitable national workers would be available for this particular job.

An examination of the naturalization laws shows that the employment of foreign workers is not considered from the point of view of permanent immigration. According to these laws, a foreigner can be naturalized provided he has not had a criminal record and is able to maintain his family. But ten years is the minimum residency required before application can be made, and even then this residence is only a necessary, but insufficient, condition for naturalization. There is no basis upon which a foreigner can make a legal claim to citizenship. As Franz has noted (1972, p. 42), "Naturalization is considered as an act of grace—and since grace is coming from God, but rarely from the state—it is not practiced vis-a-vis foreign workers unless they are married to a German."

The German Government has stated its view with regard to the naturalization of foreign workers in this manner (Federal Republic of Germany, 1975, p. 7):

The Federal Government is of the opinion that there is no necessity of providing special regulations for foreign workers with regard to the laws of naturalization. Naturalization presupposes a process of assimilation and therefore demands a time of residence which cannot be too short.

## Maintenance of the Recruitment Ban

The Federal Republic of Germany instituted on November 23, 1973 a ban on the further recruitment of foreign workers. It was justified at the time of its initiation on the grounds that there was a need to overcome the unemployment that was developing in the country as well as to leave open work places for the large number of young persons who would be entering the labor market for

---

*This provision has been considerably strengthened by a major decision of the government's Social Court on February 25, 1977. The court ruled that a local labor office was within its rights to refuse a labor permit to a non-EEC foreign worker while there were German workers in the area who were unemployed. Furthermore, the court expanded the authority of the labor offices to the point where they can now refuse labor permits for regions in the country and also for selected occupational and economic areas. The ruling would not apply to those foreigners who were members of the EEC, had lived in Germany for five years, or who had come to Germany under the provisions of special bilateral agreements. (Cf. *Der Tagesspiegel*, February 27, 1977, p. 2).

the first time. Estimates were given of a need for an additional 80,000 new jobs each year during the decade 1975-85 just to handle the German nationals coming of age and thus eligible to secure work permits. If one added to this figure the number of guestworkers' children coming of age who had immigrated to Germany prior to December 1, 1974, the total would be something like 120,000 new jobs needed in each of the 10 years.*

Two years after the ban went into effect, a report of the federal government reviewed its effects and pronounced judgment as to its future (Federal Republic of Germany 1975, p. 4):

> The Federal government will continue the engagement stop passed on November 23, 1973, even in case of a changing economic development. The engagement stop has proved an effective measure. The balance of migration has since been negative not only for the workmen, but for the general number of foreigners. This can be taken for granted that this tendency will continue. The retention of the engagement stop is justified in view of the anticipated development in the growth of the potential labor force. . . . Children of foreign workers can be given a work permit even in the present market situation if they have immigrated before December 1, 1974. This regulation will be kept in the future. If children of foreign workers immigrated after December 1, 1974, deadline, they are refused a work permit at the present time.

It should be noted that an additional aspect of this ban has been that not only the older children who have come to Germany to be reunited with their families but also the spouses of present workers are affected. They too are unable to receive work permits. Though the consequences of this ban will have, in the long run, a more severe effect upon the older children of the guestworkers, its immediate impact upon the entire family is felt, for it restricts the options for additional employment and thus additional sources of income. When data have shown that guestworkers are paying nearly one-third more in some cities for accommodations smaller than those held by German nationals, such income would be of significant import in striving to achieve a viable standard of living.

---

*This date is extremely important in its implications for the future of the second generation, born to current guestworkers in Germany. If a child had come to Germany prior to that date, he or she would be eligible upon reaching the appropriate age to apply for a work permit. If, however, the youth came into the country after that date, unless born in Germany, he would not be eligible for such a permit. The result has been that a number of foreign young persons leaving school are not able to secure work permits. They are left without employment, or they must take it illegally. Either way, they are then in a category subject to deportation, though few accounts of deportations of children of current workers have made the press. No official figures are available.

One dramatic consequence of the immigration ban of November 1973 has been the increase in the number of illegally employed migrants in Germany. Estimates placed the figure in 1975 at somewhere between 200,000 and 300,000. Prior to the ban, the numbers were small, and options for legalizing one's status were liberal. In the time since the initiation of the ban, the numbers have grown considerably.

Calling this use of illegal migrants in Germany a new form of slave labor, Federal Labor Minister Walter Arendt spoke on behalf of the government's legislative proposal for curtailing this practice. The law was passed by the German Bundestag in June of 1975 and carried a number of strict provisions and stiff penalties for those involved in the recruitment, transporting, and hiring of illegal foreign workers. Under the new law, whoever recruits foreigners without authorization from the Federal Labor Office for employment in the Federal Republic is liable for fines up to DM 50,000 and prison terms of up to three years. Whoever carries out this activity as a business for private gain can be punished with a prison sentence of up to five years. Employers who negligently or intentionally employ illegal migrants are liable for a fine of up to DM 50,000. In those instances in which the employer engages in yet further discrimination by paying the workers less than the minimum wage, there is the additional liability of being subject to a possible prison sentence of no more than five years. Deportation costs must also be borne in such cases by the employer of the illegal workers.

## Restriction of Admission to Congested Areas

For all foreigners who do not have a permanent residence permit (and most do not), it is necessary to have the temporary permit periodically renewed. Since April 1, 1975, any foreigner who seeks to have a permit renewed has stamped into his passport a list of those cities where he is no longer able to settle. This ban on admission to residence in certain urban areas of the country was instigated for the following reasons, according to the report of the Federal Ministry for Labor and Social Affairs (1976, p. 24):

> The rapid rise of the number of foreign workers prior to the recruitment ban, the increasing number of family reunions as well as the prolonged stay of foreigners have all caused a heavy strain on the social infrastructure. Despite all efforts, it was not always possible to avoid bottlenecks and social shortcomings. This is particularly true for the congested areas preferred by foreigners where sometimes every fourth worker is a foreign national. On the initiative of the Federal Ministry of Labor and Social Affairs, the Federal government and the Land Governments have therefore restricted the further admission of foreign workers into these congested areas.

The mechanics of establishing such a ban are simple: when the foreign population in a city exceeds 6 percent of the total population, a city can apply to its state government for the designation of overburdened settlement area. If the designation is granted, the city can then declare an end to all further immigration of foreigners. The control mechanism for doing so is through the refusal to grant a residency permit to those who request it. (Residence permits in Germany are not open-ended, and do not grant one the right to live anywhere in the country, or even in a certain state. They are specific to each locale, and reapplication must be made if a person moves.) When the percentage of foreigners in the population of a city goes above 12 percent, the city can of its own right automatically declare itself an area of overburdened settlement and end all further immigration. As of January 1977, five of the largest cities in Germany—Cologne, Frankfurt, Hannover, Munich, and West Berlin—had exercised their prerogatives to request such designation, had received it, and then proceeded to ban further settlement.

Though this legislation has been discussed in universalistic terms, the impact has been group-specific because there are three groups of exceptions to the regulations: those who have been in the country for five years of continuous residence, those who have married German citizens, or those who are members of the EEC. More than half of all foreign workers in the country fall into one of these categories. What the legislation does do is to work against the recent arrivals, those who are less assimilated into German society, and those from the non-EEC countries. Although the ban would apply as well, theoretically, to those persons from North America, Asia, Latin America, Africa, or any other part of the globe, its aim has been to curb the influx of guestworkers from the countries of the European South.

In examining those five large cities that have applied for the ban and subsequently exercised it, it is apparent that the pressures to use it are more often economic than social; i.e., the imperative is to preserve jobs for Germans rather than to prevent a heavy strain on the social infrastructure. Three of the five cities listed above had not even reached the 12 percent level deemed to be injurious to the social structure of the community. In Cologne, 11.3 percent of the inhabitants were foreigners, in Hannover 8.4 percent, in Berlin 9.4 percent. (Munich had 15.4 percent, and in Frankfurt 17.1 percent of the population consisted of foreigners.) What was apparent was that in the former three cities the unemployment rate of German workers was high. It was thought that to prevent additional foreign workers from coming into the area and competing for employment would be of benefit to the national labor force. As was noted in an article in *Die Zeit*, a German weekly newspaper (April 16, 1976):

> These cities have wanted to stop the influx of foreign workers now, and for other reasons than that of keeping the balance of the community: according to an official spokesman, "The arrival of foreign workers in large numbers results in unemployment for many un-

skilled German workers already living in the city. By taking this step, the jobs of many Germans at, for example, the Ford Works have been safeguarded."

The article goes on to note that the Ford Works was one of the strongest opponents to the instigation of the settlement ban for the Cologne area. The Ford Works had been heavily dependent upon foreign labor and did not wish to see restrictions placed in the way of securing labor when necessary.* (In 1975, only one of every four new employees at the Ford Works was German.) Though the Ford efforts did not succeed, the efforts of industrialists in other areas to keep open the options for further migration have succeeded. In cities like Stuttgart and Offenbach, where the percentage of foreign persons is as high as 16 to 19 percent, the ban has not been imposed. These are areas of high industrial concentration, heavily dependent upon foreign labor. It should be noted, however, that such instances are the exception rather than the rule. For the most part cities within the 6 to 12 percent range of foreign population in Germany have sought the right of prohibiting further settlement. As of January 1977, more than 45 cities in the country had instigated such a ban, including the five large cities already mentioned.

This ban on interregional mobility, aimed primarily at the migrant workers, must be juxtaposed with another ban to have a full picture of just how restrictive Germany has become with regard to the freedom of movement of its foreign labor force. Just as entire cities are allowed to declare themselves areas of oversettlement, so also are cities themselves able to make the same declarations for particular sectors within their boundaries. For example, not only has the city of Berlin declared itself oversettled vis-a-vis the rest of the country, but it has also declared three of its own districts oversettled and thus halted any further movements by foreign workers into these areas from other sectors of the city.

Taken together, these two levels of settlement prohibitions constitute an implicit assumption that the concentration of foreign workers is detrimental to German society. It also fits with the manner by which Germany addresses the integration of the foreign peoples now living in its midst. By seeking to control the aggregation of foreigners within the country, the various city and state governments are assuming that the social costs of these persons can be kept below those that would occur were they allowed to congregate and live where they

---

*As will be discussed in more detail in a later chapter, the mobility of the migrant population within Germany is a critically important aspect of their presence in the country. While Germans, for the most part, will take unemployment rather than move, it is more likely the opposite for the foreign workers. Thus as different regions expand or contract in economic activity, there exists a large pool of labor that responds accordingly. What the Ford Works feared was that in the event of a resurgent economy, the presence of the settlement ban would severely curtail their ability to find the necessary numbers of new workers.

wish. At another level, such policies are aimed at the assimilation of such workers on an individualistic basis rather than dealing with the implications of critical masses of ethnically and culturally different groups within the society.

The apparent assumption made by the various governments is that with the concentration of such groups of periphery persons, the social costs will rise and all the various manifestations of ghetto life will begin to appear. Given the current economic and political arrangements, they are correct. But the response has been, then, not to work toward the elimination of such inequalities and discriminatory practices, but rather to scatter the persons involved so as to keep the concentrations at lower and more manageable levels. The social costs of continuing a level of exploitation and discrimination and the negative effects both on the workers themselves and on the society of which they are a part are seen to be a lesser burden than the granting of benefits and rights to the workers.

It is an open question, however, just how long the assumed economic benefits of having the foreign workers in the country will outweigh the accumulating social costs to other aspects of the social fabric. When the scale is no longer tipped so strongly in favor of the economic benefits that the foreign workers have brought to Germany, a decision will be forced. The options are either to expel the workers and suffer a resultant reduced standard of living and economic growth, or to affirm the fact that literally millions of persons have been living in the country and contributing to its well-being, and should thus be encouraged and assisted in joining in the multiple ways of participating in the life of the society.

When one compares the aims of the ban on settlement in certain areas with the other expressed intent of the German government to facilitate the reunion of the workers in the country with their families, an immediate contradiction arises (Stark 1974, pp. 9-16). While further immigration of foreigners is prohibited, one finds statements such as the following in a report of the federal government (Federal Republic of Germany 1975, p. 13):

> The Federal Government does not wish to instigate policies that would make the coming of the families of the foreign workers to Germany more difficult. The Government considers the so far appointed waiting time of one year together with the proof of an adequate place of residence as necessary and sufficient preconditions.

The consequence of such a position is that while families are welcome, they are not welcome for at least a year, nor are they welcome in cities where the bans are in effect, and perhaps they are also not welcome in certain sectors of cities.

In the face of such policies, the foreign worker who wishes to bring his family to Germany confronts severe obstacles. First, if he lives in a city with the ban, he has to move to another city if he wishes to have his family come, though again he cannot move to another city where the ban is in effect. Second, those workers who have not been in Germany for a sufficient period of time (generally three years) will not receive permission to change jobs, thus restricting the area within which they are free to look for housing. Third, if the worker is in a city that has an internal ban on settlement in certain areas, he must move out of those areas where his people are gathered, where there would be come cultural and ethnic continuity for the newly arrived spouse and children, and where there is housing available for his family, even if at exorbitant prices. He must seek lodging in an area of lower concentration, one where few other foreigners are living and one where housing may be difficult to locate and even more expensive to secure. Couple this with the fact that the new arrivals cannot receive work permits and the financial burden takes on additional meaning. The cumulative impact of these obstacles is that if one wishes to have a reunited family, it will be achieved more in spite of official pronouncements of the government than because of them.

## Encouragement of Repatriation

In the context in which migration from the European South to the industrial countries of the North has been officially interpreted, the benefits for the sending countries would not only accrue while their workers were away through the gaining of skills and the sending of remittances, but with the return home of the workers the sending countries would gain a work force with industrial skills and values. German policy still subscribes to this position and describes repatriation as a positive aspect of the North-South labor migrations. As a government report (Federal Republic of Germany 1975, p. 22) noted:

> It is one of the main aims of the Government's foreigner policy to make clear to the foreign workers themselves that their return to their native countries is a chance for themselves as well as for the economic and social development of their native countries. This chance consists in the organized utilization of the knowledge and abilities acquired in the FRG. The Federal Government considers the professional and social reintegration of workers who want to return and have returned to their native countries as highly important. For years, the Government has emphasized the possibilities of utilizing the return movements in terms of developmental policies. As in the past, the Government will support contacts with the native countries, and will give impulse and support to the development of new reintegration models.

The above statement must be seen in the light of developments in Germany related to the rise in unemployment and the depth of the recession which for only the second time in the postwar period resulted in an economic downturn. In this post-1973 period, there has been a growing antagonism toward the foreign workers. In April 1976, *Die Zeit* published a poll reporting that more than half of the German workers surveyed believed that the unemployment levels were caused by foreign workers taking employment possibilities away from the native population. With sentiments such as these, it is little wonder that at least for reasons of national political gain, leaders would suggest that the government does encourage repatriation. It has the ring of benevolence in terms of Germany's relations to the European South and it assuages the anxiety of the native work force with regard to the government's sensitivity to their condition.

A call for the government to involve itself more actively in efforts to assist workers who wish to return home was made in June 1975 by a national political figure in the opposition coalition. The state premier of Baden-Württemberg, Hans Filbinger, called for the government to begin offering cash bonuses to foreign workers who would leave the country. Arguing that the scheme was necessary to relieve the unemployment in Germany, he suggested that it be voluntary and that no worker be forced to accept it. The financing of the funds would come from the accumulated social security and unemployment benefits paid in by the worker. These could be given back in a lump sum at the time of departure, a practice not now in effect.

The reply of the government was contained in their 1975 status report on the foreign workers in Germany, in which current policies were explicated and defended (Federal Republic of Germany 1975, p. 17):

> The Federal Government does not consider it necessary nor justifiable in terms of public finance to offer financial attractions out of the public funds in order to support the return of foreign workers to their countries. Also, it is not planned to suggest changes in the current legislation concerning the compensation rates so far as the social security system is concerned. Measures supporting and facilitating the return and professional reintegration of foreign workers into their home countries—with a view of general development—are not affected by this regulation.

While this was the official response to the call of the political opposition, the government did make the following announcement six days after the statement by Filbinger (quoted from a June 10, 1975 United Press International account of the Labor Ministry press briefing):

> The West German government said today it will continue its policy of repatriation of foreign workers to make more jobs available for Germans. The government will intensify talks with the sending countries about repatriation programmes to help the homecomers in settling down again in their home countries. The government rejected a proposal by the conservative Christian opposition party (CDU) to give individuals cash bonuses to encourage them to go home. Informed sources said the government's aim was to reduce the number of foreign workers to 1.5 million. Schemes being considered to reach

this goal include exceptional regulations to enable foreign workers wishing to return home to collect the percentage of pension due to them. The Government would also support development aid projects by which jobs can be created for returning workers in the countries concerned, a ministry spokesman said.

The proposal and the response to it by the government are examples of political jockeying. The call by Filbinger could be anticipated, given that he was premier of the state with the second largest concentration of foreign workers, or one-fifth of all foreign workers in the entire country. It was politically expedient for such a call to be made, both in his role as a member of the political opposition and his role as premier. He could respond to political sentiments of his own constitutents as well as prod the government to have to deal with the growing anxiety and uncertainty in the country regarding the place of the foreign worker in the economy.

From the government's point of view, the news briefing provided by the Labor Ministry was necessary, both to indicate that the government was sensitive to the voice of the opposition (though the means of supporting repatriation appears as its own proposal rather than that of Filbinger) and was attempting to deal with the foreign worker question. At the level of public imagery, it would appear that the two sides were nearly identical in their agreement that efforts should be made to assist the foreign workers who wished to return to their homelands. But as the report cited earlier makes clear, the government was, in fact, not about to release pension funds for the purpose. As of January 1977, there was still no official government policy to support repatriation other than through verbal encouragement.

## Family Allowance Payments

On January 1, 1975 the Federal Republic of Germany instituted a series of tax reform measures. The goal of these measures was to instigate a more progressive tax scale so that those with lower incomes would have less withheld from their checks, while the opposite would be true for those with higher incomes.

One other aspect of these reforms that bears particular import for this study relates to the creation of a system of family allowance payments. Prior to January 1, 1975 the tax laws were such that a tax payer claiming support of one or more children was allowed to deduct a certain amount from the gross income prior to the computation of the tax rate. (This is the procedure used at present in the United States.) With the reforms, the deduction procedure was eliminated and a new family allowance was instigated whereby payments are made (direct cash transfer) from the government to each recipient who has responsibility for the support of one or more children. Such payments are available to all children in the country at a uniform rate and are payable regardless of parents' income. The monthly allowance rates are as follows: DM 50 for the first child (approximately $25); DM 70 for the second child (approximately $35); and DM 120 for each additional child (approximately $60).

A distinction is made in this legislation between those children who are residing in Germany and those who are residing elsewhere. There is a second and lower scale for the latter group. The monthly payments for those children of eligible recipients who are not living in Germany are as follows: DM 10 for the first child (approximately $5); DM 25 for the second child (approximately $12); DM 60 for the third and fourth child (approximately $30); and DM 70 for each additional child (approximately $35). In commenting upon this differential scale, the Ministry of Labor and Social Affairs has noted (n.d., p. 1):

> The Federal Government considers it only fair that families who have their children with them in the Federal Republic of Germany and who have to bear the high cost of living here should also receive a higher family allowance than families whose children are living in their home country (except for employees from EEC countries). It expects that foreigners will provide the same living conditions for their children who live in the Federal Republic as German employees provide for their own children.

The creation of this program has been one of major importance for the welfare of children in Germany as well as for those who have remained in their home countries. The level of funding from this program reached more than DM 11 billion in 1976 (approximately $4.5 billion)! Table 3.9 indicates the magnitude of the program as well as the distribution of funds according to the nationality of recipients.

Within the legislation creating this program are reflected not only the humanitarian concerns of providing for the welfare of children, but the political concerns inherent in any such program of providing funds with few or no means tests. Of particular concern at the time the legislation was being prepared was the question of whether the allowance would be an incentive for the foreign workers to bring their children to Germany in order to be eligible for the payments. It was decided that a two-part policy could be implemented that would negate any such incentive. The first part was referred to earlier—the providing of payments to children who do stay in the home countries. If this was to be the carrot, the stick was created through regulations in the tax structure. Regulations were enacted to provide that foreign workers whose children remained in the home country would receive a higher net income than those who brought their children to live with them in Germany.* Table 3.10, prepared by the Fed-

---

*In interview after interview federal officials expressed to the author the concern over the possibility of large numbers of children of foreign workers currently in Germany coming to join their families. Given that these children do have the right to come to Germany and to join their parents if the parents have met the residence and housing require-

TABLE 3.9

Distribution of Family Allowance Payments, by Nationality, January 1-June 30, 1976

| Nationality | Total Number of Parents | Total Number of Children | Families with Children in Germany Parents | Families with Children in Germany Children | Families with Children in Homeland Parents | Families with Children in Homeland Children | Payments (in thousands of DM) May/June 1976 | Payments (in thousands of DM) January 1 through June 30, 1976 |
|---|---|---|---|---|---|---|---|---|
| German | 6,453,260 | 12,026,940 | 6,453,260 | 12,026,940 | — | — | 1,680,673 | 5,090,380 |
| Turkish | 348,957 | 933,934 | 106,004 | 236,337 | 242,953 | 697,597 | 114,947 | 337,977 |
| Yugoslav | 151,990 | 312,317 | 63,211 | 95,734 | 88,779 | 216,583 | 32,544 | 95,051 |
| Italian | 103,902 | 215,090 | 72,021 | 136,381 | 31,881 | 78,709 | 43,778 | 102,666 |
| Greek | 85,367 | 144,910 | 51,080 | 91,066 | 34,287 | 53,844 | 17,170 | 52,366 |
| Spanish | 43,767 | 85,236 | 27,746 | 51,125 | 16,021 | 34,111 | 10,162 | 30,729 |
| Portugese | 29,822 | 59,944 | 16,129 | 26,631 | 13,693 | 33,313 | 6,736 | 20,162 |
| Austrian | 27,927 | 50,952 | 22,197 | 37,778 | 5,730 | 13,174 | 7,350 | 22,167 |
| Dutch | 22,717 | 42,618 | 13,615 | 25,227 | 9,102 | 17,391 | 6,261 | 18,951 |
| French | 11,257 | 18,114 | 5,004 | 8,447 | 6,253 | 9,667 | 2,537 | 7,551 |
| British | 4,585 | 8,090 | 4,452 | 7,826 | 133 | 264 | 1,150 | 3,447 |
| Swiss | 2,292 | 4,199 | 2,210 | 4,023 | 82 | 176 | 595 | 1,796 |
| Belgian | 1,999 | 3,464 | 1,426 | 2,476 | 573 | 988 | 487 | 1,490 |
| All others | 42,704 | 75,702 | 41,382 | 73,584 | 1,322 | 2,851 | 10,658 | 33,318 |
| Total | 7,330,546 | 13,982,510 | 6,879,737 | 12,823,842 | 450,809 | 1,158,668 | 1,935,048 | 5,818,051 |

Source: Federal Labor Office, Federal Republic of Germany, Division of Family Allowance Program, 1976.

TABLE 3.10

Family Allowance, Tax Rates, and Net Disposable Income for EEC and Native German Workers Compared with Non-EEC Workers in the Federal Republic of Germany

| Children | Family Allowance (in DM) | Tax Rate (in DM) | Net Disposable Income (in DM) |
|---|---|---|---|
| Non-EEC workers |  |  |  |
| In Germany |  |  |  |
| Two | 1,440 | 1,874 | −434 |
| Three | 2,880 | 1,874 | +1.006 |
| In homeland |  |  |  |
| Two | 420 | 105[a] | +315 |
| Three | 1,140 | 105[a] | +1.035 |
| EEC and German Workers in Germany |  |  |  |
| In Germany |  |  |  |
| Two | 1,440 | 1,874 | −434 |
| Three | 2,880 | 1,874 | +1,006 |
| In homeland |  |  |  |
| Two | 1,440 | n.a.[b] | n.a. |
| Three | 2,880 | n.a. | n.a. |

[a] Arbitrary tax figure established by Ministry.
[b] data not available.

Source: Ministry of Labor and Social Affairs, Federal Republic of Germany, "Continuous Reporting System on Migration: A Report to the Organization for Economic Cooperation and Development," Bonn, 1976.

---

ments, there is the possibility of more than one million children entering the federal Republic. The group for whom the greatest concern was expressed was the nearly 700,000 Turkish children who are potential immigrants. No evidence has been found that there exist at present with the federal government contingency plans for such necessities as schooling, medical care, and additional housing for these children. The consensus appears to be that such an influx of tens or hundreds of thousands of Turkish children is not likely and to begin planning would only stir anxieties in the native population. It is a situation of assuming that a potentially explosive condition is better left alone and if it does occur, one deals with it in the aftermath.

eral Ministry for Labor and Social Affairs, is based on an annual gross income of 19,200 DM.

The net effect of the regulations in the family allowance program is to encourage the foreign worker to maintain his family in the home country. Again one confronts the fact that the public pronouncements contradict programatic realities. While statements are made by the government favoring the reuniting of families and the integration of these families into German society, the tax structure provides a tangible disincentive for this to happen. The foreign worker essentially must pay a surcharge to be with his family while the native worker does not.

While the five areas of foreigner policy described above all impinge upon the foreign worker in Germany and hinder both his personal well-being and his opportunity of integration into German society, they by no means exhaust the regulations and guidelines by which the lives of foreign workers are governed. There are additional rules governing housing, education, political expression, civil rights, and occupational alternatives. These will be taken up in later chapters.

With what has been presented thus far, it should be evident that the policies governing the lives of the guestworkers in Germany are confused and contradictory. *The continual slippage between the pronouncements of a concern for integration and well-being of the foreign workers and the realities of policies that tend to produce opposite outcomes can only reflect the deeper ambivalence of the Federal Republic toward the foreign workers.*

The cumulative impact of these and other regulations make the life of the guestworker full of stress. The difficulties are plentiful: the lack of residential mobility; the lack of opportunity to live among friends and relatives; never knowing how long one will be even tolerated, let alone welcomed; having to cope with a set of employment regulations that restrict personal mobility as well as deny opportunities for employment to spouse and children; and finally, confronting the stark realization that real financial barriers are placed in the way of a basic human right to be reunited with spouse and children. The outcomes engendered by these policies belie much that is said and done by the government under the theme of the integration of the foreign workers into German society. The policies and practices that are currently in force can more realistically be said to both create and sustain the institutional marginality of the guestworkers.

# 4

# THE TURKISH CONNECTION

They have come to Germany by the tens of thousands. They have come from the large cities of Ankara and Istanbul and from small villages of a few dozen people. They have come from the shores of the Black Sea and from the Mediterranean Sea. They have come from all five regions of Anatolia. They have come from all 67 districts in the country, some sending thousands, others a few hundred. They have come to Germany as guests to work. Together with their families, they now number more than one million persons, or more than one quarter of all foreigners in Germany.

The first of what was to become a continuing and swelling stream of Turkish workers into the Federal Republic of Germany began in 1956 when 12 Turkish workers and their families were brought to Kiel for vocational training. These workers were part of a program to enhance German capital investment in Turkey through the training of local workers to become foremen in industrial enterprises. The program did not work, the training folded, and the workers soon found employment in the dockyards of Hamburg, Bremen, and Lübeck (cf. Abadan-Unat et al. 1976, p. 27).

The numbers of Turkish workers who went abroad in the period from 1956 through 1961 remained minuscule. In 1961 the total emigration of workers was slightly less than 4,000 (van Velzen 1974). In the period immediately after that, a series of events both in Europe and in Turkey itself began to drastically change the size of this migration flow. In Turkey, fundamental political changes were materializing with the overthrow of the Menderes regime by the army in 1960. As described by Adaban-Unat et al. (1976, p. 28):

> The army seized power and the multiple party system came to an end. In a way the Revolution of 1960 facilitated labor migration to

Germany. Article 18 of the new constitution explicitly granted the right to travel abroad to each Turkish citizen. . . . The following years saw further developments in the government's involvement in labor migration which was still almost entirely directed towards Germany. . . . In 1960 the State Planning Organization was established and made directly responsible to the Prime Minister. . . . The first Five Year Development Plan, drafted in 1962, was implemented in 1963. For the first time concerned officials decided to encourage the migration of Turkish workers deliberately and incorporated their design in a State document: the First Five Year Development Plan (1963-1967) cites both "population planning" and "the export of surplus manpower" as measures for attaining the Turkish goal of a set growth rate.

The previous chapters have provided an analysis of the economic forces that were beginning to coalesce and grow in Western Europe during this same period. With the 1961 closing of the border between East and West Germany, and at a time of continuing expansion of the economy, Germany was forced to go afield to seek the manpower necessary for its boom economic growth. In 1961 Germany and Turkey signed a bilateral labor recruitment agreement with general stipulations for recruitment, employment, and wages. Turkey signed similar agreements in 1964 with Austria, the Netherlands, and Belgium; in 1965 with France; with Sweden in 1967 and Australia in 1968. Less comprehensive agreements were implemented with the United Kingdom in 1961 and with Switzerland in 1971. A 1973 agreement with Denmark was rescinded when Denmark entered the EEC.

An important component of all these bilateral agreements was the clear stipulation that recruitment procedures were to be the prerogative of the Turkish Employment Service and the respective officially recognized host government or employer asociation representatives. This was a point of mutual agreement. Turkey did not wish its workers to be recruited through private arrangements and thus face higher risks of exploitation and discrimination; the host countries were under pressure of their union organizations for fear such private contracts would undercut the current wages of national workers. Thus, apart from those workers who first entered the host countries as tourists, found work, and then sought to normalize their status are those who entered illegally.\* Turkish workers who went to the industrial North were assisted both by the

---

\*A figure of 87,104 is cited by Abadan-Unat et al. (1976, p. 16) as the number of workers who went abroad on their own initiative between 1967 and 1975, found work, and then secured a work passport through the Turkish Employment Services. This same source also suggests that a figure of 10 percent as the number of illegal Turkish workers presently in the EEC is a conservative one.

Employment Service in Turkey and the official agency of the host country. Table 4.1 provides data on all workers sent abroad through the Employment Service between 1961 and 1975.

The requests for labor sent by the industrial countries to the Employment Service were of two types, nominative and anonymous.* The former was a request by name for a specific individual, the latter for simply a category of workers to fill a particular employment opportunity. Between January 1965 and the end of December 1975, a total of 238,255 workers were sent abroad at nominative request, 33.8 percent of all Turkish workers sent abroad. As a consequence, the Employment Service was able to exercise no control over more than a third of all workers who left the country, because the bilateral agreements stipulated that nominative recruitment requests were to be honored by Turkey.† Male or female, skilled or unskilled, urban or rural—all such considerations were beyond the scope of the authority of the Employment Service. This was a factor that played some considerable havoc with the planning estimates of the Turkish government in projecting its manpower needs and resources. During the years of the mass immigrations into Germany (and 85 percent of all Turkish workers who did emigrate went to Germany), the German recruitment office was taking 75 percent of all skilled workers Turkey was sending abroad, and most of these Germany took under the nominative procedure. Between 1965 and 1975 Turkey sent 199,546 skilled workers abroad, or more than 34 percent of all skilled workers in the entire country. Of these, 149,754 went to the Federal Republic of Germany (cf. Abadan-Unat et al. 1976, p. 22).

It was only with respect to the recruitment of workers to fill the anoymous demands that the Employment Service of Turkey was able to exercise some control and attempt to implement some aspects of the manpower policies it had envisioned with the initiation of its five-year plan. The rules for the allocation of workers to fill the anonymous requests were quite specific (Abadan-Unat et al. 1976, pp. 9-10):

> 1) Applicants from under-developed regions according to the classification of provinces by the Turkish State Planning Organization are entitled to a priority of two years, applicants from developing regions, a priority of one year, and those from urban regions have no priority. This means in effect that on the day such job seekers open a file with the Employment Service, their names are placed on the waiting list as if they had registered a year or two previously.

---

*The past tense is used here advisedly. With the immigration bans of 1973 and 1974, recruitment requests have dwindled to practically nothing. Germany requested less than one thousand in 1974, and none in 1975 and 1976.

†Three groups of workers were placed off limits to recruitment by any means. These were the coal miners from Zonguldak, the workers in the Kirikale armament factories, and ship builders from certain ports in western Turkey.

TABLE 4.1

Turkish Workers Sent Abroad through the Employment Service,
by Year and Country of Destination

| Host Country | 1961-66 | 1967 | 1968 | 1969 | 1970 | 1971 | 1972 | 1973 | 1974 | 1975 |
|---|---|---|---|---|---|---|---|---|---|---|
| Federal Republic of Germany | 168,991 | 7,199 | 41,409 | 98,142 | 96,936 | 65,684 | 65,875 | 103,753 | 1,228 | 640 |
| France | 88 | — | — | 191 | 9,036 | 7,897 | 10,610 | 17,544 | 10,577 | 25 |
| Austria | 4,973 | 1,043 | 673 | 973 | 10,622 | 4,620 | 4,472 | 7,083 | 2,501 | 226 |
| Switzerland | 504 | 215 | 97 | 183 | 1,598 | 1,342 | 1,312 | 1,109 | 770 | 229 |
| Netherlands | 6,598 | 48 | 875 | 3,404 | 4,843 | 4,853 | 744 | 1,994 | 1,503 | 32 |
| Australia | — | — | 107 | 970 | 1,186 | 879 | 640 | 886 | 1,138 | 189 |
| Belgium | 13,917 | — | — | — | 431 | 583 | 113 | 265 | 555 | 59 |
| United Kingdom | 8 | — | — | 4 | 536 | 1,289 | 82 | 116 | 133 | 64 |
| Others | 16 | 442 | 43 | 108 | 4,360 | 1,295 | 1,381 | 3,030 | 1,826 | 2,955 |
| Total | 195,095 | 8,947 | 43,204 | 103,975 | 129,575 | 88,442 | 85,229 | 135,820 | 20,211 | 4,419 |

Sources: Abadan-Unat et al., Migration and Development (Ankara: Ajans-Turk Press, 1976), p. 11; Organization for Economic Cooperation and Development, SOPEMI Continuous Reporting System on Migration (Paris: OECD, 1976), p. 41.

2) Fifteen percent of all annual allocations of anonymous demands are set aside from members of Village Development Cooperatives (VDCs). In addition to paying an initial membership fee, workers sent to Europe by a VDC are formally obligated to invest a set amount of their savings in VDC activities.

3) Fifteen percent of all annual allocations of anonymous demands are reserved for officially designated "disaster areas" where the local socio-economic structure has been shaken by an earthquake, landslide, severe drought or epidemic of plant disease.

Table 4.2 provides data on the numbers of workers sent abroad under either the nominative or anonymous recruitment procedure. As is evident, with the tightening up of recruitment, the host countries began more and more to use the nominative procedure for recruitment. The post-immigration ban numbers, small as they are, reflect that the host countries have become quite particular in their designation of desired workers. (There is no way of knowing how many of these workers were in fact new to Europe or were already in Europe but seeking to legalize their status with a nominative recruitment.)

As was also the situation with Yugoslavia noted earlier, there has been a considerable drain of skilled workers from Turkey to the countries of the European North. While the precise dimensions of this drain are difficult to ascertain, the general contour is more than clear.* Yugoslavia has exported more than 50 percent of all its skilled workers. The comparable figures for Turkey are between 33 and 35 percent of all its skilled workers. In both instances, the absence of tens of thousands of such workers from the home countries has had a considerable impact upon the ability of these countries to undertake their own developmental programs.† Just prior to the immigration bans of 1973 and 1974, Yugoslav President Tito presented legislation that would have drastically reduced the number of skilled workers allowed to leave the country for work elsewhere. The initiation of the immigration bans essentially accomplished the purpose for him.

---

*One main reason for this difficulty is that there are some differences between the classification schemes used by Turkey and those of the countries of the North. The situation appears to be one of Turkey granting skilled status to occupational groups to which the countries of the North are willing to grant only semiskilled or even unskilled status.

†As Aker (1975, p. 475) notes, there is an additional dimension to this drain of skilled manpower that is critical to the developmental potential of Turkey. All candidates for employment in Germany must have a minimum of an elementary school education. Thus the whole of the Turkish adult population in Germany, save for some wives who have come to join their husbands, has a minimum of a primary school diploma. Furthermore, about 20 percent of all workers have education beyond the primary school level. When one juxatposes these data against the figure of 55 percent of the adult population in Turkey being illiterate, one sees immediately how serious is the drain of these workers from Turkey, for they represent not only a major proportion of the skilled labor force, but also a major portion of the literate population in the country.

TABLE 4.2

Emigrant Turkish Workers Sent Abroad through the Employment Service, by Year, Country of Destination, and Nature of Contract

| Host Country | 1965-71 Anonymous | 1965-71 Nominative | 1972 Anonymous | 1972 Nominative | 1973 Anonymous | 1973 Nominative | 1974 Anonymous | 1974 Nominative | 1975 Anonymous | 1975 Nominative |
|---|---|---|---|---|---|---|---|---|---|---|
| Federal Republic of Germany | 284,002 | 103,520 | 42,296 | 23,579 | 76,840 | 26,953 | 784 | 444 | – | 640 |
| France | 5,492 | 11,632 | 2,921 | 7,689 | 8,768 | 8,776 | 5,502 | 5,075 | – | 25 |
| Austria | 7,096 | 13,277 | 2,677 | 1,795 | 1,703 | 5,375 | 600 | 1,901 | 67 | 59 |
| Switzerland | 1,102 | 2,608 | 16 | 1,296 | 36 | 1,073 | – | 770 | – | 229 |
| Netherlands | 15,552 | 1,860 | 657 | 87 | 1,734 | 260 | 293 | 845 | 1 | 32 |
| Australia | 2,884 | 258 | 180 | 460 | 315 | 571 | – | 555 | – | 189 |
| Belgium | 1,661 | 1,014 | – | 113 | – | 265 | – | 113 | – | 59 |
| United Kingdom | 9 | 1,855 | – | 82 | – | 116 | – | 1,826 | – | 64 |
| Others | 469 | 5,782 | – | 1,381 | – | 3,030 | 1,199 | 340 | 1,238 | 1,816 |
| Total | 318,267 | 141,806 | 48,747 | 36,482 | 89,401 | 46,419 | 8,342 | 11,869 | 1,306 | 3,113 |
| General Total | 460,073 | | 85,229 | | 135,820 | | 20,211 | | 4,419 | |
| Percent | 69.2 | 30.8 | 57.2 | 42.8 | 65.8 | 34.2 | 41.3 | 58.7 | 29.9 | 70.1 |

Sources: Abadan-Unat et al., Migration and Development (Ankara: Ajans-Turk Press, 1976), p. 15; Organization for Economic Cooperation and Development, SOPEMI Continuous Reporting System on Migration (Paris: OECD, 1976).

It should be noted that something similar would have soon been needed for Turkey. Though the country had sent one-third of all its skilled workers abroad, the waiting lists compiled in the Employment Services indicated that another 301,294 skilled workers had made application to go abroad at the time the bans were established in late 1973.* The combined total of those who were working outside the country and those skilled workers who wished to do so was more than 500,000, a staggering 85 percent of all skilled Turkish workers. (Parenthetically, at the time of the ban there were also more than 700,000 unskilled workers who had applied to go abroad. If all those who wished to go abroad had been able to do so, Turkey could have hypothetically sent 1,750,000 of its workers abroad, or 12 percent of its entire labor force of approximately 15,000,000 workers.)

As one might anticipate, both on cultural and religious grounds, it has been the males who have migrated from Turkey to the European North. Eighty-two percent of all Turkish workers who went abroad between 1961 and June 1975 were male. Were it not for the fact that the Federal Republic of Germany recruited large numbers of female workers—90 percent of all female workers who did leave Turkey—the number of male workers would approach 98 percent of all Turkish workers abroad. With the continuing rise in family reunions since the 1973 ban and the number of female workers who have dropped out of the labor force but remained in Germany, the estimates are that as of January 1976, there were approximately 280,000 adult Turkish females, or 27 percent of all Turkish persons in Germany. The other two categories among the 1,070,000 Turkish persons in the Federal Republic totaled 195,000 children and 595,000 males (cf. International Catholic Migration Commission, *Migration News*, 1975, p. 37). Table 4.3 provides data on the numbers of Turkish workers sent abroad through the Employment Service between 1961 and 1975 according to their country of destination and their sex.

Integral to the various development plans prepared by Turkey has been the exportation of a certain portion of its labor force. It was assumed that Turkey would reap the benefits of a returning industrial work force given training and experience by someone else. This, however, has failed to materialize. One reason appears to be that efforts have failed to increase and create rural development through the exportation of rural workers. The eight most rural and least developed districts of Turkey together contributed on the average no more than 1 percent of the workers who emigrated. On the other hand, the city of Istanbul alone was sending between 15 and 20 percent of all workers (cf. Abadan-Unat et al. 1976, p. 17).

---

*Germany continued for one year beyond the beginning of the immigration ban to accept names of potential immigrant workers from Turkey. At the time it finally requested no further names from the Employment Service, more than 1,200,000 names were available, or 8 percent of the entire Turkish labor force.

## TABLE 4.3

### Turkish Workers Sent Abroad through the Employment Service, by Year, Country of Destination, and Sex

|  | \multicolumn{5}{c}{Host Country} |||||
|---|---|---|---|---|---|
|  | FRG | France | Austria | Switzerland | Netherlands |
| **1961-67** | | | | | |
| M | 144,685 | 88 | 5,848 | 598 | 6,634 |
| F | 31,505 | – | 168 | 121 | 12 |
| **1968** | | | | | |
| M | 30,099 | – | 668 | 73 | 874 |
| F | 11,310 | – | 5 | 24 | 1 |
| **1969** | | | | | |
| M | 77,472 | 184 | 918 | 162 | 3,404 |
| F | 20,670 | 7 | 55 | 21 | – |
| **1970** | | | | | |
| M | 76,556 | 8,992 | 10,511 | 1,458 | 4,840 |
| F | 20,380 | 44 | 111 | 140 | 3 |
| **1971** | | | | | |
| M | 52,162 | 7,856 | 4,285 | 1,227 | 4,790 |
| F | 13,522 | 41 | 335 | 115 | 63 |
| **1972** | | | | | |
| M | 48,911 | 10,572 | 3,291 | 1,134 | 670 |
| F | 16,964 | 38 | 1,181 | 178 | 74 |
| **1973** | | | | | |
| M | 79,526 | 17,467 | 4,943 | 1,312 | 1,980 |
| F | 24,267 | 77 | 2,140 | 845 | 14 |
| **1974** | | | | | |
| M | 1,187 | 10,544 | 1,939 | 538 | 1,487 |
| F | 41 | 33 | 562 | 232 | 16 |
| **January–June 1975** | | | | | |
| M | 214 | 18 | 145 | 57 | 22 |
| F | 23 | 1 | 52 | 33 | – |

There simply has not developed the direct rural to foreign emigration the planners had anticipated. What has happened, instead, is that an intermediate step has occurred in the migration chain. Rural workers migrate first to the urban areas and from there they emigrate abroad. Kudat and Özkan (1976, pp. 31, 40) cite data from their sample of more than 2,000 workers showing that 17.7 percent of their respondents emigrated from villages, 25.3 percent from

Table 4.3 continued

| Australia | Belgium | UK | Others | Total | Percent |
|---|---|---|---|---|---|
| – | 13,917 | 8 | 458 | 172,236 | 15.66 |
| – | – | – | – | 31,806 | |
| 106 | – | – | 43 | 31,863 | 73.8 |
| 1 | – | – | – | 11,341 | 16.2 |
| 962 | – | – | 108 | 83,210 | 80.0 |
| 8 | – | 4 | – | 20,765 | 20.0 |
| 1,172 | 430 | 512 | 4,328 | 108,799 | 84.0 |
| 14 | 1 | 51 | 32 | 20,776 | 16.0 |
| 833 | 578 | 1,232 | 1,279 | 74,242 | 83.9 |
| 46 | 5 | 57 | 16 | 14,200 | 16.1 |
| 478 | 111 | 69 | 1,339 | 66,575 | 78.1 |
| 162 | 2 | 13 | 42 | 18,654 | 21.9 |
| 659 | 256 | 106 | 3,003 | 109,252 | 80.1 |
| 227 | 9 | 10 | 27 | 27,616 | 20.2 |
| 736 | 535 | 104 | 1,807 | 18,881 | 93.4 |
| 402 | 16 | 9 | 19 | 1,330 | 6.6 |
| 79 | 36 | 63 | 1,121 | 1,755 | 88.4 |
| 110 | 3 | 1 | 7 | 230 | 11.6 |

Source: Ubadan-Unat et al., Migration and Development (Ankara: Ajans-Turk Press, 1976), p. 12a.

towns, and the majority (57 percent) from urban areas, though 43 percent of the total sample were rural born. It is also the case that the rural population of emigrants was overwhelmingly male (82 versus 18 percent). As could be anticipated, migration for rural women is not easy. It is the urban sectors that contribute more nearly an equal proportion of men and women (52 to 48 percent), or 87 percent of all women who have emigrated.

Given the fact that the urban workers are more skilled, literate, and mobile than their rural counterparts, one can anticipate that few if any of these workers would wish to settle in rural areas upon their return. Further, Kudat and Özkan (1976, pp. 69-77) report that even those few workers who have emigrated directly from the rural areas do not wish to return and settle there. They too have become urbanized. The difficulty this represents for Turkey is that the forces of emigration have contributed to the depopulation of rural areas on a long-term basis and thus severely hindered the ability of Turkey effectively to implement rural development programs, a key, as Power (1975) has noted, both to the lessening of unemployment and the creation of a more balanced development process throughout the country. In geographic terms, it is eastern Turkey that is most rural and also declining in working age population, while the opposite processes are at work in western Turkey.

It is possible to say, though with a bit of overstatement, that the internal processes at work in Turkey mirror some of the international pressures the country faces. It is not far from accurate to note that Turkey itself is experiencing a widening gap between its center and periphery areas. It is, as it were, a double compounding of the problem Turkey faces in seeking to modernize and develop its society. Not only do there exist gross imbalances in the regional development within the country, but the country as a whole is in a gross imbalance with those of the European North. The question of whether these disparities can be overcome is central to the future relations Turkey will be able to develop with the countries of the North. That the contours of such relations are more than simply an interesting academic problem is made clear by the negotiations Turkey and the member states of the EEC have had regarding the conditions under which Turkey would be granted membership.

## THE TURKISH ASSOCIATION WITH THE EEC

Among the most important developments in the foreign policy of the EEC and one that affects most directly the Federal Republic of Germany are the agreements of the Community with Greece and Turkey, generally known as the Accords of Athens (effective November 1, 1962) and Ankara (effective December 1, 1964).* Much of their significance lies in the effort to combine economic assistance, in the form of tariff preferences and loans, with eventual economic integration into the Community. The goal of these agreements is stated in Article 2, Part 1 of each Accord:

> It shall be the aim of the Association Agreement to promote a continuous and well balanced strengthening of commercial and eco-

---

*The author has drawn particularly upon the accounts of Turkey's relation to the EEC by Abadan-Unat et al. (1976), Ettinger (1965), and Valier and Ilkin (1975).

nomic relations between the parties, with full regard to the need to ensure the speedier development of the Turkish [Greek] economy and the raising of the level of employment and the living conditions of the Turkish [Greek] people.

Turkey had applied for associate membership in the EEC in July 1959, and the Turkish Association Agreement was signed in September 1963. As Varlier and Ilkin (1975, p. 426) note, with regard to the thrust of this agreement:

> The Ankara Agreement aims at establishing closer economic and commercial links between the member States of the Community and Turkey, thereby maintaining and strengthening the existing political links. The Agreement also includes as an ultimate objective Turkey's entry in the EEC as a full member. Another objective is to assist Turkey in her efforts to develop her economy and raise the standards of living of her people. This is not only an end in itself but also a means of ensuring that the links, either existing or to be established, between the EEC and Turkey will be permanent, leading eventually to Turkey's full membership in the EEC.

The agreement, which became operative in 1964, established the policy that both Turkey and the EEC were to consider, after a period of five years, whether Turkey should merely extend the period of preparation for full membership for another six years or whether she could enter into a transitional period that would lead to full membership. The primary objective of this first five-year phase was stated as follows (European Economic Community 1963): "Turkey shall, with the help of the Community, strengthen her economy in order to be able to take on the obligations which will devolve on her during the transition and final stages." The degree to which Turkey successfully met this criterion would determine movement into the transitional phase or the prolonging of the preparatory phase for another six years.

In the aftermath of the mixed Parliamentary Council of the EEC that met in Ankara in September 1968, Turkey was deemed prepared to enter into the transitional phase with no further delay. During this phase would come the gradual introduction of a customs union proper, based on reciprocal agreements between Turkey and the EEC. The unilateral aid of the EEC given to Turkey during the preparatory stage would cease. In November 1969 the full Membership Council of the EEC met in Brussels and drew up the conditions Turkey was to meet during the transition phase in order to qualify for full membership. The Turkish Parliament accepted the propositions on July 6, 1971.

A major, if not the key, component of this stage was to be the implementation of procedures leading to the full and free movement of Turkish workers within the EEC. This effort was to span a ten-year period from December 1, 1976 to December 1, 1986, during which period the EEC would commit itself to the removal of migration barriers and the implementation of policies to ensure the Turkish workers treatment without discrimination and guarantee them the same wages and working conditions as the citizens of the EEC.

But events have not gone as they might have. The recession in Western Europe, the immigration bans imposed by the industrial countries, and the reservations of the sending countries as to the detrimental effects of exporting their labor have all led to second thoughts about the feasibility and desirability of the full and free migration of Turkish workers throughout the EEC. As Abadan-Unat et al. (1976, p. 38) noted:

> Germany, first and foremost, alarmed by recession and domestic unemployment, raised objections; but the prospect of hundreds of thousands of Turkish workers flooding the labor market has been causing deep general concern. In Turkey, too, reservations have arisen practically on the eve of what might prove to be a mass exodus of manpower, of skilled manpower especially. Economic development through industrialization would then stall, a national cirsis would ensue. At the present, moreover, Turkey is not in a position to institute the system of social security benefits domestically—unemployment payments, for example—which prevails in EEC countries and which workers from these countries arriving to hold jobs in Turkey would, according to accepted rules of reciprocity, be within their rights to demand.

The consequence of this complex and interlocking set of circumstances was that the negotiations for the movement of Turkish workers within the EEC took place against a background of ambivalence at best, and at worst, a strongly negative view on the part of some EEC members. In preparing for the negotiations, Turkey developed a "Preliminary Report on the Gradual Introduction of Free Circulation of Manpower between Turkey and the EEC." This proposal divided the realization of manpower circulation into a three-stage process (Abadan-Unat et al. 1976, p. 39):

> *Stage 1*: (December 1, 1976–December 1, 1982) Continuation of policies governing the dispatch of Turkish workers abroad which are not in effect, i.e., maintenance of host country demand recruitment. Establishment of a "Directorate of Employment in the EEC Member States" to cooperate with various recruitment offices in handling manpower demands and allocations. Combination of recruitment offices of those EEC countries with whom Turkey has concluded bilateral labor agreements into a "Liaison Office of EEC Countries." Replacement of extant labor and social security pacts with a new, uniform agreement between Turkey and the Association Council of the EEC—an agreement to abolish all measures prejudicial to Turkish workers in their pay scale, working conditions, or freedom of movement and assuring them priority of placement over migrants from third countries presently supplying EEC member states with manpower.

*Stage 2*: (December 1, 1982-December 1, 1986) Admission of nationals from EEC member countries to occupy job vacancies in Turkey on demand. Transformation of the "Directorate of Employment in the EEC Member States" into an "EEC Office for European Coordination-Directorate of Domestic and Foreign Employment."
*Stage 3*: (Starting December 1, 1986) Implementation of free circulation of manpower between Turkey and EEC member states in accordance to regulations approved by the Council of the European Community and valid at that date.

The negotiations that occurred during November and December of 1976 on the matter of this movement of Turkish labor within the EEC ended with each side granting some concessions, but neither side able to have its way entirely. From the EEC point of view, the goal was the setting aside of the question of free movement of foreign workers and working toward an integration of Turkey on a gradual basis into the EEC outside the traditional labor agreements that have existed among Community members. In short, the goal was to begin to bring Turkey into membership without bringing in the Turkish workers. From the view of Turkey, the right of free and full circulation of manpower was the critical issue, more so than the lowering and removal of tariffs on agricultural products which the EEC wished to stress.

An interim agreement between Turkey and the EEC was reached on December 21, 1976. The agreement had several key points (*Die Bonner*, December 22, 1976). It provided that for the indefinite future, there would be no suspension of current immigration bans by the countries of the EEC; that Turkish workers in EEC countries would have the right, after three years of employment, to switch positions within the same occupational category, and after five years, the right to switch occupational categories; that in any future recruitments of foreign workers by the member states of the EEC, Turkey would have a priority; and that a long-term economic aid package would be provided by the EEC member states to Turkey so as to increase employment opportunities and generally enhance home development.

The newspaper account from which these four points are summarized, as well as several other articles, made it clear that all four points were essentially those proposed by the EEC. The Turkish foreign minister was quoted as saying that while he accepted the present proposals, he was hopeful that in the near future the EEC would be more conciliatory and would grant manpower concessions. He is said to have called the free circulation of labor the "pillar of the Association." Reaction of the EEC officials was muted. The Dutch foreign minister, Van der Stoel, expressed the view that with the present agreement concluded, a foundation had been laid for further cooperation on problems of mutual concern.*

---

*Almost simultaneously with this chill in EEC-Turkey relations, the governments of the nine EEC members voted for the admission of Greece, over the objections of the EEC

Though the question of the free and full movement of Turkish workers within the EEC is an issue of paramount importance to resolve prior to the entrance of Turkey into the EEC, there are several other matters that need to be mentioned as well. These all relate to the current conditions in Turkey, conditions that indicate that Turkey is essentially an underdeveloped country. The problematic nature of being underdeveloped is severe in and of itself, but to place such a country in full partnership with the member states of the EEC raises concerns that become international in scope.

TABLE 4.4

Per Capita National Income of the EEC,
Turkey, and Greece, 1974
(in U.S. dollars)

| Countries | Per Capita Income |
|---|---|
| Germany | 3,739 |
| France | 3,403 |
| Italy | 1,987 |
| Netherlands | 3,159 |
| Belgium | 3,286 |
| Luxembourg | 2,641 (1971) |
| Greece | 1,327 |
| Turkey | 563 (1973) |

Source: O. Varlier and S. Ilkin, "The Role of International Migration within the Turkish Planning Perspective," in International Conference on Migrant Workers, ed. A. Kudat and Y. Özkan (Berlin: Wissenschaftszentrum, 1975), p. 401.

Council itself. The vote on Greece notwithstanding, there is clear evidence of an increasing reluctance on the part of the EEC members to take in additional nations. In articles on the matter, both in the *International Herald Tribune* (March 2, 1977) and in the *Munich Merkur* (February 21, 1977), no mention was made at all of the eventual full partnership of Turkey. Both articles, however, did mention the inevitability of Spain, Portugal, and Greece becoming full members. As the *Merkur* noted, "In any event, the EEC has no option but to accept at least three new members, though with long transition periods which, as in the case of Portugal, might extend until 1990." The total omission of Turkey as a potential full member suggests that its eventual status within the EEC may be, at best, that of an associate member (cf. Haworth 1977, p. S1).

In assessing the position of Turkey in relation to the other members of the EEC, several sets of data are helpful. One such comparison can be made on the basis of the per capita income of Turkey with that of the EEC countries, shown in Table 4.4.

Turkey is clearly the lowest of the countries in per capita income. In fact, it has less than one half that of Greece, a country also in associate status with the EEC and considered to be underdeveloped itself. The gap, however, between Turkey and those countries with high per capita incomes is even more pronounced. The gap between Turkey and Germany is nearly 700 percent; between Turkey and France slightly more than 600 percent; and between Turkey and Belgium just under 600 percent.

A second aspect of the comparison between Turkey and the EEC countries, and one that has a strong correlation with the just cited data is shown in the structures of the different economies. As may be seen in Table 4.5, the economic structure of Turkey is at a considerable variance from those of the EEC member states.

While the ratios of the agricultural to industrial sectors in the EEC countries are in the range of 1 to 4 to 1 to 8.5, the ratio for Turkey is 1 to 1. The share of industry in the EEC countries varies between 32 and 47 percent, whereas this sector contributes less than 25 percent in Turkey. These data help to explain the prior table on per capita incomes, in that the agricultural sector is quite large

TABLE 4.5

Sectoral Contribution to 1974 Gross Domestic Product in Countries of the EEC and Turkey
(percent)

| Countries | Agriculture | Industry | Construction | Services |
|---|---|---|---|---|
| Germany | 6 | 47 | 7 | 40 |
| France | 6 | 36 | 10 | 48 |
| Netherlands | 8 | 32 | 7 | 54 |
| Belgium | 4 | 35 | 7 | 54 |
| Italy | 8 | 34 | 7 | 51 |
| Luxembourg | 5 | 42 | 6 | 47 |
| Turkey | 24 | 24 | 7 | 45 |

Source: O. Varlier and S. Ilkin, "The Role of International Migration within the Turkish Planning Perspective," in International Conference on Migrant Workers, ed. A. Kudat and Y. Özkan (Berlin: Wissenschaftszentrum, 1975), p. 402.

in Turkey and is one that produces relatively little income. Further, it is a sector that in 1973 engaged 8.8 of the 13.9 million employed workers in the country. Sixty-four percent of the labor force is involved in a sector of the economy that produces only 24 percent of the gross domestic product. Table 4.6 provides data on the distribution of the working populations in the EEC countries and Turkey, a further indication of the structural dissimilarity between Turkey and the EEC member states.

TABLE 4.6

Distribution of the Working Population in
EEC Member States and Turkey
(percent)

| Countries | Agriculture | Industry | Others |
|---|---|---|---|
| Germany | 10.2 | 48.2 | 41.6 |
| France | 15.8 | 40.4 | 43.8 |
| Netherlands | 7.9 | 41.3 | 50.8 |
| Belgium | 5.6 | 44.9 | 49.6 |
| Italy | 22.5 | 41.8 | 35.7 |
| Luxembourg | 12.1 | 45.3 | 42.6 |
| Turkey | 63.4 | 11.7 | 24.9 |

Source: O. Varlier and S. Ilkin, "The Role of International Migration within the Turkish Planning Perspective," in International Conference on Migrant Workers, ed. A. Kudat and Y. Özkan (Berlin: Wissenschaftszentrum, 1975), p. 406.

Agricultural production, of course, is inherently unstable and a precarious prop for a nation's entire economy. The vicissitudes of the weather combined with the essentially primitive methods of farming still used throughout much of Turkey mean that the ability of the government to plan and implement developmental schemes is always somewhat tenuous. Furthermore, such fluctuations hinder the possibilities for smooth and sustained economic growth. With agricultural exports accounting for 63 percent of all exports from Turkey (1973) and the pressure for imports continuing to rise, the uncertainty of Turkey's ability to function in international exchange is apparent.

## POSTSCRIPT

In international agreements regarding the exportation of the country's labor force, Turkey has conformed to the policies dictated by the recruiting countries. With the mass migrations of the 1960s and early 1970s, an episode of the past and not likely to recur in the foreseeable future, Turkey has little with which to bargain for the admission of additional numbers of its workers. Nor does it have means by which to influence those who are presently abroad to return home.

The prospects are not encouraging for Turkey so far as utilizing the exported labor as a part of its own development efforts is concerned. It has essentially lost the discretion to choose whether or not to continue to emphasize this aspect of its planning goals. While faced in this dilemma by a two-edged sword—unemployment at home and its skilled workers abroad—it has now to confront the reality of no longer being able to count on the exportation of some percentage of its workers, nor in the long run, on the continual high levels of remittances that have been a major factor in keeping the Turkish economy afloat. The options are few. Abadan-Unat et al. (1976, p. 41) suggest the following as the most feasible alternative:

> Under present circumstances and with a judicial eye on the [Employment Service] waiting list which now contains more than a million names, it would be in Turkey's best interests to insist upon the rigorous rotation system of migrants abroad which was originally envisioned as long as ten years or more ago, but never achieved. It is likely that their insistence, however, would be too late: Host countries are currently bending their efforts toward the assimilation of their existing foreign labor force, precluding the chance to work abroad for many still eager to depart from Turkey.

It is precisely this latter point, that of the immigration countries' making efforts at assimilation, however minimal and half-hearted they may be, that in the long run will prove a major factor in the inability of Turkey to modernize and develop itself. The amelioration of working conditions and the regularization of the status of the workers in Europe through the granting of indefinite residency permits may well influence those Turkish workers already abroad to stay in Europe in very large numbers and for long periods of time.* If these workers do remain in Europe throughout their productive years and bring their families to join them, the likelihood of their gradually adopting European lifestyles and modes of consumption will minimize their propensity to return home (cf. Kudat and Gitmez 1975, p. 18; Kudat and Özkan 1976, p. 91). It will also minimize their interest in or need for the sending home of remittances. If Turkey loses this most important source of foreign exchange, the economy will

---

*In the two years (1974 and 1975) since the immigration ban, OECD (1976a) estimates that a total of 80,000 to 90,000 Turkish workers left Germany and returned home. This is a figure comparable to the average return in one year prior to the ban.

quickly accumulate huge deficits and the country will find itself in a dire financial situation, one not unlike that of almost all Third World countries.

The conclusion is not an optimistic one. Just as Turkey for years supported the exportation of its workers and was unable to mobilize effectively what benefits were to accrue from this through remittances and some experience with Western industrial life, so now, 20 years later, it faces the possibility of remaining essentially as it was then—still underdeveloped, still with high unemployment, still with a small skilled work force, and still with few internal resources by which to change its condition.

# PART II
## SOCIAL POLICIES AND SOCIAL CONDITIONS

# 5

# ECONOMIC CONDITIONS AND LABOR POLICIES

In the period immediately after World War II, the countries of Western Europe faced a major problem in how to rebuild their economies and provide employment for their people. The transfer from war- to peacetime production, the absorption of hundreds of thousands of soldiers back into occupational slots, and the need to recreate markets and distribution mechanisms, all mitigated against an early and sustained recovery of the economies. In Germany the problems were particularly acute, with entire cities demolished, little or no capital available for investment, and large gaps in the labor force due to war-related deaths. But as was soon to become evident throughout Europe, recovery was swift and employment opportunities abounded.

A state of nearly full employment was reached in the Federal Republic within six to eight years after the war, except for West Berlin which was held back by its geographic isolation and the year-long 1948 Soviet blockade of land and water routes into the city. The economic expansion of Germany made possible the absorption of millions of Germans from the former Eastern Territories as well as from East Germany; and while these immigrants helped to sustain the growth of the country, their presence also had the effect of hiding a problem in the German population structure.

Succinctly, the challenge to the continued prosperity of the Federal Republic came from the fact that the country did not have sufficient numbers of its own citizens to fill all the occupational positions continuing to open up as the economy continued to expand. The population structure of Germany was badly skewed. As a result of two wars, both in terms of actual deaths and children not born, Germany had evolved a lopsided demographic structure with large numbers of children and elderly, but relatively few persons in their working years. Between 1962 and 1972, for example, the population increased by approximately 4 percent, but the working population decreased during the same period by 6.6 percent, or a loss in one decade of more than 3.2 billion working hours. Had Germany not experienced two wars in a space of thirty years, there would have been minimally an additional 2 million persons of working age in the population (Nally 1976, p. 2).

The problem, then, for Germany in the 1960s was no longer one of full employment (for between 1960 and 1970, Germany's unemployment level was consistently below 1 percent), but one of how to sustain the process of continued capital accumulation and economic growth. Between 1950 and 1970, the annual rate of economic growth in the Federal Republic averaged slightly over 6 percent (cf. Giersch 1971). A growth rate of this magnitude combined with extremely low unemployment rates and a decline in the number of employable persons meant that Germany had but one solution if it wished to continue to sustain its economic miracle: it had to increase its labor force, and this could only be accomplished through the importation of workers from outside Germany. It is not surprising, therefore, referring back to Table 3.1 and Chapter 3, to find an increase in the number of foreign workers from 329,356 in 1960 to 2,595,000 in 1973. (The fact that it dropped by 439,000 in the period from 1973 to 1975 is another matter that will be taken up shortly.) Nikolinakos (1975, p. 9) has argued that foreign labor was the absolutely essential component that undergirded the continued economic growth of Germany:

> It must be furthermore underlined in this context that the full- or overemployment state due to a steady growth was only possible in the capitalist countries because of the import of foreign workers. For otherwise, recession, stagnation, and consequently, unemployment would have been the result. The governments would have been forced in this case either to introduce planning methods in order to control the situation or to try to find outlets abroad for private capital. It is in this sense that I have spoken in another context of the guest-worker as the "saviour of the system." Saviour in the sense that he has guaranteed growth and full employment and in so doing has guaranteed the smooth functioning of the system.

Yet another aspect of this increased pressure on the German economy to locate additional workers came from the fact that the effective workweek for German workers dropped considerably between 1960 and 1970. For union workers, the decline was 7 hours, from 43 to 36 hours per week. Though the union decline was nearly 20 percent, this was not the national average, as only between 16 and 20 percent of all German workers were unionized. For the total work force, the decline was somewhat less, though still appreciable, that is, from 44.1 to 40.4 hours per week (cf. Kleindorfer and Kudat 1974, p. 3; Kudat and Özkan 1976, p. 65). The impact of such declines in the number of labor hours available from the native labor force is clear: the approximate loss in working hours for a five-day week in 1970 as compared with 1960 would total, holding the total labor force constant at 1960 figures, nearly 9,700,000 hours, or the weekly labor of an additional 240,000 workers. Combining this figure with the lost manpower due to the demographic imbalances, it is clear why the foreign workers have become, indeed, the saviors of the system.

## FOREIGN LABOR AND GERMAN ECONOMIC CONDITIONS

In view of the labor shortages in Germany and the threat that such shortages represented to the continued prosperity and growth of the German economy, German officials began a program of active recruitment to bring in foreign labor to fill the gaps. In countries throughout the European South, the Federal Republic established between 500 and 600 offices for the recruitment of laborers. Germany clearly perceived it advantageous to bring in guestworkers to mine its coal, sweep its streets, build its buildings, make its cars, and do all the other myriad tasks foreign workers have done. The foreign workers were sought after and actively courted to come to Germany, a fact that firmly counters the claim that foreign workers came to Germany of their own accord to take jobs away from native Germans. *The fact that foreign workers are in Germany is not the consequence of random events and their own strictly private decisions. They are in Germany as the result of policies made at the highest levels of the German government.*

Bodenbender (1976, p. 1) has termed the period of the rapid growth of the numbers of guestworkers in Germany one of "uncontrolled expansion." He dates it from 1960 through the end of 1972, a period when the percentage of foreign workers in the German labor force rose from 0.8 to 11.9 percent. He suggests that such an expansion was desired because "the employment of foreigners was an advantage for the Federal Republic of Germany as well as for the native countries and for the foreigners themselves, at first." As to the advantages for Germany resulting from this immigration, he suggests four, several of which have been alluded to above. First, the foreign workers filled the labor slots that could not be filled by Germans alone. They took over positions that structurally already existed but for which there were no German workers. "Foreign workers thus contributed," he points out, "to a high degree, to the economic development and the stabilization of the society through the increasing welfare of the people."

Second, Bodenbender points to the shortening of the workweek for native Germans which was made possible by the presence of the foreign workers. German workers were able to work fewer hours per week and at the same time experience sustained wage increases and social benefits. The third advantage for Germany was that the foreigners tended to be employed in those categories of work that German people were anxious to leave. The availability of foreign workers to take these jobs meant that there was considerable social mobility and improvement in the working and living conditions of German working people.

Fourth, the fact that for many years foreign workers paid in through their taxes much more than they received in turn through social services and use of public facilities meant that they were helping to subsidize these services and facilities for the German public. Since the reuniting of families and the increased birth rates are quite recent phenomena, there was a period of time when the demands of the unaccompanied foreign worker on the German social infrastructure, and his needs, were minimal. For perhaps a decade or more, the employment of foreign workers meant an improvement in the quality of life for the German citizen through the availability of tax funds neither he nor his countryman had paid.

In itemizing the benefits to the sending countries of the European South, Bodenbender (1976, p. 3) suggests three:

> 1. The sending countries had the possibility of exporting a considerable part of their relatively high unemployment to the Federal Republic of Germany. This was not only an economic advantage for these countries, but also meant a diminution of the social pressures resulting from such unemployment.
> 2. For the sending countries, the employment of their citizens in Germany meant a rich source of German money by way of a steady flow of remittances. . . . This contributed significantly to the economic development of the sending countries.
> 3. For the workers themselves, the employment in Germany normally meant the overcoming of extreme poverty and no opportunities. For even the position of unskilled worker in Germany meant a tremendous advance compared to their previous existence.

From this list of advantages it might appear that it was possible to carry out such migrations with few or no social costs or dislocations; however, Bodenbender points out that such reasoning was short-term in its outlook and made possible only by the energetic economic expansion of the 1960s. There were advantages at first, to be sure, though it is less certain that they accrued to the sending countries in the same magnitude as they did to Germany.

A second phase in the relation of foreign workers to German economic conditions was termed by Bodenbender the "consolidation phase." It is in the period between January 1973 and the end of 1975 that a series of events permanently changed the manner in which foreign workers came to be viewed in Germany. The oil embargo, the subsequent four-fold increase in the price of crude oil, the recession which eased only slowly, the unemployment of more than one million German workers, and the growing awareness of the impact of the foreign workers and their dependents upon German society, all led in the same direction so far as the future of foreign workers in Germany was concerned: no new workers were to be allowed to come and those that were already in the country could either continue to work or leave the labor force permanently.

Bodenbender suggests that the consolidation phase had three distinct parts. The first stage was initiated by the Federal Ministry of Labor and Social Affairs and directed exclusively at German employers. Employers who hired foreign workers were to be taxed at a rate of DM 1,000 for each non-EEC worker recruited for them by the German Labor Office. This was an increase of DM 700 over the old figure of DM 300. In addition, regulations were instituted to strengthen housing regulations and codes applicable to those companies housing their foreign workers. These rules were implemented to further increase the cost to the employer of seeking out foreign labor. The final portion of the effort at discouraging employers from taking on additional foreign workers was that criminal sanctions for the illegal recruitment or employment of foreign workers were considerably strengthened and made more severe.

The second stage in the efforts of the government to further consolidate the numbers of foreign workers in the country came in November 1973 with the ban on admitting any additional foreign workers to the country. The number of new workers after this ban went into effect was reduced to a trickle and the labor market in the Federal Republic became, save for new workers from EEC countries, a closed system. As was noted in Chapters 3 and 4, the results were dramatic. For Turkey, as an example, the number of new workers coming into Germany in 1973 was 103,753, but in 1975 there were only 640 who received first-time German labor permits.

The final set of activities undertaken during the consolidation phase resulted from efforts of the German government to ease the increasing unemployment of German workers. These efforts included the option of a German worker to take over a position held by a foreign worker at the time the labor permit of the foreign worker expired; the refusal of work permits for family members who came into Germany after November 30, 1974; and the passing of laws allowing cities to forbid further in-migration of foreign workers or their families, once the number of foreigners in the city's population reached a certain percentage. It should be noted that all three of these regulations were not applicable to workers from other EEC countries. The measures were in large part aimed at stopping further in-migration of workers from the European South as well as to inducing foreign workers to leave the German labor market, if not leave the country altogether. There is little doubt that the policies had the desired effect, at least in concert with the ban on further in-migration. In the first 24 months after the initiation of these measures, the number of foreign workers legally employed in Germany dropped by 439,000.

Though Bodenbender takes his analysis no further in terms of assessing the post-immigration ban effects, it appears that a third phase has evolved. Having consolidated (and constricted) the numbers of foreign workers as well as their options for employment, housing, and geographical mobility, there has emerged what might be termed a phase of "structural ambivalence." Long-term decisions on the future of the foreign workers in Germany are being postponed and ignored. With a course set neither toward the integration of the foreign workers into German society nor toward their eventual return to their homelands, there developed a set of social policies that leave ambiguous and ill defined the position of foreign workers in Germany (cf. Müller-Meiningen 1977, p. 14).

The basis for this indecision on the part of the German government and those in the industrial sector is that the fundamental economic role of the foreign worker has not been acknowledged. There continues to be the quiet and seldom discussed belief that somehow and at some time, the foreign workers will gradually disappear and leave Germany again to the Germans. While official publications and policymakers note that the German economy at present needs a baseline of at least 1,500,000 foreign workers to function effectively, there is no pronouncement that such a need will extend for the foreseeable future. Rather, the official attitude is that while there are millions in Germany today, they will all be gone before long.

The cumulative effect of such benign neglect is that the social policies toward the foreign workers continue to reinforce their marginality in German society. Be they the economic policies discussed in this chapter, or those of housing and political rights to be analyzed in the following two chapters, the end results all point in the same direction—Germany is neither ready nor willing to stake out a clear direction for its relations to the foreign workers and their families. Instead, public pronouncements emphasize the need for some minimal level of integration of the foreign workers into German society, but simultaneously the social policies ensure that such integration does not occur. The consequence of having consolidated the numbers and options of foreign workers so as to provide additional employment opportunities for German workers bears witness to the fact that the foreign workers are still thought of in large measure as an expendable manpower supply.

While the consolidation measures were being implemented, there seemed to be little realization that the use of economic restrictions was not an all-encompassing means by which to resolve the conditions generated by the presence of the foreign workers. The social conditions of the families, the thousands of teen-agers barred by law from gainful employment, and the birth each year of more than 120,000 children into the families of guestworkers could not be set aside or resolved by simply imposing greater restrictions. Direct responses to these situations were passed over in favor of indirect manipulations with work permits and residency requirements. The missing component in the consolidation phase was the creation of social policies which would have given guidance for the future of the workers and their families as well as responded to their current predicaments. The absence of such policies has reinforced the ambiguity and marginality of their present position in German society.

## FOREIGN LABOR AND GERMAN SOCIAL CONDITIONS

The effort by Germany during the consolidation phase to use economic policies as an indirect level upon pressing social conditions among the foreign workers and their communities did not work. The irony is that by avoiding the underlying social conditions (for to address them would mean the articulation of a direction for the ensuing social policies), these conditions will now exert an important influence upon the economic future and social well-being of Germany, citizens and guestworkers alike. There appear to be four broad areas in which present social conditions among the guestworkers will have a systemic impact upon German society and economy.

The first of the four areas in which current conditions among the foreign workers will influence the German economic marketplace is that of family migration. Whereas in 1961 only 20 percent of all foreign workers had members of their families with them in Germany, by 1975 that figure had risen to more than 50 percent. In fact, at the beginning of 1976, the foreign population was divided almost evenly between family members and workers, slightly more than two million in each category. Since 1970, over one million family members have immigrated to Germany. More than half that number came in the first two years after the labor ban (550,000). The Federal Ministry for Labor and Social Affairs estimates that there still remain in the home countries of the European South an additional 300,000 spouses and 1.1 million children, all of whom could be potential immigrants to Germany (Bodenbender 1976, p. 7). Again, such figures do not include spouses and children from EEC countries. A final consideration here is that unmarried workers who are working in Germany may marry in their homelands, thus adding new candidates for German immigration. At present, 26 percent of the male and 32 percent of the female foreign workers are unmarried.

A consequence of this rapid increase in family migrations into Germany is that the number of births to foreigners is quickly going up. In 1965, there were 38,000 births to foreigners living in Germany, or 3.6 percent of all live births in the country. In 1970, the figures reached 63,000 or 7.8 percent, and by 1975, the number of live births to foreigners was 130,000, or nearly 20 percent of all live births in Germany. If present trends continue, and there is every reason to expect them to do so, there will be more than 1.25 million births to foreigners during the next decade. The implications of this situation, for housing, education, or social services, are seldom discussed. Current German social policy is void of specific efforts to address the situation.

The second set of social conditions within the foreign communities which will have an impact upon economic life in Germany is that resulting from the concentration of foreign workers and their families in particular urban areas. The fact that in Frankfurt, for example, slightly more than 17 percent of the population are foreigners and that nearly 50 percent of all live births are to foreigners cannot help but shape the characteristics of future labor stocks. Furthermore, such a concentration may also have ramifications in terms of the decision of German citizens to leave the city, the support of the city for housing renewal and enforcement of housing laws, the rate and types of juvenile delinquency, and other manifestations of the social problems arising from concentrations of persons left on the margins of the society.

The implications of these first two sets of conditions lead to a third consideration: that the regional concentration of foreign workers and the increased numbers of dependents will hasten the formation of isolated enclaves within the urban areas. With more than 2 million foreign dependents in Germany and the opportunities of this group to interact with German society and German culture generally minimal, both because of employment and linguistic barriers, the foreigners naturally and inevitably seek companionship and community among their own ethnic groups. This process is also being exacerbated by the growth of those foreign groups whose cultural and social patterns are more distinct and different from those of Germany. In the early years of the immigrations into Germany, the largest group was the Italians, who shared with Germans both a common religion and clear identification as Europeans. In 1968, nearly a quarter (24 percent) of all foreign workers in Germany were from Italy. By 1976, the ethnic structure of the foreign communities in Germany had changed significantly, with 27 percent of all foreigners being from Turkey and the Italians comprising only 15 percent of the total. Although southern Italy may be classified economically as part of the European South, workers who come from that area are, nevertheless, Catholic and European and have certain cultural characteristics in common with the residents of Munich or Stuttgart. The same cannot be said of the Muslim villagers from eastern Anatolia.

The above should not be misunderstood as implying that the creation and sustaining of ethnic ghetto enclaves in German cities is a positive good and one to be supported. Rather, the point is that as the social and cultural distances between Germany and some of its newer immigrant worker groups grow wider, the pressures toward ethnic concentration and isolation will intensify. In the absence of strong and vigorous efforts on the part of German officials to give foreigners the opportunity to choose and experience as much integration as they desire, the countervailing tendencies toward ghettoization will continue to mount.

The final set of conditions that will affect the structure of economic activity in Germany is that arising from the schooling and vocational training of the foreign children. The broader aspects of this situation will be taken up later in this book (Part III). For the present, however, it is enough to note that while there are more than 400,000 foreign children in German schools, fewer than 40 percent leave high school (*Hauptschule*) with a diploma. The consequence of not attaining this degree means that, for all practical purposes, the individual is confined for the working years to an unskilled, menial occupation. With no credentials and no formal vocational training, these tens of thousands of young second-generation foreigners have little chance in a society where the demands are always growing for greater technological sophistication and training in the labor force (cf. Schrader et al. 1976, pp. 83-110).

## FOREIGN LABOR AND THE GERMAN EMPLOYMENT MARKET

Taking together the four social conditions outlined above—the considerable increase both in family migrations and the number of births to foreigners, the increasing concentration of foreign workers in particular urban areas, the tendencies toward greater ghettoization of the foreign communities within German cities, and finally, the lack of educational/vocational skills or credentials among the young foreigners—implications for the German labor market are unavoidable.

While the employment ban of 1973 has had the desired impact of preventing further in-migration of new guestworkers to Germany, it has had the unanticipated consequence of increasing family migration. This family migration comes at a time when no new work permits are to be issued, not even to wives or working-age children who migrated after the ban. The fact that there are literally tens of thousands of foreigners in Germany who could work but are prohibited from doing so will have to influence Germany's future decisions on where to seek additional labor as it is needed. This group of foreigners constitutes a reserve labor force of some magnitude. Were the ban lifted, Germany would be able to draw upon persons who are already in the country, have had some experience with the German language, and perhaps have attended German schools. Bodenbender (1976, p. 10) estimates that in the first 24 months after the ban went into effect, 40,000 foreign juveniles immigrated to Germany and were barred at the legal age of employment from receiving a work permit.

The need of Germany for this labor supply may become quite acute as the German working-age population continues to decline. (Without the addition of the births of foreigners, Germany would at present be below the rate needed to sustain its present population.) To couple this fact with the continued steady growth in the German economy implies that additional labor inevitably will be necessary (cf. Daniele 1971; Nikolinakos 1975, p. 1).

The dilemmas inherent in this analysis, however, are sobering in their implications. The first is that matter of what to do with/for/to the large number of young persons who are of the legal age to seek employment but are barred from doing so because they entered Germany after November 30, 1974. How is Germany to handle 40,000 or more foreign young persons who are forced to remain on the absolute margin of the society? If the other components of Germany's reserve labor force—for example, German women not now working, or German youth coming of employment age—take up the positions created by economic growth and the retirement of older workers, the problem may be further intensified. Germany cannot realistically risk thousands of foreign youths going perhaps five or ten years without a legal option for employment.

Another problem posed by the presence of foreigners who cannot now work is that even if new positions do open up and Germany lifts the ban so that they are able to obtain employment, these people may not have the training and credentials that will make them competitive, and probably will not if present circumstances hold. *There seems to be in the making in Germany a new subproletariate.* This group would form an underclass, not only in the sense of supporting the higher positions and mobility of German workers (cf. Hoffmann-Nowotny's concept of Unterschichtung noted earlier), but a class of workers who would not be able to compete in an industrial country for anything but the most menial and undesirable jobs. Further, as the number of such job opportunities holds steady or even decreases, this group of workers faces periods of intermittent work interspersed with long periods of unemployment. The question of how Germany, a country that experienced less than 1 percent unemployment for the entire decade of 1960 through 1970, will respond to a permanent class of frequently unemployed persons is a matter not yet being addressed in any of the literature surveyed for this chapter. Not only is Germany experiencing some degree of unemployment due to structural realignments and modifications in the German economy (Getler 1976b, p. C3), but also the development of structural unemployment due to the presence of large numbers of persons barred from employment at present and not likely to be competitive for employment in the future.

There are several additional factors that further compound and exacerbate the situation of those foreign workers who possess few if any of the skills necessary for more than the least desirable tasks. One of these factors is that within the next decade, the children from the so-called *geburstenstarke Jahrgänge* (baby-boom years) will be moving into the labor market. This is the lower end of the bimodal population distribution that has arisen in postwar Germany. As this large group of children and now young adults continues to move through the early years of the life cycle, it is putting tremendous pressure on the educational system as well as on the employment sector. There are neither enough places for these young people in the universities and technical schools nor in apprentice and regular employment slots. It is estimated by the Federal Ministry for Labor and Social Affairs that during the decade 1977–87, there will be an additional 80,000 German young people coming of age each year to go into the employment market (Bodenbender 1976, p. 11). The implication is that within 10 years, nearly one million slots will have to be found for these new workers, either through the replacement of retiring workers or through the creation of new jobs in the German economy. Combining the number of German youth coming of employment age with the number of youth who are from guestworker homes (that is, foreign youth who arrived in Germany before the ban and are thus entitled to seek work permits), the total goes even higher. Bodenbender suggests a yearly figure of 45,000 foreign children who will come of age and legally be entitled to seek employment in the Federal Republic.

Yet another group of persons who have come into Germany and who also add competition and pressure to the labor market are those Germans who are being repatriated from Poland. With the signing of the recent bilateral agreement between the Federal Republic and Poland, whereby Germans in Poland may immigrate to Germany in exchange for cash and industrial goods, the number of persons taking advantage of this opportunity has reached nearly 100,000. Of this group, approximately 30,000 are of working age and will seek employment in the Federal Republic.

The final group of persons who exert pressure upon the current German labor market are the nearly 1 million unemployed German workers. Unemployment in Germany has in the post-1973-74 oil embargo and recession period averaged between 4.0 and 5.5 percent of the labor force (Federal Labor Office 1977). For a country that had practically no unemployment for an entire decade (1960-70), this situation is viewed as intolerable for economic as well as political reasons. It is the presence of this group that has influenced policies with regard to work opportunities for the foreign workers. As noted earlier, foreign workers are now subject to regulations that allow an unemployed German worker to "bump" a guestworker from his position at the time his work permit expires. Though few German workers have availed themselves of this opportunity, it nevertheless emphasizes the relative status of German versus foreign workers in the pursuit of new employment.

All told, the various groups that are pressing for employment in Germany make clear the need for the German economy to continue to grow and prosper. If it does not, there will arise for the first time in more than a generation in Germany the prospect of sustained structural unemployment that will have an impact upon all sectors of the society. Adding the nearly 1 million currently unemployed workers to the yearly figure of 125,000 new German and foreign youth seeking employment for the first time and the more than 30,000 Polish immigrants means that in the next five years, Germany is faced with the need of locating 1.6 million employment slots for potential workers. (Of course, these figures do not include the reserve labor force of German women not now working nor those immigrants who are currently denied work permits. Were all those of working age given the opportunity to work, Germany, as a conservative estimate, would need 2 million new slots in the next five years.)

The implications of this pressure for employment upon the foreign workers, who are at the very bottom of the labor hierarchy, are clear. First, it can be anticipated that economic mobility for the foreign workers will be very slow in coming. As the data from Kudat and her colleagues in Berlin made clear, even after four years of employment in Germany, the mobility of foreign workers was negligible (Kudat and Özkan 1976, pp. 47-65). It appears safe to assume that this will continue for the foreseeable future as well. Second, it is not immediately apparent that the German government will grant work permits to foreigners now in the country who are currently denied such permits. With the pressure of hundreds of thousands of Germans without work, the policy decision arises of whether to open the labor market to yet additional persons or to retain the present exclusions and then have to deal with the social costs and problems generated by such exclusion. As of the present, this decision appears not to have been made. The rate and strength of economic recovery in Germany over the next several years may well be the determining factor.

A third ramification of this current employment situation is that those guestworkers who have remained in Germany may find that their position becomes more and more precarious as large numbers of Germans continue without work.* The necessity of gaining employment may well force German workers to accept downward mobility and take on positions thought to be "dirty work" and thus reserved for foreign workers. (Much the same situation has occurred in the United States when recessions forced whites to accept employment in areas previously relegated to black workers [cf. Rist 1972]).

A final implication to be noted here is that this situation may create intense social conflict and reaction among the children of the present guestworkers. It will be this second generation of foreign workers who have lived their lives in Germany, attended German schools, and assimilated to a high degree the industrial values of mobility, economic success, and material well-being who will resent and find intolerable the perpetuation of a second-class and politically impotent status. Their reference group will no longer be the people in the villages from which their parents emigrated. but rather, their German peers. They will not assess their status in the light of the social hierarchy in rural Turkey or Yugoslavia, but in terms of urban Frankfurt, Berlin, or Munich (cf. Diakonisches Werk der Evangelischen Kirche 1976, pp. 17-22). To recognize that their daily lives are constricted and perpetually influenced by discriminatory practices cannot but move them into a position of tension and conflict with the present German social system. Bodenbender (1976, p. 13) sees these developments as the "fuel for a social time bomb."

## GUESTWORKERS AND THE TRADE UNIONS†

In assessing the socioeconomic position of the foreign workers in Germany, the obvious conclusion is that these workers are overwhelmingly members of the working class. Moreover, within the working class, they tend to form the lowest stratum, being highly concentrated in the unskilled or semiskilled positions. Further, the proportion of manual workers among the foreign workers is proportionally far higher than it is among native workers (Castles and Kosack 1973, p. 83). Though the data are now several years old, Table 5.1 from the Federal

---

*The U.S. Department of State *Annual Labor Report, 1976, Federal Republic of Germany* provides the following information on the duration of unemployment for German workers (1977, p. 64):

> A breakdown by length of unemployment showed that 161,000 or 17.9 percent of those unemployed in September 1976 had been unemployed for over one year; this figure compared with 16.8 percent in May and only 9.6 percent one year earlier. The number of unemployed who had been without a job for over two years was 38,700 in September, 1976, 25,900 over the level recorded one year earlier.

†Special acknowledgment is given to the work of Castles and Kosack (1973), especially pp. 118-79, in the preparation of this section.

Labor Office provides, for various immigrant nationalities, the socioeconomic status of both male and female workers. As such, it clearly substantiates the point of foreign workers being on the very lowest rungs of the occupational ladder in Germany. But as has been noted here several times, this was only to be expected, given the conditions under which these workers were brought to Germany and the jobs for which they were recruited. They did not come to challenge the social and economic mobility of German workers, but to ensure it.

It is important here to note the social class perception and awareness of the foreign workers, whether they are conscious of their working-class position, whether they possess a consciousness of their status in the occupational hierarchy and the means by which their position is perpetuated, whether they seek to give expression to their understandings through organized union activity, or not. Furthermore, it must be asked whether foreign workers are used as a means for exploiting schisms between unionized workers and themselves in confrontations with employers.

Castles and Kosack (1973, p. 117) have spelled out in detail the implications for the trade-union movement of the presence of large numbers of foreign workers within the same broad class strata. They note:

> Historically the most important working-class institutions in Western Europe have been the trade unions. Their policies and activities with regard to immigrant workers remain highly significant, even though there is today a widespread lack of confidence in the traditional trade unions, with their highly bureaucratic structures.
>
> The way in which immigrants develop an awareness of their class position (or alternatively, fail to do so) and the extent to which they participate in the activities and institutions of the working class are of great importance. Class consciousness and class activity do not only affect the lives of the immigrants and their position in society. These factions are also important in determining the impact of immigration on society. Given the volume and the importance of contemporary migratory movements, the development of class consciousness among migrant workers may even help to shape class relationships and the outcome of class conflicts for the whole of society.

These same authors posit that there are seven quite specific sets of social conditions unique to the foreign workers, which distinguish them from indigenous workers. These conditions are viewed as not only affecting the occupational position of the foreign workers, but their relations to others in the labor force as well. They are also said to be permanent rather than transitory in nature. They list them as follows (Castles and Kosack 1973, pp. 118-27): traditional worker hostility to immigrant labor, language barriers between worker groups, differences in industrial experiences and cultural backgrounds, motivation for working, qualifications, segregated work-situation, and differential legal positions and political rights.

TABLE 5.1

Socioeconomic Status of Guestworkers in Germany, by Nationality and Sex, 1968 and 1972
(percent)

| Nationality | Non-manual 1968 | Non-manual 1972 | Skilled Manual 1968 | Skilled Manual 1972 | Semi-skilled Manual 1968 | Semi-skilled Manual 1972 | Unskilled Manual 1968 | Unskilled Manual 1972 | Apprentice 1968 | Apprentice 1972 |
|---|---|---|---|---|---|---|---|---|---|---|
| **Men** | | | | | | | | | | |
| Italian | — | 4 | 13 | 12 | 37 | 46 | 48 | 37 | — | 1 |
| Greek | — | — | 7 | 8 | 53 | 58 | 37 | 31 | — | — |
| Spanish | — | — | 15 | 13 | 44 | 49 | 38 | 34 | — | — |
| Portuguese | — | — | 12 | 12 | 43 | 50 | 43 | 36 | — | — |
| Turkish | — | — | 16 | 16 | 38 | 47 | 43 | 35 | — | — |
| Yugoslavian | — | 5 | 55 | 41 | 27 | 35 | 14 | 19 | — | — |
| Other European | — | 3 | — | 20 | — | 45 | — | 31 | — | 1 |
| Other foreigners | 35 | 38 | 20 | 28 | 22 | 18 | 12 | 10 | 6 | 6 |

| | | | | | | | | | | |
|---|---|---|---|---|---|---|---|---|---|---|
| Percent of labor force by socioeconomic status | 8 | 8 | 20 | 21 | 36 | 41 | 34 | 28 | 2 | 2 |
| Women | | | | | | | | | | |
| Italian | – | – | – | – | 34 | 49 | 63 | 43 | – | – |
| Greek | – | – | – | – | 37 | 52 | 60 | 45 | – | – |
| Spanish | – | – | – | – | 34 | 44 | 59 | 48 | – | – |
| Portuguese | – | – | – | – | 35 | 43 | 60 | 49 | – | – |
| Turkish | – | – | – | – | 33 | 44 | 62 | 50 | – | – |
| Yugoslavian | – | 14 | – | – | 29 | 45 | 58 | 37 | – | – |
| Other European | – | 6 | – | 2 | – | 47 | – | 44 | – | – |
| Other foreigners | 50 | 73 | – | – | 15 | – | 18 | – | – | – |
| Percent of labor force by socioeconomic status | 12 | 17 | 3 | 3 | 30 | 41 | 53 | 38 | – | – |

Source: Federal Labor Office, Federal Republic of Germany, Repräsentativ-untersuchung '72 (Nürnberg: Federal Labor Office, 1973), p. 67.

Of particular importance with regard to these conditions is the fact that they create a serious problem for the labor unions in their relations to the guestworkers; for in the end, the structural and sociopsychological conditions that separate the two groups tend to force the trade unions to choose between class solidarity and national/ethnic identity.*

For the trade unions in the countries of the European North, the potential conflict of interests between the immigrant workers and the indigenous union workers can be a severe obstacle to the building of class solidarity and a unified workers' movement. On the one hand, the local workers fear that an influx of guestworkers will keep wages depressed, provide an alternative labor force at the time of strikes, and allow the owners to reap extra profits through not having to provide the same union benefits to foreign workers. It is for these reasons that unions have frequently opposed immigration, a stance perceived to be in their own self-interest.

But there are problems for the unions in their support of a restrictive policy. On the one hand there is the ideological matter of nationalism versus internationalism, or at a slightly more pragmatic level, of the unions being representatives of all workers, and not simply those of a particular nationality. On the other hand, the unions face the issue of whether to maintain some manifestation of national identity in their membership and thus tolerate the exploitation of foreign workers who are not unionized. It is this latter situation that in the end also tends to weaken the unions, for the use by employers of cheap labor undercuts union demands for higher wages and better working conditions.

Castles and Kosack (1973, p. 128) have given a succinct statement of the problem faced by the unions:

> The trade unions find themselves in a dilemma. It may seem logical to oppose immigration, but once there are immigrant workers in the country, it is essential to organize them—not only in their own interests, but also in the interests of the rest of the workers. If the unions oppose immigration initially and even continue to do so, they may find that the immigrants do not trust them and are unwilling to join. Where this happens, the unions have the worst of both worlds. Not strong enough to prevent immigration, their attempts to do so only serve to alienate the new workers from them. The result is the weakening of the unions and the deepening of the split in the working

---

*It is a situation not dissimilar from that experienced by the trade unions in the United States, though in that instance the consideration has been race rather than nationality. The problem of the American unions has been to choose between class solidarity and racial solidarity. The question has been one of whether class superseded color, or vice versa. The answer in the United States has traditionally been the latter, that color is a more important determinant than social class in shaping economic relations and the basis for group solidarity (cf. Rist 1972).

class. Thus there is a potential contradiction between trade union policies toward immigration on the one hand and policies toward immigration workers once they are in the country on the other.

But as these authors note in their survey of the trade-union movements in Germany, Switzerland, France, and England, there is one matter on which all trade unions have agreed: that the immigrant and national workers should receive equal pay for equal work. This is, of course, not only the humanitarian view to hold, but also one that is necessary in the self-interests of the unions. To tolerate differential wage scales for a sizable segment of the working class is a direct threat to the stability and viability of the union movement. The very solidarity of the union movement in these countries depends upon their not being forced into competition with the potentially cheaper labor offered by the guestworkers. With a parity of wages, the employers lose this particular economic incentive to turn away from the national labor force in their pursuit of profits.

On a closer examination of the actual relation of the trade unions to the immigrant workers, the ambivalence of the unions toward the new arrivals becomes apparent. When the discussions within the unions first began in the late 1950s and early 1960s, there was the expected concern of what impact such workers would have upon the economic conditions of the union workers. As Richter (1970, p. 1) has noted: "In the early phase of the discussions the question was, above all, whether the foreign workers might be used to force wages down." The prevention of such a situation became a matter of concern to the unions and they lobbied extensively in governmental circles to ensure that it did not happen. The unions were successful in this effort, and in the bilateral labor agreements that Germany signed with a number of the labor-exporting countries the principle of equal pay for equal work was clearly spelled out. It was a union victory and one that helped to reduce the suspicion and antagonism that the unions held toward the guestworkers. A consequence was that the German trade-union movement did nothing to prevent labor immigration in the years when it first got under way.

It must also be noted that not only did the unions support no formal or official actions to prevent the entrance of new workers, they also made sporadic efforts on behalf of the foreign workers. In 1964, for example, when Federal Chancellor Erhard called for longer working hours on the part of German labor so as to minimize the need for foreign workers, the cause was enthusiastically taken up by management, who supported this position out of fear of not being able to control the nonunionized foreign workers as well as they could the unionized national labor force. A number of articles appeared in employers' association newsletters citing social and economic problems caused by the guestworkers. The employers' associations also gave much publicity to a poll taken by the Wickert Institute of Göttingen which reported that 64 percent of German men and 70 percent of the women were willing to work longer hours if this would prevent the employment of foreign workers (*Das Volk*, January 4, 1965).

The unions, on the other hand, vigorously fought against these proposals, not the least out of suspicion that they were made exactly at the time when the unions were negotiating for a reduction of working hours in a number of industries. Suspicious that the chancellor, in conjunction with the employers' associations, had used the threat of bring in more foreign workers as a pretext to rebuff union objectives, the unions noted that the idea of additional work by German workers to alleviate the need for foreign workers was unrealistic. The foreign and national workers were not concentrated in the same sectors and occupational areas of the economy; thus, two hours extra as a draftsman or mechanic would not alleviate the need for street cleaners, dishwashers, hotel porters, and unskilled heavy construction workers.

The result of this campaign by sectors of the government and the employers' associations was that the union efforts for a shorter work week were seriously hampered. The ability of the unions to combat the prejudice and xenophobic attitudes introduced into this instance of industrial politics was minimal at best. Many workers came to believe that they were indeed threatened by the introduction of foreign workers into the German economy and supported demands for longer working hours. The encouragement of the industrialists to have the workers take on longer hours was in some instances successful (cf. the employers' association newspaper *Bildzeitung*, March 31, 1966). The best the unions appeared to manage was the tack that the foreign workers were a necessary but unfortunate imperative of the current economic conditions in Germany.

This last argument, that the foreign workers were necessary to the continued expansion of the German economy, was a persuasive one in making German workers willing to tolerate foreign laborers. The fact that German trade unions have in the postwar period seen themselves as a means to achieve as much as possible within the current economic structures has meant that they support those practices that will enhance the strength and well-being of the German economy. Their role has been not to transform the economic system or to change the basic modes of production, but rather to ensure that union workers receive substantial benefits from the present arrangements. As Castles and Kosack have noted (1973, pp. 129-30):

> Realizing that they were not strong enough to stop immigration, the unions tried to pursue a realistic policy which would be most effective in preventing a split in the working class. It should also be remembered that the German trade union movement has reformist aims, which are directed towards getting the best possible conditions within the capitalist system, rather than securing working class control of the productive apparatus. In this context, a policy which was favorable to the prosperity of German industry could also be regarded as being in the long-term interests of the workers and unions.

With the acceptance of the principle that foreign workers were an economic necessity to the prosperity of Germany and thus to the prosperity of the

German workers, the German trade unions began to make a number of efforts on behalf of the foreign workers (see, for example, German Federation of Labor 1973). As the unions had been successful in their campaign to have the guestworkers receive equal pay for equal work, so they were also successful in their efforts to have the employers provide housing for these workers. The government has made the provision of housing by German employers a stipulation in all bilateral agreements with the labor-exporting countries. As a result, the Federal Labor Office found that by 1968, nearly a third (31 percent) of all male guestworkers were living in company-owned hostels (Federal Labor Office 1973, p. 102). And while the percentage of workers differed according to their nationality, ranging from 15 percent of the Greeks to 41 percent of the Portugese, it was nonetheless evident that this provision of housing was an important contribution to what little well-being workers experienced during the first years of their presence in Germany.

Another area in which the unions were active on behalf of the foreign workers was in the dissemination of information. Special offices were set up in some unions to distribute materials to the workers and to assist them in learning about industrial practices in Germany. This was accomplished through establishing training courses, providing newspapers and information sheets in the native languages of the workers, organizing German language courses, and placing foreign worker representatives on the union councils so that these representatives could report back to their fellow guestworkers on current matters that affected them. In assessing this broad range of services and means of assistance provided to the foreign workers by the German trade unions, Castles and Kosack (1973, p. 130) came to the conclusion that "The German unions have probably done more than those of any other country to integrate the foreign workers into the labor force, and have even taken on welfare functions going beyond normal trade union tasks."

While the conclusion of Castles and Kosack is perhaps accurate in comparison with the actions of the French or British unions toward foreign workers, it is still the case that the guestworkers in Germany remain on fringes of union activity and influence. While the foreign workers are encouraged to join the unions, there are a number of restrictions on the manner in which they may participate and the actual power they may exert. For example, while foreign workers are allowed to vote in work council elections, there are some unions that do not allow them to stand for office if they come from a non-EEC country. Furthermore, while the foreign workers are theoretically protected from retaliation under the Alien Act (for example, possible deportation) for any political activity they undertake that is legitimately sanctioned within their union, there are sufficient examples to cast doubt on the actual protection they do enjoy. The strikes at the auto plant in Lippstadt in September 1969 and the Ford plant in Köln in 1973 have resulted in foreign workers' losing their employment and thus being deported.

In the light of these efforts on behalf of the guestworkers, be those efforts strenuous or restrained, it is interesting to note what the impact has been on attracting new members from among these workers. Such data are difficult to locate nationally because of sporadic reporting on foreign worker membership to national union headquarters from the various unions. Nevertheless, an approximation does emerge. Kudat and Özkan (1976, p. 65) have reported that while the proportion of native workers in the Federal Republic who belong to unions varies between 16 and 20 percent, the corresponding figure nationally for Turkish workers is estimated to be 27 percent. These same authors also note that the percentage of Turkish workers in West Berlin who are union members is even higher than that of the national average, though no precise figure is offered. Their survey indicated that the longer a guestworker remains in Germany, the greater the likelihood of that worker being a union member. They also found that within their sample there were no variations in union membership based on geographical differences (rural, village, or city) in the home country. Somewhat older data reported by Geiselberger (1972) indicated that for the six largest national groups of guestworkers in the Federal Republic (Turks, Yugoslavs, Italians, Greeks, Spanish, and Portugese), their membership in unions was estimated for 1970 at 22 percent. This same source also termed the number of foreign workers serving on work councils at that time as "minuscule."

One would have reason to speculate, given the precarious position of the guestworkers in the Federal Republic, that they would turn in large numbers to the unions as one means of defense against the uncertainty they face in other parts of their lives. Unions can be viewed as one sector of the society in which the workers have someone else speaking on their behalf and in which they have some protection in numbers. The fact, then, that only one of every four foreign workers is a union member can perhaps be explained by the following reasons. First, there are many positions for which foreign workers cannot gain union protection because unions are not active in these occupational areas. Two examples would be in the areas of agricultural work and public services (hotels, cafes, restaurants, and so forth). In both the labor turnover is extremely high, which hinders the organizing and sustaining of union activity (cf. Kleindorfer and Kudat 1974, p. 10).

A second reason for the current rate of union membership among foreign workers is that union membership does not provide the job security it does for national workers. Unions cannot stop deportation for non-work-related reasons, nor can they prevent employees from not renewing work permits, again making the worker subject to deportation.* In short, the foreign workers may be subject to loss of employment regardless of union membership. Moreover, the foreign workers may realize that they could not necessarily count on the national work-

---

*Castles and Kosack (1973, p. 163) cite an instance in which the unions could not prevent the firing of 15 Spanish workers in Bad Homburg, but did protect them from deportation as they sought new jobs.

ers to go out on strike on their behalf even though they as foreign workers have done so for the national workers (Castles and Kosack 1973, p. 162).

Third, beyond the matters of access and job protection, there remains the question of utility. Is union membership worthwhile to foreign workers when joining offers little more than structural marginality? To be a member, but at the same time not to be a member in the way that nationals can, may readily be interpreted by foreign workers as an affront that they can just as easily pass by. When political participation and leadership posts are restricted, if not excluded completely, the range of benefits available to foreign workers inside the unions may be perceived as less than the financial and social costs.

In view of such constraints and barriers, it could be anticipated that the foreign workers would organize their own independent trade unions, or at least more informal worker organizations or associations. If established channels of communication and institutions are not open, why have the guestworkers not created new ones that would be responsive to their needs and aspirations? The answer is in two parts. The first is that the laws governing union organization within Germany place the foreign workers in a precarious position.* On the one hand, the federal constitution protects the right of all persons in Germany to organize unions, Thus foreign workers could if they desired, create their own union. However, the "catch-22" in this situation is that there are also laws that prohibit political behavior on the part of all foreigners in Germany. Furthermore, it is the personal discretion of the officials responsible for the administration of the Alien Act of the Federal Republic that determines what is or is not political behavior. Foreign workers who do wish to organize and create a union or workers' association continually run the risk that an official will deem such behavior political, or not in the best interests of the Federal Republic of Germany, and thus justify deportation.

The adaptation of the foreign workers to this situation can be generally characterized as working within German unions to promote their self-interests in Germany, but to organize themselves (with the blessings of the German government) to create employment opportunities in their home countries. One such organization is the Association of Turkish Workers which has offices both in Bonn and in Ankara (cf. Didzoleit 1977, p. 5). This organization seeks to enlist Turkish workers to invest their savings in projects in Turkey that will increase industrialization, provide employment, and provide a high rate of interest for the individual worker. Such projects, often supported as well by the Federal Republic with the hopes that the creation of jobs in Turkey will both lessen the migration pressures and entice workers now in Germany to return to their homeland,

---

*This topic of legal and political rights of foreign workers is examined in detail in the following chapter, "Civil and Political Rights." This present discussion is but a brief overview of the situation faced by guestworkers.

are created, organized, and directed by the investors in the Association. Such organizations find support in Germany, not only from the German government for the reasons listed above, but also from the unions for the reason that the efforts are all directed toward the home country and the labor conditions there. These associations are not a challenge to the German unions on domestic issues. As such, they fit within the general scheme of German trade unionism which ensures that unions are noncompetitive.

If on the one hand there are legal and political hindrances in the way of immigrants organizing themselves into trade unions, there is the alternative consideration as to the ultimate impact of such fracturing within the union movement. Castles and Kosack (1973, p. 179) applaud the fact that such independent unions have not arisen, for they see them as a direct threat to the solidarity of the working class. They note in this regard:

> But on one vital question all workers have common interests: on the need for working-class unity in the struggle for better economic and social conditions. The unions' failure to defend immigrants' interests on day-to-day issues, and their lack of success in integrating immigrants into the labor movement does not concern the immigrants alone. In the long run, failure to represent the immigrants also means failure in representing indigenous workers. A real improvement in the situation of the working class cannot be based on the continued exploitation of its weakest section; for this breeds poverty and competition, which endangers the conditions of all workers.

A diametrically opposite view is propounded by Nikolinakos for the reason that he believes the German unions restrict themselves to the support of the native workers. Thus it is his position that the foreign workers must organize, recognizing the risks inherent in doing so, for otherwise they remain politically impotent and open to the repressive measures of the government. His assessment of German unions and their relation to the guestworkers is noted in the following (Nikolinakos 1975, p. 15):

> Trade unions are deeply rooted in their nationalistic way of thinking which is evident in their attitude toward foreign workers. It is here that the contradiction between the internationalization of the labor force and the mode of production on the one hand and the national character of the trade unions on the other becomes often acute. For while the trade unions claim to represent also the interests of their foreign members, in reality they are obliged to represent the interest of the native workers. While it is true that they have gone so far as to impose the equality of native and foreign workers as regards wages in order to protect the native workers, nevertheless in other respects they have accepted the discrimination system against foreign workers. In the present stage they limit themselves to declarations of protest, but actually are not doing anything to protect foreigners against

the repressive measures of the government. If one reads between the lines of certain statements they have made about the necessity of limiting the number of foreign workers and of taking measures to better the infrastructure for guest-workers, one can detect the same attitude that is prevalent among the working class, namely, that foreigners should go back home as they are not needed any longer.

Whether one tends to accept the Castles and Kosack solidarity-of-the-working-class argument or that of foreign worker self-interest advanced by Nikolinakos, the premise from which each begins is the same: the German trade unions have not been able to afford the occupational protection or avenues for participation within the unions to foreign workers that they have to German workers. Castles and Kosack argue that in spite of such limitations, the foreign workers have no realistic alternative. They must use established means to advance their objectives. The fracturing of the labor movement into foreign and native worker unions is viewed as a no-win situation.

Nikolinakos, alternatively, assumes that established channels and union procedures are frequently a hindrance to the foreign workers and, in fact, thwart their aspirations in the economic and labor marketplace. He believes that they must go it alone, clearly articulating their own self-interests, either forcing an accomodation with the German national unions in order to prevent continued competition between unions, or beginning their own negotiations and contractual arrangements with employers on matters that they as foreign workers deem most important. In either case, the foreign workers would benefit and secure better working conditions and more equitable treatment for themselves. Exercising these options would put the foreign workers in a win-win situation, provided one notes the caveat that the administrators of the Alien Act do not define these activities as political, and thus grounds for deportation. In practicality, however, it can be assumed the actions will be seen as political and thus organizing foreign workers into a union becomes a high risk proposition.

In assessing the current situation there are several points to be made. First, guestworkers have joined German unions and at a percentage rate higher than that of national workers. At the same time, nearly three of every four foreign workers are not unionized and are thus bereft of whatever advantages may accrue from union membership. Second, unless they are willing to risk the loss of work and subsequent deportation by organizing a foreign workers' union, there is no realistic option for the workers but to work with the German unions. It is a reality that in spite of the minimal assistance and enforced marginality that confront a foreign worker within a German union, the union movement still represents the major if not sole institutional setting, other than the churches, where their concerns are acknowledged. The options are few or nonexistent for the foreign workers to find other institutional settings that will encourage their membership and act on their behalf.

In sum, the foreign workers and the German unions need one another. With nearly 13 percent of the labor force in Germany comprised of foreign workers, it is shortsighted on the part of the unions to ignore and isolate them. Furthermore, the German union movement is weakened by the exploitation of the foreign workers. If there is no unity among the German and immigrant workers, the losses in terms of strife, unemployment, and economic uncertainty will not be restricted solely to the latter group. For the guestworkers, there is an imperative of finding an institutional setting from which to speak out on economic and social conditions that affect their lives. The unions are one of the few places where this is possible, even if it is in a limited manner, for in the absence of organization and collective action, the foreign workers stand as isolated and solitary persons in a strange land, exposed to exploitation by those who, in the first place, had asked them to come.

# 6

## CIVIL AND POLITICAL RIGHTS

The present economy of the Federal Republic of Germany cannot sustain itself without foreign labor. At the same time, however, the issue remains unresolved as to whether this indispensable group of guestworkers should be understood as an additional transitory source of manpower or as new immigrants into the society. The result of this prolonged indecision by German officials has had ramifications in many areas of the social, cultural, and political life of the country. Questions of integration, of assimilation, and of the degree to which Germany should support the ethnic pluralism it now experiences within its borders are all left unanswered. The fate of more than 4 million persons remains unresolved.

If the obvious is finally acknowledged within the political and governmental sectors of Germany, that is, that the foreign workers are absolutely essential to the current standard of living and economic structures of the country, then the issue is one of charting policies that either tend toward the integration of the migrants or a perpetuation of their marginality. If the decision is made to support their integration, and no other realistic alternative appears open to Germany, then it is imperative that an appropriate legal foundation and framework for such integration be established.

Alternatively, if one is less optimistic that Germany will actively support the integration of the foreign workers, then at the least the formal legal statutes and policies should not hinder what integration might be achieved in other ways. The law is the formal means by which rights and liberties of the inhabitants of a nation are explicated, and the basis upon which one has recourse to protection from abuses; in short, it is a major determinant of how the inhabitants of a country are treated. So long as there are laws and regulations that maintain the marginality and second-class status of one group of persons within a country, it is not possible to speak meaningfully of their integration.

In this chapter an attempt will be made to assess whether the legal and administrative system in the Federal Republic is oriented toward the facilitating or hindering of the integration of the foreign workers. By examining both legal texts and administrative guidelines governing the civil and political rights of foreigners in Germany, explicit instances of support for either marginality or integration can be isolated. What becomes apparent is that while one might generally categorize the laws regarding foreigners as benign, it is immediately evident that there exists a great deal of administrative discretion and latitude in how the laws are interpreted and administered. It is this lack of specificity in the protections and rights accorded to the foreigners that allows abuses and questionable practices to occur. When civil and political rights are relegated to a dependency upon administrative discretion, the possibility arises that private prejudices will become public policies.

Added to this situation of administrative discretion is the fact that the legal rights of the guestworkers residing in the Federal Republic are scattered through a maze of international agreements, state and federal laws, precedents established by court rulings and procedural details; thus, it becomes extremely difficult to know precisely what are the legal rights to which the guestworkers are entitled.* The more differentiations made (for example, whether the foreigner comes from an EEC country, whether he has resided in Germany for at least five years, and whether he is married to a German citizen), the more difficult it becomes to untangle the web of restrictions, regulations, and stipulations, to say the least. Little wonder that one finds frequent accounts of foreign workers who, in absolute bewilderment and confusion, were deported or brought before a judicial hearing for reasons of which they had not the slightest idea. With an admitted degree of trepidation, the following is an effort to elaborate upon the civil and political rights of the foreign workers in Germany.

## CONSTITUTIONAL PROVISIONS

Article 3 of the federal constitution (*Grundgesetz*) expressly forbids discrimination because of "sex, race, language, country of origin, descent, beliefs, and religious or political suasion." It is unfortunate there is not an explicit men-

---

*It should be noted that this chapter will focus only on those laws and regulations that are German in origin and meant for the Federal Republic of Germany. There are, of course, international treaties which emanate from the EEC and are binding upon the FRG regarding the treatment of foreign workers, but they are not included in this discussion.

Rochcau (1975, p. 3) enumerates six such international treaties: The Universal Declaration of Human Rights, The Declaration of the Rights of the Child, The European Convention of Human Rights, The European Social Charter, The Convention Concerning Migrant Workers, established by the International Labor Organization, and Recommendations Concerning Migrant Workers, established by the International Labor Organization.

tion as well of ruling out discrimination based on nationality. It is understandable, however, for considerable emphasis is placed upon the distinction between rights that are available to all inhabitants in Germany and those reserved only to German citizens. Nationality becomes an important criterion for certain prerogatives and constitutionally guaranteed liberties. Interestingly, this distinction is evident in the very first article of the constitution.

Article 1: Freedom of Assembly
(1) All German citizens have the right to assemble peaceably without weapons, and this without permission or registration.

Further examples would include:

Article 9: Freedom of Alliance
(1) All German citizens have the right to form unions or associations.
Article 11: Freedom of Movement
(1) All German citizens will enjoy complete freedom of movement within Germany.
Article 12: Freedom of Choice of Occupation
(1) All German citizens have the right to freely choose their occupation, place of work, and training center.
Article 16: Extradition
(2) No German citizen may be extradited to a foreign power.

It should be noted that while the constitution does not expressly forbid the granting of these same rights to foreigners who are residing in Germany, it does provide the grounds upon which such rights may be either restricted or denied to those who are not German citizens. Maintaining the distinction between general rights and reserved rights has meant that there do exist differences in the degree to which the German constitution protects all who live in the country. The discretion left to officials as to how these rights are to be interpreted has further widened the distance between those who are and who are not of German citizenship. A number of bureaucratic and legal obstacles separate the two groups, and the fundamental legal apparatus for the creation and preservation of such obstacles is the Alien Act.

## THE ALIEN ACT

The most important law concerning the rights of foreigners in the Federal Republic is the Alien Act of 1965 with amendments passed on April 28, 1975 (*Bundesgesetzeblatt* 1). This law provides the fundamental guidelines for immigrating to and working within Germany. While the basic constitutional laws of the country do not entitle persons, other than in EEC countries, the unrestricted right to enter, the Alien Act defines who else is allowed to enter as follows

(Article 1, Section 2): "Everyone is a foreigner who is not German in the sense of Article 116, Section 1 of the Constitution." This section defines German citizenship as follows:

> With the provision that this may be changed by other laws, everyone is a German citizen in the eyes of the Constitution who holds German citizenship or who, as a refugee of German descent or spouse or children thereof, has fled to the Federal Republic of Germany from areas included in the Third Reich as existing on December 31, 1937.

According to Section 1, paragraph 1 of the Alien Act, every foreigner who wishes to enter and remain in the Federal Republic for a given length of time, and in a status other than that of tourist, must be granted a residence permit (*Aufenthaltserlaubnis*). The second sentence of this paragraph reads: "The residence permit may be granted if the presence of the foreigner does not adversely affect the interests of the Federal Republic of Germany."

A guideline such as this, general and undefined, gives great discretionary powers to those who administer the Alien Act. By not defining "adversely affect" or "the interests of the Federal Republic of Germany," the interpretations may be as many and as different as the persons who must make the decision on whether or not to grant the permit (cf. *Welt der Arbeit* 1976, p. 28). It must also be noted that the person receiving a residence permit is not necessarily entitled to keep it until the expiration date. It may be revoked for the same reason that in another instance it would not be granted at all. In the end, there is not entitlement either to the residence permit or to its retention once issued.*

The only official guideline available to those administering this act is the following, taken from the "General Administrative Regulations Concerning the Alien Act" (Roghan 1976, p. 87):

> When the residence permit does not have to be denied because of probable impositions on the interests of the FRG, the authorities shall decide upon the matter conscientiously after appropriate evaluation. Besides personal factors, also political and economic factors, as well as the interests of the labor market, are to be considered.

The guidance in these regulations is as broad and vague as the provision of the act itself. Again, it is the discretionary judgment (*Ermessen*) of the authorities that implements such a guideline.

---

*There is a variety of other reasons, as well, for which a residence permit can be revoked. As examples, begging, violation of residency restrictions, and violations of the "free democratic foundations" of German society are listed as sufficient reason for the permit's being revoked.

Those foreign workers who, prior to the labor hiring ban, came to Germany to look for work were generally required to have a labor legitimacy card in order to be allowed to enter the country. This card, issued in the home country by the German Labor Office when the worker had secured a contract for employment in Germany, was sufficient for the granting of entrance into Germany. When the worker had reached his destination and established his residence, he was then required to apply for the residence permit. If the labor contract was in order and the worker had reported to his new employer, the permit was granted. (Stipulations such as this were always present in the bilateral labor agreements Germany signed with countries of the European South.) If the labor contract was revoked by the employer or the worker, the residency permit likewise could be revoked and the worker could be subject to deportation. No data could be found to indicate how often such deportations occur for this reason, but one account is provided by Özkan (1974, p. 13), taken from a 1967 judgment of the Superior Court for Administration in Münster:

> The employee by not informing the employer about his change of workplace has violated the existing prerequisites for granting a visa and informing us by that act that he is not willing to conform to German law. The employee knew that his residency was only valid so long as he was employed by restaurant owner L. . . . Because of the large number of foreigners working in the FRG, such practice represents a dangerous development for the domestic order. The only effective way to stem this danger is through extradition at the mere instance of such a violation.

The residence permits granted to foreigners are valid throughout the Federal Republic, subject to certain limitations and restrictions, most notably those of time, location, and forbidding of business activity (*Gewerbeausübung*). On the time dimension, the initial residence permit will be for a period of one year. At the end of that time, and if all prerequisites have been met, it will be extended. After a period of five years, the authorities have the discretion to issue a permanent residence permit, though foreign workers can anticipate that certain restrictions will stay in effect for them even if such a permit is granted. The alternative to a permanent permit is one for a specific time, generally three to five years. While it has been generally the case throughout Germany that upon the completion of five years of uninterrupted work in the Federal Republic, the foreign workers receive favorable consideration for permitting longer stays, this has not always been the case. Özkan reported that in 1974, the immigration police of Bavaria wrote to several hundred Turkish workers stating that it was no longer feasible to extend their residence permits since they had already spent five years in the country. Some workers had been in the FRG for periods up to eight years. The case was taken to court and is still pending more than three years later.

The location restrictions have been briefly mentioned in Chapter 3 and will be taken up again in the next chapter, on housing policies. Briefly stated, the issuance of the residence permit can carry the restriction prohibiting the foreign workers from taking up residence in those urban areas which have been declared congested due to a certain percent of foreigners already in residence there. As will be analyzed more fully, it is apparent that there are a number of serious problems associated with this restriction, not the least important being the prevention of family reunions and the generation of illegal migration in order to locate new employment.

The provisions for entrance into the Federal Republic of foreigners from the member countries of the EEC are quite different. Article 48 of the Treaty of Rome binds each of the signators to the opening of their respective borders in an almost unlimited fashion to citizens of member states. The residence permit requirement is still in effect for EEC nationals in the Federal Republic, but they have three months in which to come to Germany to locate employment and housing without having to have the residence permit. If work is located, the residence permit is to be automatically issued for a period of not less than five years. No work permit is needed, as EEC nationals enjoy in this regard the same opportunities and options for employment as do German citizens. The only grounds upon which the residence permit can be revoked, and the author has personally found no such instance in which it has happened in Germany, is for acts committed against "public safety and order" or against the "interests" of the Federal Republic.

One other broad area in which the regulations and guidelines regarding the residence permit for foreigners are noteworthy is in the area of marriage and birth of children. The marriage of a foreigner with a German partner influences the position of the residency permit. This is so primarily because of Article 6 of the constitution which states that there are special protections which marriages are to enjoy, most notably, the protection of the marriage from interference by the state. These protections are accorded not only to the German partner but to the non-German national as well.

Though the protections of Article 6 have made the rights of foreigners married to Germans more secure in the sense of their being allowed to remain in Germany and not be so easily deported, there has still been considerable discretion in how such protections are interpreted by German officials. In fact, the discretion was thought too broad. New restrictions on the freedom of authorities concerned with the status of foreigners married to German nationals were contained in special legislation passed in March 1973. Until this time, when deportation hearings came up for a foreign male married to a German female, it was the position of the authorities that the spouse either followed the deported mate or dissolved the marriage (Strange 1973, p. 73). One clear example of this line of administrative thinking was evident in the following 1969 decision of the Superior Court for Administration in Lüneburg (cited in Özkan 1974, p. 15):

Even though married to a German citizen, and even though his children were raised in the German environment, the plaintiff is not protected from deportation.... The resettlement is not too much to ask of the plaintiff's wife, since at the time of marriage with a "guest-worker," it must have been clear to her that he would have to return to his homeland sooner or later. One does generally expect of a German wife that she will follow her husband abroad.

This particular decision reflects two policies that were changed with the 1973 legislation. The first was that such administrative opinion was defined as being in violation of the constitution, for it did not grant the special protection to marriage that is a constitutionally guaranteed right of all persons married and living in Germany. The second aspect of this decision that was no longer allowable in deportation hearings was the distinction between the status of German men married to foreign women and German women married to foreign men. The status of the former marriage was seen to be higher than that of the latter marriage. Thus there were no reservations about deporting a foreign male married to a German female and expecting the female to follow her husband out of the country. This precedent came from Paragraph 13.54 of the German Civil Laws which gave to the man, but not the woman, the right to decide where the family was to live. The 1973 legislation invalidated this paragraph and now both partners have the right to choose where they wish to live. Thus, if a wife chooses to remain in Germany, the courts must take this into consideration in any deportation hearings, for to deport the man would then be to take away special protections granted under Article 6.

With the 1973 changes in the laws, the reasons for the deportation of one spouse of a German-foreign marriage must be specific, important, and based upon evidence presented in an open hearing. The intent of such procedures is to ensure that the discretion of the administrative officers is not given free rein, but that the constitutional guarantees are adhered to. Rojhan (1976, p. 89) suggests that it would now not be far afield to assume that those who live in the Federal Republic and wish to maintain their marriage in Germany itself will be able to do so.*

As of January 1, 1975, children born to a German-foreign marriage automatically have German citizenship. This is independent of whether the German

---

*Several authors have noted that with these legislative changes that seek to protect the marriages of German nationals and foreign citizens, there has arisen some concern as to the abuses this is bringing. Rojhan (1976, p. 89) cites a statement of the Bavarian Office for the Administration of Foreign Workers that they are investigating the allegation that some German women have begun to marry foreign workers for money so that the foreign workers are entitled to remain in Germany. In fact, there is concern that this has become a bit of a scandal with women marrying a foreigner one day, being divorced the next, and marrying for a second time on the third day, and so on.

spouse is husband or wife. But prior to this date, the child received German citizenship only if the father was a German national and no citizenship was granted if the German parent was the mother. The basis for this change in the regulations regarding the granting of citizenship came as a result of a constitutional supreme court decision which rendered the view that granting of citizenship only in the case of German fathers was discriminatory and thus unconstitutional. The court decision has been seen as an important step in the process of creating equal status before the law for German women. There is nothing in this legislation that prohibits the child from holding dual citizenship, should it be granted by the country of the non-German spouse.*

Yet another aspect of the Alien Act with regard to the conditions under which a foreigner is to be granted a residence permit concerns the considerations by which it can be revoked and the person deported. Paragraph 10 of the Alien Act provides for deportation of a foreigner for any of 11 reasons, ranging from violation of police reporting requirements to serious traffic violations, from illegal employment or change in employment, to political behavior not in the interest of the Federal Republic. Grounds for deportation may also be based on the destruction of public security and order. For example, the city of Forscheim ordered deported a 42-year-old Turkish male worker because of his involvement with his landlord's since-divorced wife. The Alien Office in Forscheim based its decision on the assertion that the Turkish worker had ruined a German marriage and had thereby endangered public morals. A newspaper account of the hearing noted (*Stuttgarter Zeitung*, October 10, 1968):

> The Government of Oberfranken also remarked that an intimate relationship between a German married woman and a foreign worker provided sufficient reason for the deportation of the foreign worker involved. The Mayor of Forscheim envisioned an "invasion of foreign customs," from which "the German people require protection."

According to Paragraph 13 of the Alien Act, if a foreigner is ordered deported, that person is to be taken into custody until the time deportation can be effected (*Abschienbungshaft*), and the custody can last for as long as a year. (This is in contrast to the maximum length in Austria of two months or in the Netherlands and Belgium where the maximum provision is one month. Switzer-

---

*One aspect of this situation regarding the granting of citizenship to children of German-foreign parents is that citizenship in Germany in this instance is based upon lineage. It is quite different from the situation in France and the United States where any child born in the country, regardless of the nationality and citizenship of the parents, is automatically considered to be an American or French citizen. This becomes particularly important in the case of the more than 100,000 children born in Germany each year to the parents of foreign workers. Though born in Germany, they have the citizenship only of the home country of their parents, and not of their new residence, Germany.

land and France have no provision for such custody in their deportation regulations.) There remains in the German regulations an unresolved contradiction between the guidelines for the treatment of aliens to be deported and the fact that the Federal Republic is a cosigner of the European Extradition Agreement, Article 16-IV. This article notes that a person may not be imprisoned prior to deportation for more than 40 days, and then only if there is strong suspicion of a criminal act having been committed. Özkan (1974, pp. 18-19) cites an example of detention of over 10 months and another of a full year. While there have been several calls for reform of this regulation, including one from the German National Federation of Unions which stated that the period of imprisonment should be no more than three months and then in only the most extreme cases, they have to date been to no avail. Predeportation detention for a period up to a year is possible with any deportation order.

A final section of the Alien Act that is relevant to the matter of residence relates to the issuing of a foreign passport (*Fremdenpass*) to any person who does not possess a valid passport or a suitable substitute. According to Paragraph 4 of the Alien Act, German authorities have the right to issue such a foreign passport when one is requested by the person involved. The most frequent instance of this request comes when the home country has revoked the passport for political reasons or when the person has inadvertently let the passport expire and then faces the possibility of deportation for failure to have a valid passport. Though used rather infrequently, this foreign pass can also be issued to those persons in the Federal Republic who seek political asylum. Such a pass is valid for the person until the time of locating housing and employment, when the person must apply for the regular residence permit as a foreigner and is subject to the rules and regulations discussed in this chapter. The granting of political asylum is used rather sparingly by the Federal Republic in contrast to such countries as France or Italy (Özkan 1974, p. 22). Of the 33 Turkish persons who requested such asylum during the 15-year period from 1953 to 1968, nine were granted (Özkan 1974, p. 23).

## POLITICAL RIGHTS

Although the agreements signed when Germany joined the EEC stipulate a number of reciprocal political rights that all citizens of member states enjoy and share in common, it is more accurate to say that the granting of political rights is an internal and domestic activity as opposed to one found in principles of international law. The Federal Republic of Germany is under no obligation to grant political rights to non-German citizens unless it has made explicit treaty agreements to do so. This is really quite the same situation with other countries as well. The degree, manner, and variety of political expression allowed in any nation-state is generally a matter decided internally by that state. (Again, if international agreements are signed, such as the Helsinki Agreement of 1975, that stipulate countries will provide certain liberties to their own citizens and they do not do so, the basis arises for considering political rights as an international as opposed to exclusively internal affair.)

The Federal Republic has signed and ratified a number of international agreements relating to the granting and protecting of political rights, such as the Convention for the Protection of Human Rights and Basic Freedoms, proposed by the European Council in 1950.* Likewise, it has ratified two major United Nations agreements, the International Agreement about Civil and Political Rights of December 1966 (*Bürgerrechtskonvention*) and the International Agreement about Economic, Social and Cultural Rights, also of December 1966 (*Sozialrechtskonvention*).

In the ratification of the former agreement Germany chose not to ratify certain subsections of the document, specifically, Article 19 (Freedom of Opinion), Article 21 (Freedom of Assembly), and Article 22 (Freedom of Association and Coalition). With the latter agreement, Article 2, Paragraph 2 (Forbidding of Discrimination) was not ratified because the German government interpreted it to mean that the signer was to extend "every social, political, and economic right that is now granted to the German portion of the population to the whole population at once." This was rejected on the grounds that the granting of political rights to foreigners was an evolutionary process that requires step-by-step concrete actions as opposed to broad declarations that could not be successfully implemented (Rojhan 1976, pp. 90-91).

But as for those laws and regulations that are specific to the Federal Republic of Germany, it is apparent that foreigners are granted political rights in only a limited way. The first, and perhaps most basic, democratic right is the right to vote. Only German citizens have the right to vote for members of the Parliament (Paragraphs 12 and 16 of the Government Election Law, *Bundeswahlgesetz*), for the state legislatures, and for city councils. There have been some cities in Germany, most notably those in Hessen and North Rhine-Westphalia, which have granted foreigners the right to vote for local community advisory boards. However, such opportunities for foreigners are few and far between, being the exception rather than the rule. (It should be noted that Sweden is the only country of the European North that at present grants formal voting rights to foreigners, and this at the level of elections of city councils.)

While several German critics have assailed current election procedures for the exclusion of foreigners from participation in the electoral process (Özkan 1974, p. 32; Borris 1974, p. 256), there are others who seriously question whether their inclusion is possible within the current framework of the German constitu-

---

*It must be noted with respect to the foreigners, however, that in this accord the granting and monitoring of political rights of each of the cosigners was determined to be an exclusively domestic affair. The Convention stated: "None of the points listed above can be interpreted in a manner that those points prohibit the chief signers to control or limit the political activities of foreigners."

tion (Rojhan 1976, p. 91). While the German constitution does not specifically mention that voting rights are to belong exclusively to German citizens (Article 38), it does state (Article 20.2) that the power of the state comes from the people and such power is expressed during voting. Furthermore, "people" in this instance are defined as "native citizens" and not all those who reside in the nation. By inference from this Article, it is apparent that the German people are the final possessors of state power and it is only they who may grant, modify, or restrict the power of the state.

In several of the states, the foreigners are explicitly forbidden by language in the state constitutions from possessing the right to vote in state elections. However, even in those states where such prohibitions are not explicit, it is required by the federal constitution (Article 28.1) that for all state and city elections, the principle of homogeneity must be followed; that is, "The constitutional order in each of the states must be in accordance with the basic principles of the republican, democratic, and social legal state, in the sense in which these are expressed in the basic Constitution."

The constitution does, however, grant the right to foreigners, in conjunction with German citizens, to create on the community level advisory boards or foreign councils. The composition and function of these organizations differ in several ways from organizations to be founded by German citizens (cf. Tomuschat 1974, p. 97). For one thing, it is mandatory that there be German representatives on the councils, most frequently these being representatives from city agencies and officials having responsibility for foreign worker problems, for example, social welfare, housing, labor unions, and charity organizations. The foreign representatives are sent by unions that have migrant members, by charity organizations working in the foreign workers' community, by foreign workers' councils, or by informal neighborhood groups in the foreign community. This "foreign parliament" seeks to gain information on the social and cultural problems of foreign workers and their families so as to be able to send recommendations to the city agencies, city officials and, in some instances, to the city council for legislative action.

If the constitution forbids the right of voting to foreigners on the ground that voting is an expression of the political will and only German citizens are to decide that will, what of other forms of political expression? Might the passing out of pamphlets by foreigners be considered a building of the political will? What if foreigners stage a demonstration, go on strike, or form political associations? The constitution gives a differential answer to this matter. As was noted earlier, the constitution reserves some political rights only for German citizens, while it extends other political rights to all who are living within the boundaries of the Federal Republic. In this latter group, one finds those rights of all men (the *Menschenrechten*) to consist of the freedom of press and opinion (Article 5.1), and freedom of association (*Koalitionsfreiheit*, Article 9.3). For German citizens are reserved the political rights of freedom of assembly (Article 8.1), freedom of association (Article 9.1), and freedom to organize a political party (Article 21.1).

Rojhan (1976, p. 93) makes the point that if the constitution of the Federal Republic of Germany does not expressly grant specific protections and rights, it does not forbid restrictions on any nonspecific freedoms. While the federal or state legislators are free to grant political freedoms and rights to foreigners through the passage of a simple legislative procedure, as was done in expanding the foreigners' rights of assembly and of association, so also by this same legislative machinery can rights be restricted or reduced. An important provision in this area, and one frequently cited by those who would introduce legislation for the restriction of rights, is Article 6, Paragraph 2 of the Alien Act. This paragraph indicates that the political activities of foreigners can be limited or suspended "when such activity disturbs the public order and safety or interferes with the political will of the Federal Republic of Germany or other such important interests as may be apparent to the Federal Republic of Germany."

No specific definition of political activities is provided, nor are there guidelines that spell out the limits of public order and safety. The question arises, for example, of whether attending a rally is as political as organizing one. While it is realistic to assume no guidelines could be drawn to cover all such instances, the consequence is that the decision on the activities of the foreigner reverts to the discretion of the administrator in charge.

In an effort to elaborate upon the criterion mentioned in Article 6, Paragraph 2 of the Alien Act, the very next paragraph of the same article seeks to provide some specificity as to what activities could be considered as contrary to the interests of Germany. They include those activities contrary to international law; those activities that threaten the democratic foundations of the Federal Republic of Germany; and those activities that are directed at promoting parties, associations, or movements outside the jurisdiction of the Federal Republic of Germany and whose principles are contrary to the free democratic foundations of the constitution. It is an open question, particularly with regard to the latter two groups of activities, whether any additional clarity has been provided as to the distinction between acceptable and unacceptable political behavior on the part of the foreigners.

In order to avoid possible criminal sanctions and deportation, foreigners must follow the guidelines in this section of the Alien Act, avoiding activities that are examples of the behavior that could be considered disruptive of the public order and the interests of the country: demonstration against heads of state or against representatives of one's home country, or public criticism of one's home country; agitation within industrial firms; or distribution of pamphlets and brochures in front of universities or along streets with heavy traffic.

It would not be an exaggeration to suggest that such restrictions in the end imply that political pragmatism and political opportunity for the government in power become sufficient reasons for the restriction of political rights for foreigners. The foreign policy of the present government determines which international relations are of most importance and therefore should not be disturbed. Perhaps this is no different from what one should expect, given that international relations are part of the political milieu in which governments operate and in which they seek to make alliances and agreements to their own benefit. But the implication is that the rights and freedoms of some persons within the country are then determined in part by the elusive and ephemeral status of current foreign policy. Further, Germany as a democratic society blinds itself to the consideration of whether the political behavior of foreigners within the country is just and worthy of support.

In sum, a foreigner in Germany confronts a host of political rights and restrictions. It is useful now to focus on several of these areas in more detail, for it is in the closer assessment of these areas that a clearer picture may emerge as to where the foreigner stands with respect to his political expression.

## Freedom of Expression

The constitution of the Federal Republic in Article 5.1 grants the freedom of expression to all persons in the country, foreigner and German citizen alike, stating that "Every person has the right to express his opinion in words, written material, and in pictures and also to publish and distribute these materials." While there are legal scholars who take this constitutional guarantee in its most literal sense, others argue that in the context of other portions of the constitution, not all freedoms of expression are open to foreigners (cf. Rojhan 1976, p. 94).

The view that this article does not grant the absolute right of expression to foreigners is based on the reserved rights of German citizens to participate in the political process and to seek to influence public opinion and will. The exclusion of foreigners from this process means that in those circumstances in which they would seek to do so, they are in violation of the reserved rights of German citizens. For this reason it is argued that foreigners can be restrained from exercising certain freedoms of expression. The view is essentially that since the struggle over the direction of political opinion is a basis for the development of the political will, foreigners are not allowed all freedoms of expression, for the freedom of political expression is reserved only for German nationals.

The alternative view is one that argues that the basic rights of the constitution are general rights and take precedence over reserved rights. Further, it is argued that the specific restrictions placed on the political participation of foreigners by Article 6.2 of the Alien Act must be subservient to the general rights as enunciated in the constitution. Were the Alien Act a part of the general law, then the restrictions would be allowed. But so long as the general protections afforded to all persons take precedence, due to their presence in the basic constitution, the special restrictions of Article 6.2 of the Alien Act cannot limit the basic freedom of expression of non-German citizens.

No concrete examples have been found of this issue being resolved one way or another, either in constitutional law cases or in hearings for deportation based on the limitations of Article 6.2. While Özkan (1974, p. 36) cites the example of an American citizen who was denied a residence permit in 1972 on the basis of his organizing a demonstration against the Vietnam War in front of the U.S. Consulate in Schweinfurt, he does not provide sufficient detail on the case to learn whether the constitutional question was or was not raised. On the basis of the record of discretionary adjudication of deportation hearings, one can only assume that until the constitutional question of freedom of expression for foreigners is clearly enunciated and clarified, the use of Article 6.2 of the Alien Act as justification for deportation will continue.

## Freedom of Assembly and Association

According to federal legislation passed on July 24, 1953, every person in Germany has the right to organize and take part in public assemblies. Further legislation on August 5, 1964 granted the right to form associations. However, since both of these liberties are granted by legislative and not constitutional authority, the position of the foreigner is not protected by general law. Thus freedom of assembly and freedom of association for foreigners must be in accordance with the restrictions of Article 6.2 of the Alien Act. Both assembly and association can be forbidden to foreigners should such activities be deemed political in nature or threatening to the interests of the Federal Republic.

According to decisions rendered in administrative hearings, German authorities have the right (Article 6.2) to take action against foreigners, either individually or collectively. The latter is possible because foreign associations have a weaker legal position than do German associations, particularly if such foreign associations organize, support, or participate in political activity aimed at either foreign or domestic issues. Foreign associations can be prohibited, according to Paragraph 14 of the Law of Association (*Vereinsgesetz*) if such associations "endanger or violate important interests of the Federal Republic of Germany."

One set of restrictions on those clubs that are engaged in various forms of political activity, but have not been banned by the authorities, is to require that they provide names and addresses of all members, that they indicate all sources of income that support the association activities, and that they be able to account for the expenditure of all association income (Paragraphs 19 and 20, Law of Association). Neither foreign associations not involved in political activity nor German associations are required to provide such information (cf. Özkan 1974, p. 37). What could not be learned in relation to this regulation, however, was upon what critera and by whom decisions were made as to what constituted political versus nonpolitical behavior on the part of the foreign associations. Again, with that vagueness and lack of specificity that continue to obscure precisely what freedoms are or are not available to foreigners, one can only assume that the final judgments are made in the name of administrative discretion.

## Freedom to Create a Political Party (Die Parteifreiheit)

The constitutional supreme court, in a decision on whether Article 21.2 of the German constitution forbids foreign associations to become political parties, has ruled that it does so and that foreign political associations do not have such freedom. Since the majority of members and directors of foreign associations are themselves foreigners (and consequently not German citizens), they do not meet the qualifications of Article 2.3 of the law regarding the formation of a political party (*Parteiengesetz*).

Political parties that are already in existence have the right to decide if they wish to have foreigners as nonvoting members.* Such foreign members, if they do join an established political party under these conditions, may not seek office in the party, according to the federal election laws, Article 22.1 (*Bundeswahlgesetz*).

These restrictions on the participation of foreigners in established parties and the creation of new parties by foreigners are based on the constitutional principle that the participation in the political process is a component of the building of the political will of the people, and only German citizens are reserved the right to participate in this building of the political will. The constitution mandates that there be a connection between the nationality of the participants and the efforts of the political association. Both must be German.

## Freedom of Association (Die Koalitionsfreiheit)

The freedom of association, as enunciated in Article 9.3 of the constitution, is a freedom available to all persons in Germany, foreigners and German citizens alike. It is without restrictions. The article states: "The right to build associations in order to protect and support labor and economic conditions is for everyone and for all professions guaranteed." There is in addition to this freedom to create a union, the explicit wording that there exists the freedom to

---

*Recently some of the political parties in the Federal Republic have changed their bylaws to allow foreigners to become members. At this time the following parties allow foreign members: Social Democratic Party, Free Democratic Party, German Communist Party, and in West Berlin, the Socialist Union Party. The first two of these parties constitute the present governing coalition in Germany. The following parties do not currently allow foreigners to become members: Christian Social Union, Christian Democratic Union, and National Democratic Party of Germany. While the former two parties constitute the opposition coalition to the present government, the latter party is not represented in the Parliament. No data could be found to indicate the number of foreigners who have availed themselves of the opportunity to join those parties which are open to them. Özkan (1974, p. 34) reports that the Free Democratic Party listed only one foreign member in all of Berlin in 1974.

belong to a union, partake of all union activities, and also engage in legal strike action.

This protection becomes particularly important for those foreigners who are members of unions and engage in union protests, picketing, and strikes. So long as foreigners possess this right under Article 9.3 of the constitution, the authorities responsible for the supervision of residence permits and also for deportation based on political activity cannot act against them. The exercise of these rights is protected by general law and they are not to be abrogated or violated in the process of administering the Alien Act (Tomuschat 1974, p. 92).

How important this protection is for the foreign workers is worth stressing because it gives them certain parities with their German coworkers. By possessing the freedom to unionize and strike, foreign workers are not put in a position of being caught between unions and management over the question of the legality of their union activity. They are as free and protected to go on strike as their German counterparts. They also suffer and share the same risks. But, importantly, they do not incur additional risks by this behavior vis-a-vis the Alien Act and the discretionary decisions of the administrators responsible for its implementation.

# 7
# HOUSING: TOWARD INTEGRATION OR SEGREGATION?

Other than the economic sector of German society, there is perhaps no area in which the presence of the guestworkers is more apparent than housing. It is here that all conflicting pressures, policies, and prejudices of Germany toward the workers find expression. Further, it is here that one finds concrete evidence of the social conditions in which guestworkers live and seek to make a place for themselves and their families.

The housing conditions of the foreign workers in Germany are but an additional manifestation of the social, political, and economic marginality that they experience. The fact that the housing of the guestworkers tends to be the oldest and least desired, that it is located in the areas of cities left by the upwardly mobile segments of the German population, and that both rents and density are higher proportionally than for Germans could only be anticipated, given what we have come to know of the status position the guestworkers occupy in German society. They are in a situation comparable to that experienced many times over by other racial and ethnic minority groups who come into the metropolitan areas of center countries.

The linking of the conditions of foreign workers in Germany to those of minority groups in other countries is not spurious. A sizable body of literature has been written concerning the housing problems of minority groups in urban settings. And although the emphasis has been upon the conditions in North America and particularly the United States, there are a number of studies that supply us with valuable insights on the conditions in Great Britain, France, and Switzerland. In addition, there are numerous studies of such conditions in countries under colonial rule as well as those of internally repressive governments, such as South Africa, Rhodesia, and Brazil.

The commonality within this large corpus of research is not difficult to find: namely, ethnic and racial discrimination is such an important cause of residential segregation and of differences in the quality of available housing stocks, that the existence of a minority racial or ethnic area in a city can be taken as prima facie evidence of inequalities in the operation of the housing market. Data from the United States are particularly strong in suggesting that it would be a significant accomplishment to reduce racial and ethnic segregation just to the level of socioeconomic segregation. In other words, if the housing market were to become color-blind and simply function along the lines of discriminating by social class, a vast improvement would take place in the current living conditions of minorities. The same holds true for the guestworkers in Germany (Diricks and Kudat 1975a, p. 13).

What such an analysis implies is that discrimination within a system is predictably directed against certain groups, and that its magnitude, nature, and duration are properties of requirements within that system. The migrant workers comprise a group brought into the industrial countries of northern Europe to promote economic development; the costs of their presence to the system in terms of social capital have been kept to a minimum; and they are relegated to the lowest status positions in the society. In short, discrimination and exploitation are part of the very process that brought them to the North in the first place. The functioning of the housing market for foreign workers should not be anticipated to be different. It functions as an integral part of the entire apparatus which has brought, sustains, and profits from the efforts of the guestworkers. As Diricks and Kudat (1975b, p. 15) have noted:

> The studies dealing with the housing conditions of migrant workers have not only been extremely descriptive in nature, lacking a theoretical orientation and a methodological crux, but have also been misleading in their diagnosis of the major causes and consequences of the underlying phenomena. However, whatever theory has been developed has been removed from an overall understanding of the nature of the problem. Housing has been taken as a phenomenon meaningful in itself rather than focusing on its specific position within the overall framework of the transitory migration movement. . . . Housing is not only an area where the economic level is reproduced, but it is also an important need affecting significantly the chances the working population have of a better standard of living.

What follows in this chapter is first an assessment of the various housing policies present in Germany at both the federal and state levels, and second, an analysis of the actual conditions of housing for the guestworkers, including several differing interpretations for these conditions. Throughout the chapter, particular attention will be paid to those policies or conditions that affect the probability of either integration or segregation in the housing of foreign workers. An assessment of these two alternatives is critical to an understanding of the opportunities (and constraints) available to Germany's new immigrants. As Rose

(1969, p. 74) suggested, "It need not be stressed how important adequate housing is for the worker's health, mental balance, protection, social integration, status, and sometimes opportunities (e.g., for education of his children)."

## FEDERAL HOUSING POLICIES

As the bilateral agreements that Germany had signed with the labor-exporting countries were put in force, explicit requirements were frequently made for the German government to supervise, regulate, and mandate certain conditions in the housing of the foreign workers. Beyond these stipulations, a variety of measures and regulations were adopted by the German government of its own accord. These latter acts were less for the well-being of the workers than for the political and social implications of large numbers of foreign workers in Germany. The policies that have been adopted by the German government may be divided into four categories.

The first category concerns that set of regulations governing the housing provisions for first entrants into Germany. When new workers have been recruited by a German company to come and work in Germany, that company has been required to provide housing for the worker or show that other accomodations have been secured that meet government standards. The company housing, referred to as *Heime*, are frequently large barracks or boarding homes found in the areas of many cities where large industrial concerns are located. The housing has been built so as to be in close proximity to the work place, and though it is illegal, this proximity has frequently led to what is termed the "hot bed," or the same bed used by different workers as they consecutively switch work shifts.

An additional stipulation regarding first entrance into Germany is one noted earlier, that of workers having to certify available housing before they are allowed to bring their families from the home country to join them. While this law sought to prevent overcrowding in living quarters and ensure sufficient living space for a family, it has also had the effect of forcing any number of workers to bring their families into Germany illegally, since such housing could not be secured. Crowded conditions, in spite of regulations, became the only option for those who wished to reunite with their families. It has been exceedingly difficult to ascertain the exact numbers of family members who have come into Germany illegally and have moved with spouses into overcrowded condiions. Unless the new arrivals were caught in illegal employment or tried to register their children for education without proper papers, there would be little or no way for authorities to learn of their presence. Any number of landlords appear fully willing to cooperate covertly with the workers for a price in bringing their families together illegally.

A second category of housing policies at the federal level governs physical specifications of housing for guestworkers. Such specifications are quite explicit and are legally binding upon firms that provide housing for their workers (group housing), as well as for those in the public market who make agreements with the firms or public officials for the housing of the workers. There are two major sets of regulations that guide the provision of living quarters for the migrant workers, the first of which was issued by the Federal Ministry for Labor and Social Affairs on April 1, 1971, entitled "Regulations for the Living Quarters of Foreign Workers in the Federal Republic of Germany" (*Richtlinien für die Unterkünfte ausländischer Arbeitnehmer in der Bundesrepublik Deutschland*). The following are but a few examples of the 31 specifications included in the regulations:

For every dweller a sleeping place must be provided. Bunk beds may have no more than one bed above another.
In any living quarters with more than 50 dwellers, a separate sick room must be provided.
Each dweller must be provided with a locked cupboard in which to keep personal food items. For each two dwellers a cooking place must be provided.
Walls and roofs must be insulated.
Each new dweller must be provided with clean linens.
The washrooms must be in the same building as the sleeping areas. One wash place must be provided for each five dwellers and each wash place must provide hot and cold running water.

Further regulations were issued in June 1973, this time not under the auspices of a particular federal Office, but by the federal parliament (*Der Bundestag*). Entitled "Regulations for the Minimal Conditions of Living Quarters for Foreign Workers" (*Gesetze über die Mindestanforderungen von Unterkünften für ausländische Arbeitnehmer*), they were passed by the government to amend general housing laws and guidelines of 1934, 1959, and 1968 so as to take special recognition of the living conditions of the foreign workers. Sanitary conditions were made more explicit, cooking facilities were outlined in greater detail, and the responsibilities of those providing the housing were made more specific. It must be noted, however, that in reading these regulations, no provisions for monitoring compliance or penalties in instances of violations could be found. It may be that such items are specified in the general housing codes, but this is an important omission in a set of housing guidelines for that group of people in the society most likely to bear the brunt of discrimination and exploitation. It goes without saying that if the foreign workers were receiving inhabitable housing as a matter of course, such regulations would not be necessary.

Financial support and inducements for the building of housing for foreign workers constitute the third set of housing policies at the federal level. One set of policies spells out the basis upon which the government will provide financial aid for the establishment of hostels (or *Heime*) for workers, support which would come from the social housing budget of the government. These policies, set forth in 1971 under the title "Regulations by the Board of the Federal Labor Office for the Promotion of Construction of Living Quarters for Foreign Workers" ( *Grundsätze des Vorstandes der Bundesanstalt für Arbeit über die Förderung der Errichtung von Unterkünften für ausländische Arbeitnehmer* ), included stipulations for entering into a contract with the government, financial terms, general architectural features of the housing to be built, time lines as to construction periods, and agreements that the housing would indeed be used for the foreign workers. This particular set of guidelines contained 27 points, many with a number of subsections.

The other area in which the government has involved itself is in the financial support of housing for married foreign workers. It was first put forth in June 1967 under the title "Regulations for the Guarantee of Loans for the Promotion of Apartment Buildings for Foreign Workers" (*Grundsätze für die Gewährung von Darlehen zur Förderung des Wohnungsbaues für ausländische Arbeitnehmer* ). This policy statement outlines the relationship of the government to those who build such housing in much the same way as in the previous agreement on group housing. It also carries the additional provision of providing loans to foreign workers so that they can purchase such housing when constructed. In a sense, the government with this policy undertook support of both sets of participants in the housing field—the builders and the buyers. What could not be found was an indication of the financial support given to this and the other program for the construction of new foreign worker housing. The policy statements themselves provided no indication of the estimated support necessary for the effective implementation of the programs. Nor were such figures mentioned in the comprehensive accounts of current housing policy with regard to the foreign workers by Freiburghaus (1975), Muhlens (1976), or by Reimann (1976).

The fourth and final category of federal housing policy with respect to the foreign workers is one mentioned previously in Chapter 3, involving restrictions on further concentration of workers in specific metropolitan areas. By the authority of the federal government, cities with more than a 6 percent foreign worker population may apply to receive permission to limit further immigration of foreign workers. When the concentration of foreign workers reaches 12 percent, the cities have the right to act on their own and refuse admission to any additional workers. It is estimated that at the end of 1976, approximately 45 cities in Germany had placed such a ban on further in-migration. The total number of cities that have applied for such authority could not be determined. It is difficult to know whether any city with above 6 percent foreign population, which wishes to have the option of suspending permits for new arrivals, can essentially do so, or whether this authority is granted with some consideration of factors other than local interest.

In either event, this policy has had an important impact upon the lives of foreign workers. It has prevented desired activities in some instances, and has forced others to be done covertly. It can only be argued that this policy is beneficial to the foreign workers if, indeed, this set of restrictions does prevent the negative aspects of further concentrations and opens up new avenues for their integration into the society. There are no data, however, that show this to be the case. Rather, what one finds instead is that family reunions are hindered, job mobility is hindered, the incorporation of new arrivals into the community of foreign workers is hindered, and those children who are affected frequently find themselves in schools where their numbers are small, the teachers ill prepared to instruct them, and the services few, if any, to assist them in their transition into the German educational system. The goal was distribution and minimizing of social costs. The reality appears to be the creation of isolation, illegality, and further marginality.

The few possible positive benefits of this policy lie in the perceptions of German nationals that Germany has been effective in its efforts to integrate the foreign workers, that steps are being taken to prevent the formation of urban ghettos, and that the lives of individual workers must be better if they are not in the areas of high congestion. As will be analyzed later in this chapter, all three of these suppositions are open to dispute. There is no evidence that this policy has, in any way, had concrete and tangible positive benefits for the workers or their families.

In his assessment of the federal involvement in housing for the guest-workers, Freiburghaus (1975, p. 243) suggests that such policies are interpretable only in the light of the broader political/economic context of foreign labor in Germany. He notes that the creation of law is a political instrument of government and, therefore, the creation of law regarding the housing of the workers is a political act. He offers the following six political/economic hypotheses as a framework within which to interpret the legal dimensions of housing for foreign workers and their families (1975, p. 244):

1) The main problem is the total lack of imagination of the policy with regard to the employment of foreign workers. This policy is characterized as representative of the interests of capital, modified to a degree by so-called social considerations, which serve the purpose of avoiding internal and international conflicts.

2) The fluctuating policy toward foreign workers hinders the improvement of housing, because housing improvement requires long term and vast financial planning.

3) In the metropolitan areas of high concentration, it is well known that the provision of housing for the comparable group of the native worker population is as inadequate as that for foreigners.

4) Building of housing in the Federal Republic is carried out by private and semi-public institutions which are either profit oriented, or at least must be economically justifiable. Any government pres-

sure on the conditions of their housing allocation would require adequate financial aid.

5) The demand of foreign workers for apartments with minimal standards of quality is in the interest as well of the relevant agencies of the housing market, since they are able to profitably rent out low quality facilities until the time to be demolished.

6) Though frequently better information would benefit the foreign workers, there is no doubt but that thereafter increasing demands would escalate the already existing dilemma.

These hypotheses fit well with the contention, cited earlier in this chapter, of Diricks and Kudat (1975b). It is imperative, as they note, that in an examination of the housing conditions and policies of the foreign workers in Germany, attention be paid to the economic and political context in which the workers find themselves. In a section of northern Europe where housing is in scarce supply and great demand, the means by which the available stock is allocated cannot be assumed to operate outside such considerations as nationality, social status, political and informal social contacts. On all four items, the foreign workers would have to stand, according to prevailing German standards, at the end of the line. Even assuming that the housing policies of the government function along the lines of the formal orthodoxy regarding the workers—that they are not immigrants and will be returning home—the conclusion is to avoid investing heavily in a transient population when many native Germans are still in need of much new and refurbished housing.

## STATE HOUSING POLICIES

Within the political structure of the Federal Republic of Germany, each of the 11 states (*Länder*) is granted broad discretionary powers to set its own policies and direct its own programs, so long as they are within the boundaries of federal directives. The caveat, however, is that the discretion is not comparable across all areas of social life. While the states have considerable control over the educational policies and programs within their jurisdiction, they have much less over labor policies and economic planning. The matter of housing appears to fall somewhere between these two. The guidelines from the federal level are rather detailed, but the programmatic implementation is much more in the hands of the states. Likewise, the fact that the federal government heavily supports housing initiatives and programs in the various states does not appear to constrict their options. In fact, there appears to be something of a revenue-sharing program in operation where funds are block-granted to the states to use in their housing programs.

One state where a rather extensive set of housing proposals has been developed and adopted is Berlin, one of the three city-states in Germany. A city of slightly under 2 million persons (1.91 million) and having a legal guestworker population of 190,000 (10 percent), Berlin remains one of the largest German cities, in spite of a pronounced population decline. This decline is due both to the exodus of some workers to other parts of the Federal Republic and to the fact that the demographic structure of the city is heavily skewed toward the elderly. One of every three persons in the city of Berlin is a single woman over the age of 45.

In view of the demographic realities and the need to sustain itself as a viable economic entity, Berlin has perhaps gone further than any other state in Germany, in terms of official policy, to promote the integration of the foreign worker population. The facts can speak for themselves. Without the foreign workers and their families, Berlin would be a city essentially of the elderly and the young, but few if any workers.* Estimates by the Institute of Economic Research, a federal government think tank, suggest that Berlin will lose another 300,000 German residents by 1990, mostly due to the deaths of the older age group, but also because the net loss of people in the age group of 21-30 is averaging 3,000 persons per year (Getler 1976b). It is the guestworkers who are filling the vacuum, and it is the birth of their more than 5,000 children per year (31 percent of the total) that contributes substantially to the efforts of Berlin to maintain its population and shape a more normal demographic profile.

The governing body of the state of Berlin (*Der Senat*) has adopted a set of proposals relating to the housing of the foreign workers as a part of a broader integration program envisaging a graduated assimilation into the life of the city. This integration program (*bedarfsorientierter Integrationsmodell*) functions under the basic policy decision that the foreign workers should be integrated into the city. Berlin has thus implicitly seen itself as a center of immigration for foreign workers and their families and not as a center for the simple rotation of laborers.

The housing proposals adopted by the Berlin government can be described under three headings (cf. Knebel and Kempe 1975, p. 258). The first of these consists of proposals for the expansion of housing stock available to foreign workers either through new construction or through greater access to present dwellings. New housing has been created by subsidizing expanded quantity and quality of company-owned housing. Increased access to present housing was to be achieved by increased distribution to foreigners of both subsidized and nonsubsidized housing belonging to the city; by the purchase of real estate outside

---

*Beside the fact that Berlin is Germany's richest theater, music, and cultural center, a strong attraction of Berlin for the young is that residents of this city are not subject to the military draft of the West Germany army. This is in keeping with the four-power agreements on the demilitarized status of the city. East Germany, however, has revoked this portion of the agreements and does draft men from East Berlin.

of present areas of concentration and in future urban renewal areas (*Sanierungsverdachtsgebiete*), so as to make this housing available to the workers; and by the providing of improved counseling services for those immigrant workers seeking new accommodations.

The goal of the second set of housing policies aimed at an integration of the foreign workers is to monitor present accommodations so as to maintain inhabitable conditions. Increased supervision of guestworkers' apartments would prevent neglect of the dwelling by the owner, and closer supervision of the workers' claims would ensure that suitable housing had been located for reuniting families. It is yet too soon to ascertain if, in fact, the monitoring has had any impact upon the behaviors of either the landlords or those workers wanting to bring their families to Berlin.

The third area in which Berlin has been active in the housing of the immigrant workers has been the most important to date. It was the official halt, drafted in November 1974, and effective as of January 1, 1975, to any further movement by foreign workers or their families into three of the districts in the city. These three, Kreuzberg, Wedding, and Tiergarten, with guestworker populations of 25, 17, and 15 percent respectively, all border the downtown area of Berlin and also the wall with East Berlin. This halt, as noted in Chapter 3, was essentially a precursor to the larger ban Berlin placed on any further in-migration into the city itself as of April 1, 1976. Consequently, non-EEC foreign workers have been restricted from moving into Berlin since April 1, 1976, nor have they been able to move into three of the districts from other parts of the city since January 1, 1975.\*

It appears extremely difficult to ascertain how these bans will facilitate the integration of foreign workers into the society. The bans on moving have thwarted the legal reunification of families. Freedom of movement and oppor-

---

\*A newspaper article, intensely critical of the housing policies of West Berlin, was published in the *Frankfurter Rundschau* (April 1, 1976) on the same day as the complete ban on further in-migration of foreign workers and their families went into effect. The author of the article, Vera Gaserow, made the following assessment of both the within- and total-city ban regarding housing for foreign workers:

> The foreign families are now the ones to solely suffer under this strict order. An unsystematic foreigner social-policy is responsible for the Berlin calamity. For a long time, the city officials have been idly watching the influx of foreign workers and their families into the city and the three districts in particular. The foreign workers gravitated to these areas as the one place where they could secure housing. For the German landlords and owners, this was a unique opportunity. They demanded and got "cut throat" rents for what are now the poorest facilities in the city. They also worked to cause the German tenants to move out of the areas so that the flats could be sub-divided to accommodate more foreign workers and their families.

tunities for locating housing have been drastically diminished, particularly if the workers have been living in company-owned housing, and even if they have been in one of the three areas where the within-city ban is in effect, they are unable to leave it if they cannot find housing in other areas. Any opportunity for better housing in one of the two other areas where a sizable number of foreign workers have located is blocked. Further, the constrictions are imposing greater problems of discrimination and illegality, making the housing situation worse rather than better, and generating increasing pressure for the intervention of German authorities. This is nearly the antithesis of integration. Instead, what the immigrant have and are experiencing is greater restriction on mobility, less opportunity for family reunion, fewer options for housing, and the increased intrusion of German agencies of social control into their everyday lives. The image of integration fractures against the reality of marginality and increased isolation.

## HOUSING CONDITIONS

Any assessment of the housing conditions of the guestworker population in Germany must be made not only in the context of the specific social policies described above, but also in awareness of the general housing situation in the country. The reason this becomes important is that, unlike America or Canada, the German housing market is extremely limited. The indigenous German population does not have the flexibility in its housing choices that corresponding socioeconomic groups in the United States have. While this situation is particularly aggravated in a city like West Berlin where there is the physical impossibility of forming further suburbs, the large cities of Germany are all still in a process of recovering the housing losses experienced during the last war. The pursuit of comfortable housing consumes much of the time of those who wish to change their current accommodations. Further, securing desirable housing is seen as such a fortunate occurrence that people tend to hold on to it for as long as possible. (This in turn drastically reduces the geographic mobility of Germans in terms of moving from one city to another for reasons of employment, professional advancement, and so forth.)*

An interesting implication of the lack of housing options for German nationals is that it has hindered housing segregation of the foreigners. Were the Germans to have greater flexibility of movement within the housing market, there might well be a suburban flight such as has created de facto segregation in the United States. The reality of housing immobility has inhibited many German

---

*One indication of this residential stability and permanence of the German population is that there do not exist furniture rental agencies such as one might find in any large city in the United States.

nationals, particularly those who are aged or in lower income levels, from leaving areas where guestworkers have found housing. This is not to suggest, however, that the guestworkers have not experienced housing segregation and discrimination. They have. It is only to note that the scarce housing options facing the German population have had an inadvertent outcome of hindering still further segregation.

It appears premature to suggest that German cities have developed the typical ghetto situation seen in the United States. This is not to say that Germany, or Europe in general, has done a better job or made more positive efforts in housing the migrants. Rather, the immigration of the foreign workers is a recent phenomenon, one that for the Turkish workers is perhaps no more than a decade long. The social, political, and economic dynamics that create and sustain the conditions and infrastructures of ghetto life are evolutionary and not set in place with the first wave of migrants. With time, and the exacerbation of current conditions, the creation of minority enclaves, segregated and shunted away from the other sectors of German society, can be anticipated.

The fact that the housing conditions of the foreign workers in Germany have not become so desperate as those of many minority groups in urban America has been noted by Diricks and Kudat (1975a, p. 19):

> What makes the European ghetto different from American ghettos is not the fact that the former is not exclusively composed of particular ethnic groups, but rather its social characteristics. In the European ghetto, and particularly in West Germany, the crime rate is not higher than elsewhere in the city. Not the migrant minority, but more probably, the indigenous residents, are unemployed, desperate and relatively deprived. Within these ghettos it is not the foreign proletariate but the indigenous youth who is more a drug addict; it is not the young and healthy migrants but the old indigenous population left behind by the middle-aged mobiles who are in need of medical care. Moreover, the local authorities, as well as the central government, can effectively control service demands of the minority groups with simple policy tools [as opposed to either ignoring or suppressing them through social control].

Acknowledgment must be made of an alternative line of analysis to that presented here regarding the causes for the current housing situation of the foreign workers. While an attempt has been made here to interpret conditions in the light of the economic and political position that foreign workers occupy in German society—that is, a structural analysis—there are those who argue that the conditions must be explained in terms of the characteristics of the workers themselves—that is, a sociopsychological analysis. Consider, for example, this statement by Mehrländer (1975, p. 246):

Home life as it is understood in Central Europe might, however, have been unknown to many of those questioned when they first took up residence in the Federal Republic of Germany. Scientific studies have shown that sublimated home life, i.e., the need for cleanliness, order and decoration in the home, and the heightened desire to shape one's own home have to be interpreted in part as a direct result of industrial activity and factory discipline. Because of their socio-economic background, the majority of foreign workers will have had no opportunity to be influenced by these factors as far as accommodation requirements, way of living, and home life are concerned. In assessing living conditions, accommodation requirements and way of living among foreign workers in the Federal Republic of Germany, account should be taken of the fact that they arrive in the Federal Republic without furniture, without any concrete or perhaps with only short-term ideas on their stay here, and with a desire to return to their homelands.

With the "need for cleanliness, order and decoration in the home" absent in many of the families due to their lack of participation in "industrial activity and factory discipline," this line of analysis tends to be more than simply reminiscent of the culture-of-poverty debate that raged in the United States a decade ago. It is, as was aptly demonstrated in the American debate, a line of analysis that in the end blames the victim for the victimization and its manifestations. Thus for Mehrländer, it is not the thrust of current social policies, nor the economic and social marginality imposed upon the foreign workers, that results in their being excluded from German society, but rather that the workers are not familiar with the characteristics of central European home life and that they arrive in Germany without furniture.

This line of reasoning is taken one step further by Timur (1975, pp. 263-64). His argument, drawn from a sample of foreign workers in West Berlin, is that the following five criteria are the basis for interpreting the reasons foreign workers live in areas with high concentrations of other foreign workers and in housing that "hardly meet[s] the minimum requirements for human living conditions."

> Foreigners who come from villages where frequently much less adequate living conditions are common will be content with a lower quality housing.
>
> A survey carried out for the Berlin government in connection with a social plan for urban renewal areas concluded that foreigners were not willing to spend more than 11 percent of their net income (18 percent for Germans) for rent. However, the willingness to pay more rent tends to increase with length of stay in the city.
>
> Many foreigners do not wish to pay high rents because they send all the money they can to their relatives at home, or because they expect to

be only temporarily working here. Moreover, those foreigners who do not come from Common Market countries are very likely influenced by the current legal situation with respect to aliens and the resulting insecurity they face.

Foreigners do not have the same supply of housing available to them as have Germans. Other housing has been offered to them, however, with some complications. When a foreigner is offered a new apartment within an urban renewal area, it is done only on the basis of an adequate ratio of family members to housing size; for example, it is not possible for a foreigner (or German) with a six-member family to move into a 2-1/2 room apartment.

Those areas of the city with a high concentration of foreigners have more shops, school classes with foreign teachers, kindergartens, and day-care facilities for the foreign population. This is a reason for many foreigners to decide to move to or remain in these areas.

Though it is not worth belaboring the point, it does need to be made forcefully: the emerging debate in Germany as to the sources of the conditions of the foreign workers and their families is one that is highly similar to the debate in the United States over the conditions of the black American population. In either the German or American situation, to blame the victim rather than the structure leads to quite different implications for social policy and social action. The American debate is waning because the outcome of the contending paradigms appears to have been decided. The U.S. intellectual, political, and economic sectors have come to the conclusion that the position of black Americans is one not based on personal and private idiosyncratic characteristics, but can be ascribed to the structural position that black Americans have been forced into by powerful forces external to themselves. The debate is no longer whether black Americans deserve equity and equal opportunities in America, but rather how these goals are to be achieved and what institutional modifications and realignments are necessary for this to be accomplished. The question remains, however, to what degree the impact of this debate will influence both academic and governmental analyses of the situation of the foreign workers in Germany. To date, it is the author's personal view that the U.S. experience has been largely ignored.

## Conditions in Frankfurt

More than 110,000 foreign workers and their families live in Frankfurt, a city of approximately 650,000.* At present, 48 percent of all live births in the

---

*Unless otherwise noted, the data for this section on Frankfurt come from the excellent study conducted by Maria Borris (1974) on the guestworkers in Frankfurt. This, to-

city are to families of the migrants, the highest percentage in Germany. (Munich has 38 percent and Berlin (West) has 31 percent [Getler 1976]). The majority of all foreign workers in Frankfurt come from the five major labor-exporting countries of the European South—Greece (18.7 percent), Italy (7.2 percent), Turkey (36.1 percent), Spain (9.0 percent), and Yugoslavia (12.7 percent). More than 90 percent of the foreign workers are below the age of 45 and nearly 70 percent below 35. Seventy-seven percent of the workers are male. The highest percentage of female workers are from Greece (34 percent) and the lowest from Turkey (19 percent).

The reuniting of foreign workers and their families in Frankfurt is heavily influenced by four factors: length of residence, nationality, sex, and number of children. The longer a married worker has lived in the city, the more likely he is to have brought his spouse (84 percent of those who have been in the city for ten years or longer, 71 percent of those who have been in the city for five years, and 41 percent of those who have been in the city for one year or less). There is also considerable variation among the male workers, by nationality. While 70 percent of all Greek male workers have brought their families to Frankfurt, only 48 percent of the Spanish workers, 38 percent of the Turkish workers, and 34 percent of the Yugoslavs have brought theirs. When the female is the worker, the figures for family reunions are somewhat higher: 64 percent for the Italians, 56 percent for the Spanish, 53 percent for the Turkish, and 49 percent for the Greek female workers. Family size also has considerable influence upon the likelihood of a spouse residing in Frankfurt. Table 7.1 suggests that the larger the family, the more likely it is to have remained in the homeland.

TABLE 7.1

Location of Spouses of Foreign Workers,
by Family Size
(percent)

|  | \multicolumn{5}{c}{Number of Children} |
| --- | --- | --- | --- | --- | --- |
|  | 1 | 2 | 3 | 4-5 | 6 or more |
| Frankfurt | 76 | 62 | 49 | 37 | 21 |
| Home country | 24 | 38 | 51 | 63 | 79 |

Source: M. Borris, Ausländischer Arbeiter in einer Großstadt (Frankfurt: Europäische Verlanpanstalt, 1974), p. 19.

---

gether with the research of Kudat and her colleagues on Berlin (West), represent two of the very few in-depth studies available on the guestworker situation in single German cities.

TABLE 7.2

Housing of Foreign Workers, by Type of
Dwelling and Nationality
(percent)

| Nationality | Company Barracks/ Group Homes | Private Rooms | Private Apartments |
|---|---|---|---|
| Greeks | 22 | 20 | 58 |
| Italians | 51 | 14 | 36 |
| Yugoslavs | 73 | 11 | 16 |
| Spanish | 32 | 20 | 48 |
| Turks | 32 | 27 | 41 |

Note: N = 1963.
Source: M. Borris, Ausländischer Arbeiter in einer Großstadt (Frankfurt: Europäische Verlanpanstalt, 1974), p. 132.

Overriding all the factors mentioned above, however, are the housing conditions themselves in Frankfurt. Reunions of large families are influenced by the regulations requiring sufficient housing to accommodate those who wish to come. Such housing is neither easy to find nor inexpensive. In fact, all guestworkers face difficult obstacles, whether searching for larger accommodations, moving from a company-owned hostel (*Heim*) to a private room or apartment, or attempting to locate less expensive housing.

Foreign workers have found housing in all 16 districts of the city, though only one district—that of the *Innenstadt* in the vicinity of the train station—has more than a 30 percent foreign worker population. Borris contends that as a consequence of this dispersal, one cannot infer that there exists in Frankfurt a particular foreign quarter that might be compared to either an American ghetto or one in the classical European sense as described by Worth (1928). However, as she notes, the concentrations of foreign workers are in those areas viewed by Germans as the least desirable sections of the city and where the housing is in poor repair and slated for urban renewal. Frankfurt, then, has pocket ghettos of only a few houses, or perhaps along one street or another. It is in this sense that the housing market in Frankfurt is taking on a dual nature, one part reserved for German nationals and one part reserved for foreign workers, scattered as it may be. There are essentially three categories of housing available to the guestworkers: company-owned barracks and group houses, private furnished or unfurnished rooms, and private furnished or unfurnished apartments. Table 7.2 provides data on the distribution among these types of dwellings by the nationality of the workers.

This table, taken together with the previous data on family reunions, suggests that there are differences among the foreign workers as to their sense of permanence and anticipation of staying in Frankfurt. For example, 70 percent of married male Greek workers have brought their families to Frankfurt. They are also most likely to house their families in private apartments—a sign of an apparent desire to remain. Only 16 percent of the Yugoslav workers, on the other hand, are in private apartments and only 34 percent are reunited with their families. Most Yugoslav workers tend to live in company barracks, seemingly in anticipation of returning home after saving a large portion of their earnings. Italian workers have the advantage of being relatively close to home when they are in Frankfurt and, thus have close access to their families who remain in Italy. And because Italy is a member of the EEC, Italian workers have the guarantee of entry into Germany as often as they wish.

Length of residence in the city is another variable that influences the option of private or company housing. Those who have been in Frankfurt for seven years or longer are more likely to have private housing (61 percent versus 39 percent). For those who have been in Frankfurt for less than two years, the percentages are nearly reversed—42 percent in private housing and 58 percent in company housing.

The worker's age is also likely to influence his choice of housing. The older (s)he is, the more likely it is that the worker will be in company housing. This is due, perhaps, to the desire on the part of older workers not to uproot their families and also to save as much as is possible from their work in Germany in the last years before their retirement. For the younger workers, there is greater likelihood of being united with their families, seeking suitable accommodations and surroundings for the children, and being willing to spend more of their earnings on a higher standard of living while in Germany.

The 661 respondents in Borris's sample who chose to live in private quarters gave the following reasons: 44 percent desired better living conditions, 37 percent wanted to live with fewer other persons, 30 percent wanted to reunite with their families, and 25 percent wanted to live alone. (They were free to give more than one reason.) While these responses indicate a desire for more private and less crowded accommodations, the evidence suggests, however, that the workers living in private rooms were still in overcrowded conditions. Table 7.3 shows that the number of persons per room for the guestworkers is quite high, much higher than the national German average of .79 persons per room.

Not only, then, must the foreign workers tolerate generally overcrowded conditions (72 percent of all one-room apartments of workers have three or more persons in them, 63 percent of all two-room apartments have four or more persons in them, and so on); they may also have to put up with poor furnishings and facilities, as indicated in Table 7.4, taken from Borris's survey.

Moreover, such facilities, poor as they are, do not come cheap. While it is difficult to establish comparability between one city and an entire nation, the data provided by Borris do suggest that, at least for the foreign workers, the cost

TABLE 7.3

Occupancy of Apartments, by Number of
Rooms and Number of Persons
(percent)

|  | Number of Rooms* | | | | |
|---|---|---|---|---|---|
| Number of Persons | 1 | 2 | 3 | 4 | Percent of Total |
| 2 | 28 | 10 | 3 | 0 | 16 |
| 3 | 25 | 27 | 17 | 0 | 24 |
| 4 | 27 | 36 | 26 | 0 | 30 |
| 5 | 14 | 17 | 25 | 27 | 18 |
| 6 | 4 | 5 | 15 | 27 | 7 |
| 7 or more | 2 | 5 | 14 | 46 | 5 |

*Excluding kitchen and bath.
Note: N = 672.
Source: M. Borris, Ausländischer Arbeiter in einer Großstadt (Frankfurt: Europäische Verlanpanstalt, 1974), p. 150.


TABLE 7.4

Fixtures and Furniture in Foreign
Workers' Apartments

| Fixtures | Percent of Apartments | Furniture | Percent of Apartments |
|---|---|---|---|
| Toilet inside apartment | 42 | Clothes closet | 66 |
| Toilet on same floor | 29 | Bed | 63 |
| Toilet outside the house | 29 | Table and chair | 63 |
| Cold water | 60 | Sofa | 32 |
| Hot and cold water | 28 | Additional chairs | 10 |
| Electric lights | 92 | | |
| Gas | 44 | | |
| Wash basin | 52 | | |

Source: M. Borris, Ausländischer Arbeiter in einer Großstadt (Frankfurt: Europäische Verlanpanstalt, 1974), p. 150.

TABLE 7.5

Rental Costs for Apartments: National Data
Compared with Those for Foreign Workers,
Frankfurt, 1972

| Rent Payment (in DM) | Percent Paid Nationally | Percent Paid by Guestworkers in Frankfurt |
|---|---|---|
| Under 100 | 13 | 9 |
| 100 to 150 | 21 | 9 |
| 151 to 200 | 22 | 15 |
| 201 to 350 | 32 | 43 |
| 351 and above | 9 | 23 |
| No data | 3 | 1 |

Note: DM250 = $100.
Source: M. Borris, Ausländischer Arbeiter in einer Großstadt (Frankfurt: Europäische Verlanpanstalt, 1974), p. 152.

of housing in Frankfurt is considerably above that of the national average (Table 7.5).

Paradoxically, despite the difficulties and discriminations that foreign workers face in locating suitable housing, there exists a great deal of residential instability in this group of workers. One might expect that if a worker finally located housing after difficulties and humiliation, there would be little motivation to move again, but this is not the case. Borris notes that of the sample she interviewed in Frankfurt, half were actively seeking new accommodations with more room, lower rent, or better facilities. Only those who have given up hope of finding suitable housing have stopped looking. It is evident, too, that those living in private quarters move more often than those in company housing. (Fifty percent of the former group have moved at least twice, while 62 percent of the latter group have moved not at all.) These data tend to reinforce the suggestion that company housing is essentially for those workers who come without their families, seeking to save as much of their earnings as possible, pay as little as possible for rent, and generally place themselves outside the life and activities of German society.

Though the workers do change their accommodations in the hope of finding a more suitable setting, the evidence suggests that they are generally unsuccessful in their pursuit. A majority are displeased with their present

TABLE 7.6

Location of Living Accommodations in
Frankfurt Preferred by Foreign Workers

| Accommodation | Percent |
| --- | --- |
| In a foreign worker settlement far away from the living areas of German people | 5 |
| In a foreign worker settlement in the near vicinity of the living areas of German people | 6 |
| In a neighborhood in which German people live, but in a house in which only fellow countrymen live | 21 |
| In a neighborhood in which German people live, and in a house in which both Germans and fellow countrymen live | 37 |
| In a neighborhood in which German people live, and in a house in which only German people live | 21 |
| No answer | 10 |

Note: N = 2003.
Source: M. Borris, Ausländischer Arbeiter in einer Großstadt (Frankfurt: Europäische Verlanpanstalt, 1974), p. 159.

residence and are looking for another location.* More significantly, the workers have indicated that they are willing to pay at market rates for the accommodations they desire—an interesting refutation of the oft-repeated accusation that the guestworkers are unwilling to invest more in their present situation in Germany so as to upgrade their standard of living. These data suggest that it is not that workers are unwilling to upgrade their conditions, but that the opportunities simply are not afforded them. Furthermore, and again contrary to a popular notion, most of the workers do not want to live in a closed community of fellow foreigners.

Borris (1974, p. 159), citing data from a sample of 2003 foreign workers in Frankfurt, reports preferred living accommodations as follows: in a foreign

---

*Borris indicates that an additional 30,0000 apartments and rooms would be necessary to meet these expectations of the foreign workers. The sheer magnitude of the demand plus the reality of limited housing resources in the city suggests the constant treadmill that the workers are on in terms of locating desired housing. Suitable accommodations are just not a realistic option for more than a small percentage of the workers.

workers' settlement far away from the living areas of German people, 5 percent; in a foreign workers' settlement near the living areas of German people, 6 percent; in a neighborhood in which German people live, but in a house in which only fellow-countrymen live, 21 percent; in a neighborhood in which German people live and in a house in which both Germans and fellow-countrymen live, 37 percent; and in a neighborhood in which German people live and in a house in which only German people live, 21 percent; 10 percent of the sample expressed no preference.

In other words, the guestworkers are looking for contact and interaction with the German people. They choose integration, not segregation.*

Borris recognizes the paradox inherent in these responses in terms of the implications for the future of the foreign workers in Germany. On the one hand, this group of people has come to Germany to work, to fuel the economic growth of the country, and they increasingly choose to make it their home and place of raising their children. They prefer to live in contact and interaction with the German people, not on the margin, isolated and segregated. But the policies and conditions negate and inhibit these aspirations. Crowded together in the poorest housing in the city, facing both public policy discrimination and private prejudice, the workers live their lives with constant frustration and knowledge that in spite of their intentions, they are not welcomed. The question of how long such a situation can continue to exist in Germany remains. Borris concludes (1974, p. 162) that a resolution is imperative:

> There remains only one alternative: Either grant to these people decent and humane housing or repatriate them. But repatriation is not possible because the foreign workers are an essential part of the labor force in the economy. There only remains, then, the recognition of their needs.

## Conditions in Berlin

Foreign workers and their families began arriving in Berlin in significant numbers in the early 1960s and the number reached nearly 200,000 (10.4 percent of the population) by 1977. This number includes only the legal immigrants, but there is also a large number of illegal workers in the city. There is no

---

*Borris takes special note that a full fifth of the sample wish to live only in accommodations with German people. She terms this desire an "overidentification" and attributes it to a reaction to the experience of deprivation. An example of the sociopsychological reaction to discrimination and deprivation, the oppressed individual identifies with the source of that oppression, hoping that present miseries will ease as the powerful come to know the worthiness of the individual.

way to obtain reliable data on the size of this illegal group, but a conservative estimate of 10 percent would suggest a total foreign worker population in Berlin of approximately 220,000. Half this number are Turkish. Of the total, approximately 20,000 are of school age, another 14,000 are below school age, 118,000 are male above school age, and 48,000 are female above school age.

Certainly the growth of the foreign worker population had an impact upon the housing situation in Berlin, as Stevens and Kudat (1975, p. 209) have noted:

> Between 1960 and 1974, the pattern of behavior of foreign workers changed in several ways, all of which contributed towards making them active participants in the rental housing market. In particular, foreign workers tended to extend their stay in West Berlin and to bring members of their families with them. As length of stay increased, workers became more likely to change jobs at least once during their period of work abroad. Many of those changing jobs had initially been housed in quarters provided by their employers; unless these workers found a new job with similar housing associated with it, they would of necessity have to enter the housing market as demanders of shelter. As family members joined foreign workers abroad, the workers would again often be forced to leave employer provided accommodations and seek shelter on the open market.

A large (N = 2258) survey taken among the foreign worker communities in West Berlin in 1974 by Kudat and her colleagues shows that 40 percent of the sample had moved once and another 32 percent had had two or more moves. Of particular import is their finding that with each successive move the residential segregation of foreign workers increased. They have commented upon these results as follows (Diricks and Kudat 1975b, p. 6):

> Although one might have expected workers who have already changed houses several times to have gained a greater freedom of movement out of the concentration areas, our analysis clearly indicates the opposite. Migrants who move more frequently remain within given districts while those who move less often are more likely to change the district of their residence. The pattern is clear: the distribution of the first residence shows a greater spread over the city. The movement out of the first residence is also a movement towards greater concentration and segregation. The second and third movements simply aggravate this trend. In addition to those migrants searching for better housing within the high concentration districts in which they reside, those who have accidentally stayed away from the segregated districts during their first movement move there also, and hence the population of the "ghetto" grows. This, in the case of West Berlin, continued to the point where the city authorities prohibited new moves into high concentration areas, thus

eliminating whatever chances the workers may have had of securing the integration of their family, and thus encouraging a high incidence of moves within the concentrated districts.

What makes these findings particularly significant is that the correlations are extremely high for the Turkish population in the city. This can be attributed, according to the authors, to the facts that the Turks are greater in number, that they are more severely discriminated against in the housing market, and that they have been in Berlin longer than the other large foreign worker group, the Yugoslavs.

As with the workers in Frankfurt, there are two main reasons for workers to change their living accommodations: a change in employment and a desire to bring all or a portion of the family to the city to be reunited. It is in this latter instance that the worker must find housing that satisfies the requirement of the city administration before permission is given for the reunion. Once the family reunion has occurred, it obviously loses its importance as a reason for moving. What then begins to take precedence is discontentment with the present surroundings and a desire for a better quality environment. But as was noted earlier in the findings of Diricks and Kudat, each successive move leads to greater housing segregation and to the greater likelihood of even poorer housing than that previously occupied. This inability to improve one's housing conditions despite a high number of moves is attributed by the authors to factors outside the workers' control, such as change in employment or family reunion, discrimination and charging of higher rents, and eviction by landlords. In the sample population included in the Kudat survey, 50 percent of the first changes in residence were accounted for by either family or job change, while the poor quality of the environment and the smallness of the accommodation accounted for 50 percent of the third moves.

One way of measuring the quality of the environment in which the workers live is to assess the provision of amenities in their dwellings. As in Frankfurt, there is clear indication that the workers are living in conditions that are poor and undesirable. Table 7.7 provides an indication of what is available, and indirectly suggests why it is that workers continue to seek new accommodations.

Earlier in this chapter, mention was made of the two differing lines of analysis available in attempting to assess the causes of the formation of ghetto-like conditions in areas where the foreign workers live. On the one hand, it is suggested that the conditions evolve as the result of individual choices of the foreign workers themselves, whether the choices are to save most of their earnings, to maintain traditional customs while in Germany, or simply not to invest energy in the upkeep of someone else's property. Hemmer and Leminsky (1974b, p. 28) have supported this line of analysis:

> The Turks do not want to pay high rents. They do not care for the comfort and furnishing of their houses. Because Turkish women

TABLE 7.7

Provision of Amenities in Current Residences
of Foreign Workers in Berlin, 1974

| Amenity | Percent |
|---|---|
| Kitchen | 98.1 |
| Electricity | 99.7 |
| Bathroom | 67.8 |
| Hot water | 25.6 |
| Central heating | 10.0 |
| Bathing facilities | 24.1 |
| Furniture | 27.6 |

Source: Y. Diricks and A. Kudat, "Instability of Migrant Workers' Housing," International Labor Migration Project (Berlin: Wissenschaftszentrum, 1975), p. 28.

make it a matter of pride not to clean the staircases, they live in dirty houses. Because of their religion, they do not fight against the insects invading their houses. The smell of their kitchen disturbs the Germans. Technique, hygiene, comfortable housing, religious liberty are foreign to them. Therefore Germans run away from the areas in which Turks live. And ghettos, thus, come about.

The alternative view, most clearly articulated by Kudat and her colleagues in West Berlin, is that the housing situation of the foreign workers is best explained by discriminatory public policies, the deliberate restriction of access to certain segments of the housing market, and the quiet toleration by the authorities of the private discrimination carried on by landlords and realtors. They analyze the number of foreigners in each of the twelve districts of West Berlin. As can be noted in Table 7.8, the concentration patterns are clearly manifest for the Turkish and Yugoslav populations, the two ethnic groups that comprise more than 80 percent of the foreign population of West Berlin. While a quarter of Kreuzberg's population consists of foreigners, non-German nationals make up only 3.6 percent of the population of Reinickendorf.

One item of interest in this table is the evidence that almost one-half of all the Turkish residents live in two districts, while Yugoslavs are less concentrated and found in some numbers throughout the city. These relative concentrations would be, perhaps, even more apparent if the number of illegal Turkish workers, in particular, were added to the totals. Additional analysis of this variation will be presented shortly, but it should be noted here that the previous comments on the tendency of each additional move within the city of West Berlin to increase the concentration of the foreign worker community are borne out by these data.

TABLE 7.8

Distribution of West Berlin's Population, January 1974

| District | Total Population | Foreigners Number | Foreigners Percent | Turks Number | Turks Percent | Yugoslavs Number | Yugoslavs Percent |
|---|---|---|---|---|---|---|---|
| Tiergarten | 90,555 | 14,536 | 16.0 | 6,941 | 7.7 | 2,803 | 3.1 |
| Wedding | 166,421 | 29,140 | 17.5 | 19,028 | 11.4 | 5,004 | 3.0 |
| Kreuzberg | 154,396 | 37,893 | 24.5 | 25,275 | 16.4 | 5,547 | 3.6 |
| Charlottenburg | 181,035 | 16,269 | 9.0 | 3,890 | 2.2 | 2,652 | 1.5 |
| Spandau | 196,115 | 9,554 | 4.9 | 3,384 | 1.7 | 1,993 | 1.0 |
| Wilmersdorf | 142,044 | 9,810 | 6.9 | 1,049 | 0.7 | 1,456 | 1.0 |
| Zehlendorf | 87,076 | 5,020 | 5.7 | 435 | 0.5 | 454 | 0.5 |
| Schöneberg | 155,578 | 16,602 | 10.7 | 6,438 | 4.1 | 3,190 | 2.0 |
| Steglitz | 183,613 | 7,219 | 3.9 | 1,575 | 0.9 | 1,014 | 0.6 |
| Tempelhof | 166,040 | 5,969 | 3.6 | 1,334 | 0.8 | 1,116 | 0.7 |
| Neukölln | 279,694 | 17,397 | 6.2 | 7,792 | 2.8 | 3,582 | 1.3 |
| Reinickendorf | 245,381 | 8,929 | 3.6 | 2,282 | 0.9 | 1,737 | 0.7 |
| Total | 2,047,948 | 178,338 | 8.7 | 79,468 | 3.9 | 30,548 | 1.5 |

Source: Y. Diricks and A. Kudat, <u>Ghettos: Individual or Systemic Choice</u> (Berlin: Wissenschaftszentrum, 1975), p. 21.

The Turks have been in Berlin longer than have the Yugoslavs and have made more changes in their housing, thus increasing their concentration (Diricks and Kudat 1975b, p. 19).

A second step of the Diricks and Kudat study, beyond that of determining the aggregation of workers in the various districts of West Berlin, was to establish the relative levels of concentration in the different districts (Table 7.9). These data suggest how the Turkish and Yugoslav populations deviate from what could be expected, were there no segregation in the city and the two groups distributed in the same manner as the indigenous population. As is evident, the data suggest heavy overconcentration in three districts, slight overconcentration in one, and underconcentration in all others.

TABLE 7.9

Degree of Concentration of Turkish and Yugoslav Foreign Workers in West Berlin's Districts

| District | Expected Foreign Concentration | Turks Actual Number Census[a] 1973 | Turks Actual Number Survey[b] 1974 | Yugoslavs Actual Number Census[a] 1973 | Yugoslavs Actual Number Survey[b] 1974 |
|---|---|---|---|---|---|
| Tiergarten | 4.0 | 8.7 | 11.4 | 9.2 | 10.8 |
| Wedding | 7.3 | 23.9 | 22.6 | 16.4 | 21.2 |
| Kreuzberg | 6.2 | 31.8 | 30.8 | 18.2 | 13.8 |
| Charlottenburg | 8.8 | 4.9 | 5.8 | 8.7 | 10.4 |
| Spandau | 10.0 | 4.3 | 3.4 | 6.5 | 11.9 |
| Wilmersdorf | 7.0 | 1.3 | 1.5 | 4.8 | 3.8 |
| Zehlendorf | 4.4 | 0.5 | 0.3 | 1.5 | 0.4 |
| Schöneberg | 7.4 | 8.1 | 7.2 | 10.4 | 6.3 |
| Steglitz | 9.4 | 2.0 | 1.8 | 3.3 | 1.5 |
| Tempelhof | 8.6 | 1.7 | 1.5 | 3.6 | 3.9 |
| Neukölln | 14.0 | 9.8 | 8.8 | 11.7 | 9.0 |
| Reinickendorf | 12.6 | 2.9 | 2.6 | 5.7 | 3.4 |

[a]Census data were compiled as of December 31, 1973 from official police records.

[b]Data from the Survey were those taken from the survey of more than 2,000 foreign workers conducted by the International Institute of Comparative Social Studies, Berlin, in June 1974.

Source: Y. Diricks and A. Kudat, Ghettos: Individual or Systemic Choice (Berlin: Wissenschaftszentrum, 1975), p. 22.

Even at the level of individual residential blocks within these districts, Diricks and Kudat (1975a, p. 10) conclude that almost nowhere in West Berlin are Turks and Yugoslavs distributed in representative proportions. They then seek to answer the question of whether there are predictable characteristics of migrants living in high concentration areas that distinguish them from those guestworkers who are living outside such areas. They stated their problem as follows (1975a, p. 12):

> Whether residential segregation is to be interpreted as a need to live in a familiar environment and as a need to ease problems of interethnic communication or as a measure of unwillingness to become integrated into the social milieu or the "host" society, it can only be validated when at least some of the background characteristics of these foreign workers correlate significantly with differing tendencies of congregation in residential blocks. When such is not the case, factors external to the migrants, i.e., mechanisms prevailing in the housing market or discriminatory practices, must be viewed as instrumental in explaining the residential patterns of foreign workers. To test whether these negative findings cannot be attributed to the partial analysis applied above, and to see how much of the concentration phenomenon can be explained by the joint background variables of foreign workers, various regression models were tested.

Using the variables of years of schooling, sex, age, marital status, number of children, length of stay, knowledge of German, job mobility, total savings, number of dependents, place of birth, and place of departure for Germany, Diricks and Kudat (1975a, p. 13) concluded that *"the individual characteristics of a foreign worker bear no relationship whatsoever to the environmental aspects of his housing or of the degree of his residential segregation"* (emphasis added). Moreover, when the quality of the housing of the foreign workers was compared to the concentration patterns, it was found that the foreign workers were segregated regardless of the quality of the housing. Even when they were in the higher-income housing areas, there was little or no improvement in the quality of the housing they were able to obtain. They were still able to get only the poorest quality housing.

One important implication of these findings for the current policies guiding the restrictions on the movement of foreign workers into congested areas is that policies appear to have mistakenly assumed that the concentration of the foreign workers occurs at purely a district level. What the data of Diricks and Kudat suggest is that the segregation of the foreign workers occurs more precisely at the residential block level. If the intent of the city of Berlin is in fact to increase residential dispersal and integration of the foreign workers, then the policies must address the reality of segregation where it is most apparent and most actively promoted.

Having presented data on the presence, extent, and origins of the housing segregation that foreign workers experience while in West Berlin, there is a final matter to be considered. To what degree do the workers experience a price discrimination in their pursuit of housing? Is the housing segregation one merely of spatial separation, or is there economic discrimination as well?

The data on price discrimination might be anticipated, since housing for the foreign workers is an extension and further manifestation of the marginal position that is imposed upon them in the political, economic, and social sectors of the society. Working both from public census data and the large migrant worker survey conducted in 1974, Kudat and Stevens (1974) found that in whatever area of Berlin the guestworkers reside, they pay more for housing of a given size and quality than do native Germans. Only for large, low quality apartments are foreign workers estimated to pay less rent than Germans. For small apartments with all amenities, foreign workers are estimated to be paying from 38 to 79 percent more than Germans for comparable accommodations. For large apartments with all amenities, the excess percentage paid by the foreign workers is estimated at between a low of 1 percent and a high of 30 percent.

Perhaps, if more public housing were available to guestworkers, they would not be so vulnerable to rent gouging and discrimination in the private market. But since less than 1 percent of foreign workers are in public or "social" housing, this becomes essentially a moot question. The fact is that the foreign workers and their families are restricted almost exclusively to the private housing market and thus are indeed vulnerable to the kinds of abuses noted above. It is an open question as to whether future policies will increase or reverse the persistent housing discriminations that guestworkers now experience.

# PART III
## THE EDUCATION OF THE GUESTWORKER CHILD

# 8

# GERMAN EDUCATION AND THE GUESTWORKER CHILD: POLICIES AND PROGRAMS

As with so much of the rest of Germany at the end of World War II, the educational system was in shambles. Not only had facilities been destroyed and faculty as well as students suffered many casualties, but also education had been turned into indoctrination under the Third Reich. Thus in the immediate postwar period, the task of rebuilding German education took on physical as well as psychological dimensions. As the recent OECD review of German education noted (OECD 1972, p. 17):

> At the end of the Second World War much of Germany was physically in ruins, the country in the hands of its military occupiers, and its self-confidence gone. In those early post-war days each occupation authority tried in its characteristic way to eliminate what remained of Nazi institutions, in education as in all other facets of German national life, and to substitute in their place practices largely modelled on their own British, French, Soviet, or United States ideals. In this process, almost inevitably, serious doubt was cast upon the validity of *all* past German principles and practices in social and political life. Not only the most recent inventions of the Third Reich were marked down for dismantlement, but also many of the long established ways of doing things that dated at least from the beginning of the German Empire in 1871, even if not further back. The watchword was "democratization," and nowhere was this applied by the occupying powers with more zeal and enthusiasm than in education. "Re-education" plans were launched to teach the German people the ways of democratic governance.

While the Allies (and some educational reformers) made plans to transform the German educational system into something new and different from what it had been at any time before in its history, the strong sentiment of the German people, and the educational profession in particular, was to revert back to pre-Nazi institutional arrangements. When the Allied Control Commission in 1947 issued a series of directives that sought to provide more equality in German education through guidance services, longer compulsory school attendance, curriculum changes, and better teacher-training programs, those persons left in charge of the day-to-day operations of the German schools in most instances made little or no effort to implement them. It was not reform but reconstruction that was desired. This schism between the philosophy of the Allies and that of the German educators was perhaps nowhere more evident than in the German resistance to the directive that the schools should reconstitute themselves into a comprehensive educational system: a system that would no longer be hierarchical and selective, but one that would offer opportunities to all students throughout their compulsory period of schooling.

If one adds together the magnitude of the task, the resistance of the German educational bureaucracy, and the rather rapid restoration of self-determination to the German nation, the fate of these reform efforts was sealed. In fact, observers of the educational system in Germany have termed the two decades between 1947 and 1967 essentially decades of "non-reform" (cf. Robinsohn and Kuhlmann 1967). In virtually every Land of the nation, save for Berlin, there were no efforts at reform or assessment of the implications of reconstituting the traditional German educational system: a system that had itself accepted national socialism and propagated it. One found throughout the country efforts to rebuild German education on a model of what existed in the 1920s, or in some instances, even the years prior to 1914. The foundations for an educational system to function in the mid-twentieth century were sought in nineteenth-century perspectives. But this is perhaps understandable, given the conditions in Germany after World War II. Again citing the OECD report (OECD 1972, p. 19):

> One might with justice point out that this unwillingness to abandon institutions that had proved themselves in the past, this reluctance to embark on experiments in new social and education forms, were merely counterparts of the overriding desire of the German people for an end of the utter social collapse and grievous physical privations that had afflicted them at the end of the Second World War. What the German people longed for at this time was essentially a return to "normalcy," and normalcy was defined, not without reason, as enough food to eat, a roof overhead, some decent clothes to wear, and stability of social and political institutions. The philosophy of hard, daily toil along conventional lines dominated social political thought.

When a new German constitution was ratified in 1949, it fundamentally transformed German political institutions into those of a federalist system.

Centralization was to be minimized if not excluded altogether, and much of the domestic administration and political life of the country would function at the level of the eleven Länder. Education was one of the most important functions reserved exclusively to the Länder. Here decentralization was initiated with clear political and historical considerations in mind. If Nazism meant the centralization of education and the promulgation of a nationalist ideology, the postwar education system would be local and/or regional in character, to avoid the resurgence of nationalistic dogma.

The fact that such trends in decentralization have continued over the past three decades helps to explain the diversity in current German educational policy. Eleven different sets of institutional arrangements and policies have resulted in frequent instances of a lack of coordination, mutually exclusive and nonreciprocal credentials, and restricted mobility within the country out of fear that one's previous educational work will not be accepted toward requirements in a different Land. The social costs to Germany of maintaining such a pattern of educational organizations are becoming more and more evident. And it has been in response to this situation that most of the recent reform efforts in Germany have been mobilized (cf. Littmann 1976; Federal Ministry for Education and Science 1970; and *Bund-Länder* Commission for Educational Planning 1973).

## GERMAN EDUCATION: TRADITIONALISM AND SELECTIVITY

If education is broadly defined as having two major functions—on the one hand, that of transmitting the cultural values, beliefs, and skills thought to be important for the preservation of the society while, on the other, generating social change in the direction of assumed goals and visions of progress—German education in its present form leans heavily toward the former function. The postwar reconstruction of the Gymnasium in its classical nineteenth-century form, where Latin is still today the first foreign language for many students, where entrance is decided at age 10, where successful completion has been a guarantee of a position in the university and a subsequent high status occupation, and where the financial investments in the students are as much as 100 percent greater than for those students who do not gain admittance, suggests the degree to which traditionalism defines the German educational experience. It is also the case that, as mentioned, the social costs to the society of maintaining such an arrangement for a highly technological and industrial society are severe. In a society in which creativity, ingenuity, and technological sophistication are highly valued, the schools have mirrored a German past that was authoritarian, dogmatic, and hierarchical. Commenting on this schism between the realities of the society and the values of the schools, the OECD (1972, p. 44) has noted:

> At present, in their atmosphere, their goals, and their organization they fit more nearly the older, more primitive, early capitalistic

economic scene. Authoritarian teachers prepared the child for authoritarian employers and supervisors; drill methods of instruction conditioned him for the repetitive work to come on the farm, in the factory, or at the office; and the closing of chances for secondary and higher education to most of the population reflected the actual paucity of jobs requiring such skills. As the work-place becomes less authoritarian, and as work itself becomes more and more complex, requiring ever higher levels of skills from more and more people, the schools can no longer continue along their old lines, however successfully they may have performed in the past—as indeed in Germany, they did.

In an effort to outline more systematically the important elements in the current structure of German education, there are certain key aspects. A caveat, of course, is needed in that German education is not as homogeneous in its adherence to traditionalism as these points may lead one to believe. There are efforts at reform and, more apparent in higher education than in the elementary and secondary schools, traditional lines of authority and means of credentialing have begun to change. Even in the lower grades, the experimentation with comprehensive schools (the closest one comes to the current structure of American schools) as well as the efforts to provide an alternative approach, rather than through the Gymnasium, for university admission (*der zweite Bildungsweg*) speaks of efforts to bring the system more into line with the needs of the society. But even so, the characteristics of a nineteenth-century educational system still prevail. They may be summarized as follows:

First, *the system is characterized by the principle of selectivity, a principle which implies and implants the creation of elites.* Furthermore, the creation of such elites is done in such a manner as to reproduce and reflect the class structure of the society. The government itself has acknowledged this function of German education. The *Bildungsbericht '70* of the Federal Ministry for Education and Science noted (1970, p. 28): "With its methods of selection, the present school system helps to perpetuate the outmoded social class system." In another section of the report, the following comment is made (1970, p. 67):

> Despite manifold efforts to bring about improvements and partial reforms, the three-limb structure of secondary education [vocation, general, and university preparatory] and early selection after the fourth primary school year still have the effect of perpetuating and reproducing a social class system within the educational system. This is a problem involving the structure of the educational system and the varying educational consciousness and desire for education in the population.

If the schools do reflect and reproduce the social class system of the larger society, then one would anticipate that those who were in attendance in the more selective components of the system would be of a higher social class background. This view is confirmed by data supplied by Littmann (1976, p. 6) and the Federal Ministry of Education and Science (1970, p. 30). Littmann posits that only a quarter of all children of the appropriate age group enter the Gymnasium. Data from the federal ministry define the social class characteristics of this group and note that in the last year of Gymnasium, only 6.4 percent of the students are from working-class homes. The remaining 93.6 percent come from homes characterized as salaried employee (32 percent), self-employed (18.3 percent), civil servant (27.6 percent), and professional (12.4 percent). For the employed male population over 40, 45.2 percent are classified as working class and 8.7 percent are classified as civil servant. Thus there is an underrepresentation of working-class students by 700 percent on the one hand, and, on the other, an overrepresentation by 300 percent of children of civil servants.

What such data call into question is the contention that while the educational system is admittedly selective, it is not on the basis of social class, but on the basis of ostensibly objective measures—comprehensive examinations, final marks in course work, and the like. The fundamental premise, as Littmann (1976, p. 5) notes, has been that education is a sorting process whereby those who are most intellectually gifted gravitate toward the training offered in the Gymnasium and then university. Such a selection process has assumed that the determining characteristic has not been social class, but rather the intellectual ability and academic performance of the student. In short, the formal ideology of the system is that merit, not social class, determines advancement.

The reality, however, is something quite different. With the selection process beginning at the end of the fourth grade as to which route of secondary education a child should pursue, the criteria available for measurement of achievement are highly amenable to the influences of the home and the expenditure of private resources. As the *Bildungsbericht '70* (1970, p. 47) reported:

> In the primary school, children's attainments are still measured against standards of what is in the final analysis a specifically class educational tradition. These standards are decisive for selection after the fourth school year. Those children who are not encouraged by their parents and environment to adopt the content, forms of expression, and standards of this tradition cannot live up to these standards. Thus, the formally equalitarian primary school contributes to perpetuating the social class system.

The selectivity factor in German education as a reflection of social class differences becomes even more apparent when one examines data on the backgrounds of university students. The *Bildungsbericht '70* (1970, p. 141) reported that from a survey of 259,457 students, 30.9 percent came from civil servant families, 31.7 percent from salaried employee families, 29.5 percent from those homes where the father was self-employed, 2.8 percent from farm homes, and

5.7 percent from workers' homes. Again, the first group is overrepresented by nearly 400 percent and the latter group underrepresented by almost 800 percent in proportion to the occupation distribution of the employed male population. It is little wonder that the term *Bildungs-elite* (educational elite) has long been used, though rarely now, to describe the proper role of the university graduate in German society. The cycle is completed as the university graduate is able to compete for and attain a position in the society not open to one without the degree, insuring his/her own eventual status in the society. Just as the social class of the parents originally influenced the child's educational opportunities, now that child, grown and matriculated through the system, is able to perpetuate the status position and provide additional opportunities to his/her children.*

Second, *the school views the child as an empty vessel which must be filled with highly specified quanta of information.* As a result, the child is taught with fixed syllabi, there are regular examinations to ascertain if the material in the fixed syllabi is being learned, and continued progress through the system depends upon successful performance on such regular examinations. Failure of the examination means repeating the grade. As the structure of the educational endeavor is fixed, so also is the content (cf. OECD 1970, p. 46):

> Curricula offerings of the schools, methods of instruction and examinations are rigidly set. Within each region, what each type of school teaches and how it teaches it tend to remain constant over time, and from child to child. The child is delivered to the school to be "moulded"; the school is expected to provide a single offering of educational opportunities, to which the children's individual talents, inclinations, and interests must then adapt.

If the above statement is somewhat overdrawn, it is nevertheless true that the latitude and discretion given to an American student in high school or in the first years of college far exceeds that granted to a student in the Gymnasium. Perhaps the most a German student can anticipate in the way of discretion is in the choosing of the institution to attend—that is, a natural science Gymnasium, a modern language Gymnasium, and so forth. But once the institution is chosen, the options in it are almost nil. This situation applies not only to those students who are intent upon going to the university, but to those in vocational and gen-

---

*There is a need to acknowledge that the disjunction between university education and high status employment in the society is growing. The pressure on admission to the university is such that not all students are admitted to their fields of chosen study, and indeed, not all students are even admitted. The waiting lists for some professional fields are of such length that students must wait three to four years before a place opens to them. And even if the student successfully completes university, the guarantee of a high status position is more tenuous than previously (cf. Littmann 1976, p. 10).

eral educational courses as well. Throughout the German educational system, the curricula materials, the instructional schedules, and the examination rituals are well fixed. It is not a system prone to experimentation. The core remains inviolate; at the most, there is some tinkering along the margins.

The imagery of a child as an empty vessel fits well with the emphasis German education places upon school achievement. This achievement (*Leistung*), or how well the vessel has been filled, is carefully measured with precise instruments. Furthermore, the parameters of what is to be considered school achievement are quite narrow, essentially restricted to cognitive performance, on defined bodies of knowledge. This explains the emphasis on tests and comprehensive examinations as the means of assessment. Within the traditionalism of German education, the curriculum and means by which it is taught to the students are not open to question. If failure occurs within this system (and the system is exceptionally strenuous at the level of the Gymnasium), it is a flaw in the container that is at fault rather than the methods used to fill it.

The intense pressure that this system of education creates has invariably generated casualties among the children. One reaction that has received particular attention in recent years has been that of a severe psychological withdrawal, labeled as *Schulstress* or school stress. The presence of this reaction to the pressures of schools has been the subject of both popular and academic writing (cf. *Quick* 1976; Brockmeyer and Oelmann 1976). With the entire burden of successful performance upon the child, and the teachers, parents, and students themselves accepting cognitive success as the only standard for success in school, those children who fear failure or have already failed find no means by which to have others also accept responsibility for the situation. Frequently the reaction to this negative sanction and derogation of personal worth is psychological withdrawal, a means to try to preserve personal estimations of self-esteem.

Third, *the hierarchical status system is reinforced by differences in teacher training, salary, and advancement.* To teach at the high prestige Gymnasium, a person must have, with only rare exceptions, a university degree. Furthermore, this same training that allows one to teach in the Gymnasium also allows entrance into the teaching faculty of some teachers colleges, others specializing in social services, and finally, those offering vocational degrees (*Fachhochschule*).

Those teachers who teach in the elementary grades (*Grundschule*) receive their education in a teachers training college (*Pädagogische Hochschule*). This training is of shorter duration and less rigorous than that of the university. Teachers trained in these teachers colleges are not able to teach in the higher-paid Gymnasium but they may teach in the *Hauptschule* and the *Realschule*, the two alternatives open to the 75 percent of the students who do not attend Gymnasium. Little or no status is afforded to a teacher in the Hauptschule for it is a school providing a five-year curriculum preparing students for entry into work at the lower levels of skill and training. For those in the Realschule, the situation is only somewhat better, conditioned by the slight selectivity in the student population and the fact that the curriculum is closer to that of the Gymnasium than the Hauptschule: for example, basic subjects include German, two foreign languages, mathematics, and science. The graduates are equipped to assume the positions of middle-level civil servant, nurse, medical technician, or salesman.

Finally, *the allocation of financial resources reflects the selectivity and hierarchical status of the educational system.* Throughout the various levels and forms of education in Germany, it is abundantly clear that more money per pupil is spent on the education of students in the higher prestige schools than in the others. This differential is apparent from the moment the students leave the comprehensive and unified curriculum found in the Grundschule. The selection of the Gymnasium as opposed to Realschule or Hauptschule means an immediate difference in the financial resources made available for one's education. The *Bildungsbericht '70* (1970, p. 65) cites figures showing that the expenditure in 1967 per pupil in the Gymnasium was 310 percent above that spent on pupils in the Hauptschule.

The same situation is found when one examines the costs and expenditures related to higher education. The cost in 1968 to educate one student for one year in a medical school was DM 52,650. For that same period, the cost per student in a university was DM 13,349, while in the Pädagogische Hochschule, the expenditure per student equaled DM 7,580. Parenthetically, for those studying theology at academic institutions with university status, the yearly expenditure in 1968 was DM 2,683.

Commenting on this divergence in expenditures of public resources on the education of German students, the OECD report suggested that the impact of such differentials needs to be viewed not simply in terms of the yearly sums, but in terms of the cumulative impact as well (OECD 1972, p. 57):

> Not only do the students from wealthier homes have more public money spent on their education for each year of their secondary education, but each such student tends to receive a larger total of public educational resources over his school career than do children from lower social levels, because length of study is positively related to school type and social class level.

The impact of these four characteristics of the German educational system as it is presently constructed reinforces current social arrangements in the society. It is, as noted earlier, a system oriented toward the preservation of traditional values and beliefs. Central to this belief system is the view that education functions properly when it carefully screens and selects those who are to take up and occupy the elite sectors of the society. It is taken as a given in this educational system that at each successive educational milestone, there will be a sorting process that allows only a small percentage of the students to move to a higher level. It is also taken as a given that at each level a disproportionate amount of the available resources should be spent on the students and teachers in the highest status schools. It is an educational system that is not apologetic about the tracking mechanisms it uses to sort out and stratify the students.

It is within this set of educational arrangements that the immigrant children from the countries of the European South have come into German schools. A country that has prided itself on the severity and selectivity of its Gymnasium system is confronted with tens of thousands of Turkish, Greek, Yugoslav, Italian, and Spanish students who have neither the cultural background nor educational preparation that would allow them to participate in any but the most limited and restricted educational settings. The educational policies that have been evolved with respect to these children and the unique educational challenges that they represent must now be considered.

German education is confronted with the reality that if it allows the present system to continue as it is presently constituted, it will invariably ensure that the children of the guestworkers will for several generations to come be relegated to the underclass position now occupied by their parents. And if this does occur, there will emerge in Germany the systematic and institutional discrimination of these groups in a way that will be comparable to the condition of minority groups in England and the United States. *It will no longer be a matter of immigrants coming into the host society on the lower rungs of the socioeconomic ladder, but the deliberate intergenerational perpetuation of a prejudicial and discriminatory social system.* And the legacy of German history cannot give comfort to those who find themselves relegated to a distinguishable minority position.

## EDUCATIONAL POLICIES FOR GUESTWORKER CHILDREN

Any analysis of the current educational policies for the children of the immigrant workers has to begin with the premise that such policies are dictated by the political and economic concerns of the Federal Republic. The policies have emerged, not as the result of pedagogical principles, but in response to broader societal concerns that predetermine the role of education. In short, educational policies, prior and present, should be assessed in terms of their response to the political rather than educational problems that lie behind them. This is perhaps no different than saying that as the social and political situation of the foreign workers has changed, so too have perceptions of what constitutes an appropriate education for their children. As policies relating to other aspects of the foreign workers' role in Germany have developed, so too have the educational policies. It may sound simplistic to say there were no specific guestworker policies, educational or otherwise, when there were no guestworkers; but it is true that the policies have emerged in response to the growing presence of guestworker children in the schools.

The educational policies specifically targeted for the immigrant children can be seen as having three distinctive phases. Each phase coincides with those noted earlier in the development of the role of the foreign workers in German society. These phases were summarized with the terms "expansion," "consolidation," and "structured marginality."

What follows now is a broadly sketched outline of the educational policies operant in each of these phases. It is not possible to specity in detail all the nuances and particulars of these policies, due to the frequent variation and not infrequent contradictions among the different Länder. Policy recommendations on which there was clear Länder consensus were issued through the Standing Conference of the State Ministers of Education (*Ständige Konferenz der Kultusminister der Länder in der Bundesrepublik Deutschland*). The Standing Conference is the coordinating and policy generating mechanism created for cross-Länder cooperation in educational matters. Policy recommendations passed by the Standing Conference are not considered legally binding on each Land, but it is assumed that by agreeing to a particular position, the various Länder will introduce legislation or modify existing regulations so as to come into agreement with it. Thus a presentation of the policy recommendations of the Standing Conference represents as close an approximation as one can achieve in articulating national policy with respect to the education of the guestworker children.*

## Phase I: Policy Recommendations of May 1964 on the Instruction of Foreign Children and Youth

The ever-increasing flow of foreign workers into the Federal Republic during the 1950s and early 1960s had its repercussions, of course, in the schools; as the number of guestworkers in the country increased from 72,900 in 1954 to 985,000 in 1964, the number of their children in the schools went from less than 2,000 in 1954 to 35,135 in 1964 (cf. Müller 1975; Council of Europe 1974a). While this increase in the schools was not the dramatic, quantitative leap found in the sheer numbers of new workers, it nevertheless represented a new and heretofore unknown group of students in the German schools.

The first and foremost emphasis of the first set of policy recommendations was to extend compulsory education to cover all foreign children and youths in the Federal Republic. Until this time, there were several Länder where

---

*The term national is used advisedly, since the Federal constitution reserved the general responsibilities for education to the respective Länder. It is for this reason that reference to federal educational policy with regard to the guestworker children is inappropriate. The federal government has not the authority to establish such policy.

school attendance was not required and where only a few foreign children voluntarily came.* The basis for the establishment of this policy was articulated as a desire on the part of the Länder for "the full integration of the foreign children in the German schools in the framework of compulsory education" (Council of Europe 1974, p. 98). The emerging fear of several of the ministers in the conference was that without compulsory education, the social isolation of the children and youths would be perpetuated and they would have few or no skills for functioning in German society.

This call for compulsory education included the first formal policy with regard to bilingual education. The statements of the ministers noted that with foreign children coming into the schools and not knowing the German language, there would be a need for preclasses or transition classes (*Vorbereitungsklassen*) where German would be taught as a second language. The ministers thus established that the first education in Germany would be native-language instruction with German being taught so as to allow the children eventually to take part in German schools. The emphasis upon the instruction in the native language was, however, not merely that of maintaining the native language, but rather that of "the recognition of the need of the foreign children to maintain living ties to their homeland—its language, its culture, the way it portrays itself " (Council of Europe 1974, p. 98).

It is perhaps symptomatic of the newness of the situation and the lack of preparation of German policymakers and educators with respect to the schooling of guestworker children that nowhere in the entire policy package is any direction given for organizing and facilitating this bilingual education, or for coordinating it with the instructional program of the German schools. In short, the local educators were left to make shift as best they could. On the one hand, there were directives to provide native-language instruction with German as a second language. However, no directives were given as to how rapidly or how intensely German was to be taught so as to facilitate the movement of the children into standard German classes. Likewise, there were no guidelines on how to coordinate the native-language instruction with that in the German schools so that when the child had some minimal level of proficiency in German, he/she also had received the substantive background necessary to keep pace with German peers. The principles were established without the follow-through on how they were to be implemented. Consequently, little implementation occurred.

---

*The lack of attendance in German schools of large numbers of the children of the foreign workers has been a persistent situation. In 1975, more than a decade after this first recommendation on compulsory attendance was made, the *Deutsche Caritasverband* (a charity organization) published data that indicated only two-thirds of all foreign children who were of the appropriate school age were, in fact, attending school. In numerical figures, it represents nearly 140,000 children (cf. *Frankfurter Rundschau*, October 4, 1975). The author has been unable to locate any other data that either confirm or challenge this figure.

The thrust of these policies reflected the tightrope that Germany was already walking with respect to the place of foreign workers and their children in German society. Compulsory education was seen as the means for meeting a recognizable need, specifically the need for competence in the German language, if even the most basic aspects of life in the country were to be handled. There was also the view that guestworkers and their families would not be long-term residents in the country and thus native-language instruction, cultural education, and continued contact with native-language speakers were also called for. While the rotation principle was rejected from the very beginnings of Germany's use of foreign workers (cf. Stingl 1975), there was a complementary view that the presence of the workers did not imply a need for their long-term integration into German society. After all, they were guestworkers.

## Phase II: Policy Statement of December 1971 on the Foreign Students in the Federal Republic of Germany

As the number of foreign workers in Germany was moving toward its zenith (2,239,300) and the number of foreign worker children in the schools had climbed to more than 165,000 (cf. Mahler 1976, p. 180), the inadequacies of the prior policy statements on the education of the children became readily apparent. Thus seven and a half years after the 1964 meeting of the Standing Conference on the matter of immigrant education, another meeting was held in December 1971. In regard to this meeting Brinckmann (*Die Welt*, April 29, 1977) has noted:

> The discussion at the time revolved around two main problems, namely the question of whether foreign children should be taught in independent foreign schools or whether they should be integrated in the German school system. If it could be assumed that the guestworkers would be integrated in the political and social system of our state, the decision would obviously have had to be in favour of the integration model.
>
> But if, on the other hand, it was assumed that the foreign workers would spend no more than a few years in this country, it would be unwise to burden the children with the German school system since the training they receive there would not be recognized in their home countries.

As Brinckmann concludes, and as is evident from a reading of the policy statement issued by the Standing Conference, the ministers took the position that even if they were in Germany for a short time, foreign children should be integrated into the German educational system. The idea of establishing independent schools for guestworker children was rejected, though several of the countries with large numbers of workers and families in Germany were strongly in favor of the proposal. (Cf. Jancke 1976a, p. 329, for evidence of the fact that there are foreign governments still in favor of such an approach and that they are approximating it on a private basis with afternoon and weekend classes devoted exclusively to language and cultural instruction on the home country.)

With the policy decision made to integrate the children into the German system, the ministers established a series of structural and organizational priorities aimed at facilitating this policy goal. It was this set of priorities that was missing from the 1964 policy statements and thus severely hindered their implementation at that time. In the 1971 statement, ten policy recommendations were set forth. While it is not possible to state them all in their entirety, several of the key provisions can be summarized as follows (Council of Europe 1974, p. 100; Willke 1975, p. 361):

Foreign children who are able to follow the instruction in German schools without great difficulty are to be placed in a class that corresponds to their age or their performance level. Foreign children should not make up more than a fifth of the total number of children in any given class.

Foreign children who were not of school age when in their own country and have become of school age in the Federal Republic should attend instruction along with German children in German schools from the onset. This also applies to foreign children who enter the first grade during the course of the school year.

Foreign children with language difficulties, who according to their age should attend grades 2 to 9, are to be assigned to preparatory classes.

The preparatory classes are a constituent part of German schools. They are designed to facilitate and to speed up the process of acclimatization. A preparatory class can be organized for 15 students, speaking the same or different languages. When the number of children reaches 24, the class can be divided. The instruction is to be based on the generally applicable curricular guidelines. In the subjects of music, art, crafts, textiles, domestic science, and sports, the children in the preparatory classes and the German children can receive instruction together. After sufficient help in the German language, children in the preparatory classes are to be assigned to the grades that correspond to their age or their performance level. As a rule, children attend the preparatory classes for one year.

Compulsory school attendance is to be extended to cover foreign youths at vocational schools, those with on-the-job training periods, and unemployed youths under age 18.

There was an additional set of recommendations regarding teachers for the preparatory classes. These recommendations covered both native German teachers and those from the homelands of the children. The German teachers, according to the recommendations (Council of Europe 1974, p. 101), were to receive further training to help them to meet their responsibilities as teachers of foreign students. For the foreign teachers, the recommendations were as follows: employment of foreign teachers should be limited to those who have completed teacher training in their own or the host country; efforts should be made to retain proved teachers for an extended period in Germany; and foreign teacher-candidates signing a contract must be able to prove they have adequate knowledge of German or must commit themselves to acquire this knowledge within one year.

A final section of the statement of the Standing Conference included a reaffirmation of the right of the foreign children to receive instruction in their native language. The position was also reiterated that this instruction is most beneficial when given by a teacher from the home country (cf. Wolf 1976, p. 13). What is left unclear in this section is whether the afternoon national classes sponsored by the various embassies and consulates that have large numbers of their citizens in Germany meet this recommendation, or whether such instruction must be under the auspices and direction of the school system. The lack of specification on this point may have been deliberate, however, in order to give the various Länder flexibility in deciding how to provide such mother-tongue instruction. And further, there may have also been the recognition that the different sending countries of the European South are not all equally able to provide the teachers necessary for such a large undertaking, or may not even wish to do so.

By opting for the view that the guestworker children should be integrated into the German school system as opposed to being taught in independent foreign schools, the ministers brought educational policy into line with other facets of government activity aimed at the consolidation of the foreign workers and their families in German society. It was not that full integration was to be pursued, but the government did want the new immigrants to be sufficiently versed and acquainted with the German language to be able to function within the society. Further, such an approach fitted well with that summarized by Bodenbender (1976, p. 3) with respect to the views of the Federal Ministry of Labor and Social Affairs. It was the then (and present) position of the ministry that uncontrolled migration into the Federal Republic was an unacceptable situation and that steps needed to be taken to prevent the ethnic ghetto concentration of the foreign workers and their families. It is easily envisoned how the creation of independent foreign schools for the children with instruction, staff and curriculum oriented toward the home country would intensify the separation and distance from German society. Though neither assimilation nor pluralistic integration was thought to be the necessary or desirable outcome of placing the foreign children in the German schools, neither was an isolated and linguistically impenetrable ghetto to be fostered.

## Phase III: Policy Recommendations of April 1976 on the Instruction of the Children of Foreign Workers

Superseding the recommendations of December 1971, the Standing Conference issued a new set of policy guidelines in April 1976. These most recent ones, however, break no new ground with respect to the basic approaches articulated in previous documents. Rather, they appear to offer a more precise articulation of the earlier points. Furthermore, they continue to carry forward the twin concepts of preparation and linguistic assimilation within the German school system, while at the same time maintaining linguistic, cultural, and historical ties to the homeland. Though it appears that this policy approach presents a set of irreconcilable social goals for the children of the foreign workers in Germany, particularly those who are now second-generation, the official policy would suggest that it is both feasible and desirable. Quoting from the document (Standing Conference of Ministers 1976, p. 1):

> The point is to enable foreign pupils to learn the German language and to reach German school finals. These same pupils should also derive knowledge from instruction in their mother tongue as well as to be able to continually enlarge upon this knowledge. Such educational arrangements will play an important role in contributing to the social development of foreign pupils so long as they are in the Federal Republic. Such an approach also serves as a means for the preservation of their linguistic and cultural identity.

Thus the notion is continually reinforced that the children of the guestworkers must be able to move between two worlds (which are not culturally compatible and neither of which considers a second-generation immigrant child a full member). Here current German educational policy reflects the structural ambivalence discussed in earlier chapters. Pedagogically, it would appear that German educational policy might move in one of three directions in the instruction of immigrant children: define the children as guests who will return to their homeland and thus create an educational system that exclusively prepares them for that eventuality; define them as new Germans, exposing them to and informing them of German life, language, and customs or third, define them as hyphenated Germans and seek some synthesis of the two extremes immediately above. This last is perhaps best understood as bilingual/bicultural education.

There is a fourth policy option, one that seems untenable. This is to approach the education of the children as if two different spirits and selves were within one body. Unfortunately, this is precisely what seems to be the thrust of current German educational policy. The children are considered Germans for the period of German instruction and foreigners for the instruction of the mother tongue and life in the homeland. The current approach in German education assumes a dichotomy whereby the two cultural identities are at odds within the individual.

While it is important to call to task current German educational policy from a pedagogical perspective, it must be remembered that pedagogics is not the basis for public policy. Rather, this approach to the education of guestworker children emerges from political considerations that appear to be twofold. On the one hand, German policymakers and political leaders are confronted with the continued belief by many citizens that the presence of the foreign workers as 12-13 percent of the labor force is the main reason for Germany's unemployment and inflation. Also common is the view that the presence of the foreign workers is having a profound negative impact upon the cultural and ethnic identity of Germany. For these and comparable reasons, German authorities seek to stress that the foreign workers are not a threat to the basic cultural and economic patterns in German society. Pointing to the schools, they note that the foreign children are all being taught to one degree or another in German, and some few are even making it into the Gymnasium. The school, then, is forced to take on the role of ensuring that the differences are not so great as to exacerbate the current social distance between the foreign workers and the native population. The educational policy, moreover, apparently aims at preventing a backlash by the German people against the foreign workers and their families.

The flip side of the educational policy for these children, reflected in the mother-tongue instruction, cultural awareness of the home country, embassy-supported national classes, and so forth, is to reassure the German population that the presence of the workers and their families is temporary. Thus there is the continual emphasis that *within the German educational system*, children from Turkey, Yugoslavia, Greece, and elsewhere are receiving sufficient instruction to enable them to return with their parents and resume their studies in the home country educational system.

A sense of this dual approach to the education of the children is seen in policy recommendations found in the 1976 Conference of Ministers document. On the one hand, the following recommendations state that foreign children are to be treated like German children as far as German curriculum and instructional practices are concerned:

1.1 Foreign pupils have the same rights and the same educational tasks as German pupils.

3.1.1. Lessons in preparatory classes have the task of easing the acclimatization of the foreign pupils in the German school. Therefore the primary purpose of these classes is to impart the German language.

3.1.3. Curricula for the lessons in preparatory classes are to be based on the German curricula.

3.4. Foreign pupils in standard German-speaking classes who do not have sufficient knowledge of the German language are to be given additional instruction.

4.1. Foreign pupils are to be particularly supported in the secondary schools so that they can pass courses which are commensurate with their abilities.

Contained within this same document are, on the other hand, policy recommendations that reinforce the view that the foreign children are not German children, that they are not becoming so, and that they will be returning to their mother country:

3.1.4. If preparatory classes consist of children who all speak the same mother tongue, the subjects of instruction can be imparted by a foreign teacher in the mother tongue of the pupils.

6.1. If it is possible to gather up pupils of one nationality within the same region who are obliged to attend vocational school, then the pupils can be taught the subjects of instruction in their own mother tongue by a foreign teacher.

What is missing from the entire set of recommendations is any sense of a need to blend together these different instructional components of the curriculum. During part of the day the child is German and during other parts he is foreign. But never is the child someone who is assisted in integrating these two parts of the self. In fact, the recommendation is made that even when the child can function in German classes among German children, the option should be there of allowing the segregation of all such foreign children into a single class:

2.2. As far as is possible, the number of foreign pupils in standard German classes is not to be more than one-fifth of the total. This proportion can be exceeded if the pupils in question are foreign ones who can join the classes without linguistic difficulties. There also should be the possibility of building special classes for foreign pupils. In these classes the instruction should take place in the German language and the curriculum should be that of the standard German school.

The fact that German society still appears unwilling to acknowledge that it has become a pluralistic society in which many of its residents are hyphenated Germans finds clear expression in the structure and orientation of the schools. It is not seen to be possible to be German and also something else at the same time. Whether the "cognitive map" of the German people reinforces their public policies, or vice versa, the implications for the schools are the same: treat the foreign child as if he were, in fact, two empty vessels rather than one.

It is because of the simultaneous (and apparently contradictory) efforts in both directions that current educational policy for the guestworker children is unsuccessful. The notion that a child can be prepared to cope with two different educational, cultural, linguistic, and ethnic social systems at the same time and in total isolation, one from the other, strains beyond the breaking point any educational credibility the approach might otherwise have. To reject a bilingual/ bicultural approach for the sake of two mutually isolated and noncomplementary educational orientations can have but one logical outcome for the child: educational failure on both counts (cf. *Frankfurter Rundschau*, October 4, 1975).

The outcome in this instance of generating educational policy on the basis of political considerations is that Germany is paying a rather high cost. While it may be politically necessary to reassure the German people that the foreign workers and their families are neither so different nor so permanent as to be a threat to the well-being of Germany, the price for maintaining this view is a large number of educational casualties among the foreign youth (cf. Köhler 1976, p. 93). One can only speculate about the consequences when the social costs outstrip the political benefits of structurally segregating and perpetuating on the margins of the society tens of thousands of second-generation immigrants. The reality is that these casualties of current policies are no more transitory residents than are their parents.

## EQUALITY OF EDUCATIONAL OPPORTUNITY

The matter of equality of educational opportunity simply does not fit into the current structure of German education, whether for foreign children or native. It is hard to detect a basis for equality of opportunity in a system that is hierarchical and selective, bent on the formulation of an intellectual elite, based on a pedagogical principle of children as empty vessels, and that accepts as a given that the system will produce many losers and few winners. In such a set of circumstances the school is anything but a mobility escalator for those children who begin with fewer resources of social status, parental education, or occupational prospects.

Yet Germany, as well as the other Western democracies, has had to face up to the realization that the perpetuation of an educational system that fosters inequality is a threat to its long-term well-being and social security. As OECD (1972, p. 51) has noted:

> The principle, "equality of educational opportunity" has the attraction not only of wide currency, but also of *prima facie* congruence with contemporary economic, social and political forces. The need to tap and utilize reserves of talent if economic growth is to be sustained; the ever increasing reluctance to tolerate social systems in which a young person's future is determined largely by the social status of his parents; the urgent need to create an informed and self-reliant electorate so that democracy may survive—all these desiderata,

and others, conspire to promote the importance of equality of educational opportunity. The provision of education is tantamount to the provision of chances to serve society at a higher level and to secure some of society's higher rewards, both monetary and nonmonetary. The argument that these chances have been allocated unequally in the past, but must now be allocated more equally, is virtually incontrovertible from any standpoint other than that of unshakable belief in the beneficence of hereditary privilege.

The debate in Germany over whether and how to provide equality of educational opportunity (*Chancengleichheit*) has frequently become enmeshed in the ambiguities of the meaning of the term. As in the United States where the varying definitions of the term have multiplied and then generated their individual and quite dissimilar standards for evaluating whether equality of opportunity was being achieved (Gordon 1971, pp. 3-10), so in Germany the term can be consistent with any one of a half dozen or more interpretations (Harant 1976, p. 151). Furthermore, each of these varying interpretations has quite different implications for the organization of the school systems as well as for the goals toward which the schools are to strive. The end result of such a multiplicity of meanings is that efforts to translate them into a basis for action become extremely difficult. With no clear choice dictated by the principle itself, reform becomes stymied and neutralized.

Perhaps one way out of this quagmire of ambiguity is to approach an understanding of equality of educational opportunity, not from an abstract and theoretical position, but in terms of how it would be applicable to different modes of school system organization. In short, begin with the premise that there exist different forms of school organization and that within each, the underlying concepts of education define how equality of opportunity is to be achieved. From this perspective there are at least three distinct models of school organization, each consistent with a different interpretation of equality of educational opportunity and each premised on the existence of a different social order (OECD 1972, pp. 52-53). While such an approach does not provide the answer as to what is the most correct and true meaning of equality of educational opportunity, it does link the differing interpretations to concrete forms of social organization. Further, it provides guidance to policymakers who are functioning within one or another of these models as to how they may achieve equal educational opportunity for their students.

In the first model, the school system is organized in such a way as to allow only a very few children the opportunity to move beyond the elementary grades. The reason for such restriction on access to further education is that the society itself is static and little economic or social change is anticipated. Therefore, there is little need for educational training at higher levels, as these skills are not in demand. The positions for which further education is necessary are relatively scarce. The backgrounds of those many children who do not move beyond the elementary grades are overwhelmingly from the existing lower social class. Social and economic mobility is at a minimum. Only the rare student from a poor or laboring class background has an opportunity for secondary school education.

Equality of opportunity within the parameters of this educational system could be defined as the provision of equal access to compete for only a limited number of participants. For those who are admitted, the curriculum, the evaluation, the bases for promotion are all standardized. Thus success or failure is defined in purely personalistic terms among the few students involved; the capable will succeed, the rest will gradually fade away.

> The essence of the model is that it is designed to select and train a relatively small number of young people to man the limited number of high level positions in society. In this spirit, it may best be characterized as a school system dedicated to the principle of providing a few children with "equal opportunity to fail," its main function being to identify and promote the academically talented. (OECD 1972, p. 52)

A second model, the one that seems to fit current conditions in Germany most closely, is that of a school system within a society that is rapidly changing, highly technological, and in need of a labor force that is both flexible and well educated. It is a society in which new occupations, new avenues for personal advancement and material acquisition, and new educational skills are promoted. Talented persons from all social strata are in demand to enhance and promote the social and economic growth of the society.

For the schools, the task is one of providing to the society the diversity and breadth of talent that is needed. It is still a system in which competition is severe and the successes are few, but it is also one in which, theoretically, all will have the opportunity to compete. It is also a school system in which there are multiple options for advancement, as opposed to a single curriculum, a single set of measurements, and one criterion for advancement. With the demands of a bewildering variety of occupations to be filled, the schools respond with a number of alternatives so as to provide graduates who can take up positions in these different sectors. The fact of this multiplicity of options means that the discretion of the individual student is greatly increased. It is also recognized that not all options are of equal status and carry equal social worth. The hierarchical nature of the social structure is reproduced in the educational system as well. Consequently, different educational outcomes confer unequal status and unequal opportunities for benefiting from the fruits of the society.

The model of equality of educational opportunity espoused within this social and educational system is one of equality of inputs. That is, the system seeks to provide all students with equal access to the competitive structures within the schools so that they can then compete for unequal outcomes. And for those students who are not able to begin the race on equal terms with others, there are special programs of preparation beginning in early childhood. It is an educational system premised upon the proposition that equality of opportunity is equipping everyone to come to the starting line. Once the race has begun, it is assumed many will falter at different points along the course, with only a select few completing the entire effort. Those who do complete are all winners and the others are ascribed different statuses according to how much of the course they completed. The fact that particular groups of children disproportionally succeed or fail in this effort is believed due to the innate characteristics of the children rather than to the course over which they must compete.

A third alternative is one that represents a fundamentally different approach to schooling from either of the two previously outlined here. When a society has achieved such a standard of living for its citizens that material accumulation is no longer the be-all and end-all, that society must then adapt and develop new goals and visions. As long as accumulation and personal success are seen as synonymous with simply gathering material goods, the goals are both visible and concrete. Furthermore, the schools can easily adapt to such circumstances as they socialize the young into the worlds of work and highly specialized occupational categories. The schools function as has been described in the other two models.

When societies have developed beyond this point, the relation of the individual to both his occupation and his surrounding environment takes on new dimensions. As OECD has noted (1972, p. 53):

> The task of the schools is not merely, or mainly, to prepare children for the world of further study or work. And, although workers with skills are still needed at all levels, they are needed not as relatively passive executors of orders relayed from above, but as active participants in the shaping of their jobs, their companies, and their society.

In such circumstances, the educational experience becomes one quite different from that which exists when the linkage between education and work is assumed to be primary to the future life chances of the individual. Again, as OECD notes (1972, p. 53):

> The relevant educational model is one that emphasizes active participation by pupils in school affairs (both pedagogical and organizational); and de-emphasizes competition and develops co-operation. Not only does this model lower, or virtually abolish, the hurdles, but the competitive characteristics of the track are removed. It now becomes a sheltered area over which the runners try out and develop their varied paces, styles, and powers.

The model of equality of educational opportunity inherent in a school system organized in this fashion is one that functions on the premise of equality of educational outcomes; outcomes not in the sense that everyone leaves school with identical knowledge and skills, but that when one does leave, it is after having had equal opportunity to develop one's personal potential (cf. Husén 1976, p. 410). Warnock (1975, p. 5) has explicated the perspective in this manner:

> Everyone has an equal right to as much education as may enable him to have more if he wants it: and when he has been educated so far, he thereafter has a right to equality of opportunity for more. Whether he actually gets more will depend upon his inclinations, upon the amount of the commodity available, and the kind of competition involved in getting it.

The consequence for the society of supporting and espousing an educational system based on these principles is that traditional hierarchical arrangements and status positions become more tenuous. It is not that they disappear, for one can assume that doctors will continue to have more prestige and standing in a community than will someone who chooses to wash windows, but rather that the differences in occupational choices are personal choices rather than the workings of the schools to sort, identify, and differentially reward students on the basis of such characteristics as race, sex, social class, or ethnic background. In short, the assumption of winners and losers becomes less salient for persons whose occupational choices are based on their own decisions. In this model, one can no longer assume that persons with high status positions are in them because they were the winners in a competitive system that allocated occupational slots.*

In assessing current possibilities for educational reform in Germany and the manner in which reform can contribute to equality of educational opportunity, OECD (1972, p. 54) concludes that neither the first nor third alternative is a feasible option. Their assessment is that the debate in Germany over educational reform is essentially reducible to variations in the second alternative. On the one hand are those who look to the second model as the means to sort children more effectively and rationally into the correct educational track. The hierarchical nature of the school system remains. What occurs within it is a more systematic selection process undertaken with earlier guidance and testing techniques. Equality of educational opportunity is achieved when children are slotted correctly into the appropriate level of the hierarchy where each has the opportunity to compete among peers of comparable scholastic capacity. Edu-

---

*The single greatest difficulty behind the implementation of such an approach in terms of its being able to guarantee that a student could go as far in the educational system as he or she desired is that the commodity is not an unlimited one. Warnock recognizes this, as seen in the caveat in her statement. But the fact remains that access itself to the educational system continues at all levels to favor those of higher socioeconomic status background (cf. Husén 1976, p. 410).

cation then becomes competition among equals for the rewards and benefits available to those at that particular level.

Another interpretation of this model also finds adherents in Germany. Perhaps foremost among this group are those from the Federal Ministry for Education and Science who wrote the *Bildungsbericht '70*. The thrust of this report argues for an educational system in which the hierarchies would remain, but where there would be multiple opportunities for passing between them. Thus, in opposition to the first interpretation of the model, this group sees a benefit in great fluidity within the educational system. One is not put on a track at the end of fourth grade for the rest of one's academic career. Rather, there are numerous ways in which to move between tracks or advance to a higher educational level. The goal is to provide each student with the opportunity to go as far as that student is capable of going. It seeks not to foreclose the options to a talented child who was mistracked in the early grades, but to ensure that if the talent is there, the child will have the opportunity to exercise it. In the end, it is a view of education to promote the rise of a meritocracy.

At present, this view appears to be the overwhelming favorite among those educators and policymakers working on questions of reform in German education. Their goal seems not to disrupt the internal hierarchy in German education, but to sever the current linkage between education success and social background, and thus their aims clearly fall within the predominant concern of the second model, that is, educational opportunity as access to the higher ranks of the system, based on competence and successful competition.

## EQUALITY OF EDUCATIONAL OPPORTUNITY AND THE GUESTWORKER CHILD

Whatever the limitations and denials of opportunity a German child of low socioeconomic background may experience in the German schools, the conditions are even more restrictive and prohibitive for the guestworker children. On this group falls the full weight of the traditionalism, selectivity, elitism, and rigidity inherent in German education. In a system that has until now effectively excluded some 90 percent of German students from the opportunity for university-level education, the opportunities for foreign worker children have been even more effectively closed off, even at levels far below the university.

Data published in 1976 by the Federal Ministry for Education and Science indicate that for 1974, 282,732 or 2.8 percent of all students in German elementary and secondary education were from the five largest guestworker communities, that is, Turkish, Greek, Yugoslav, Italian, and Spanish.* Students from

---

*By the 1975-76 school year, the number of elementary and secondary students from these same five communities equaled 308,564 of the total elementary and secondary

these same communities represented 3.9 percent of all students in the comprehensive elementary grades and .046 percent of those in the selective Gymnasium. While there is no selectivity in the elementary grades, it works with a vengeance in the later years. More than 60 percent of all children of foreign workers in the appropriate age group do not complete any of the three alternatives for secondary education (Bodenbender 1976, p. 9).

While it is not possible here to catalog all the barriers and handicaps particular to the guestworker children, which they must overcome in order to succeed in the German educational system, it is possible to note several key difficulties that in large part predetermine their eventual success or failure. First and foremost among the difficulties faced by the immigrant children is the matter of language. The preparatory classes for teaching the German language are both overcrowded and frequently of short duration (Willke 1975, pp. 362-63). And to compound the situation, the classes are usually comprised of students from several different nationalities and mother tongues, students who have different ages, levels of performance, and skill with the German language are mixed together, and throughout the school year new students are entering the classes.

While on the one hand there is the tendency to push the students too quickly into the German schools, there also exists the contrary pressure in some instances of wanting to keep the children out of the German schools and maintain them in separate facilities. This tendency is most pronounced in Bavaria where there are guestworker children spending five, six, or seven years in the preparatory classes which provide the foreign children only eight hours per week in German language instruction (cf. Willke 1975, p. 364). There has essentially evolved in this Land a dual school system that has the effect of segregating the foreign children away from German schools and German children.

A third difficulty arises in the efforts to teach the child's mother tongue. The problem lies in deciding *who* should teach the child the language. On the one hand are those who suggest that it is best for German teachers to instruct the child in the mother tongue so as to be able more effectively to help the child draw the parallels to the German language. A contrary view is that teachers from the home country are most sensitive to the patterns of language development, to the way the language is actually used in the home country, and to what the needs of the child are as he seeks to retain the mother tongue while in the midst of a new language system.

In either event, the consequence is that many parents who are certain (at least at the moment) of their return to the home country choose not to send

---

school population in Germany of 9,995,525. No data were found that gave the numbers of foreign worker students in post-secondary education, though a reasonable assumption is that the numbers are minuscule.

their children to German classes, but only to those where there is instruction in the native language. As Willke notes (1975, p. 363):

> Assigned as complementary lessons in order to maintain cultural and linguistic ties between the child and his parents and with his parents' roots in the native country, these classes often become the only kind of school a child attends. Parents often prefer these classes because they offer certificates that are valid in the home country and thus facilitate the child's further training.

Yet a fourth hurdle faced by the foreign workers' children is the emphasis upon continual evaluation of student performance and competence. Not only has the foreign child no experience with coping in a school atmosphere of constant evaluation, but the foreign child also is handicapped when it comes to the preparation of class assignments. Homework plays a critical role in the schooling process. It is not uncommon for first-grade students to have regular homework assignments. Further, it is assumed by the schools that the parents will spend the necessary time, if they are interested in the future of their children, to ensure that the assignments are completed. Such an approach not only spells trouble for German children when both parents work, but it may be impossible for foreign worker children if both parents work and neither speaks sufficient German to assist in the preparation of the assignments.(See, for example, Akpinar, López-Blasco, Vink 1977, pp. 31-71.)

The assignment of heavy homework loads that depend upon parental help to complete them stems from the short (compared to American standards) school day. In Germany, the school day ends between 11:30 a.m. and 1:00 p.m., depending upon the locale. It is assumed that the child will be fed at home (there are no cafeterias in German schools) and that homework will occupy most of the child's time during the afternoon. Such an approach, clearly, is predicated upon the assumption that there is a parent at home to feed and teach the children. When the parent (usually the mother, of course) is not at home, the child must accommodate by going to a neighbor or a grandparent or perhaps a day-care facility. But the point is that the homework is not done, nor are the parents able to assist when they are not in the home. It is the middle-class family in which the mother is not in the work force that is the norm for such a system. As the *Bildungsbericht '70* noted (1970, p.69):

> In secondary education, lessons take place as a rule during the morning. As far as homework is concerned, the younger pupils especially are dependent on help from their parents. Parents can only offer help in general when at least one parent has been sufficiently educated and does not have a full-time job. Expensive extra lessons are necessary on a frighteningly large scale in order to help a growing percentage of children get better marks or prevent them from having to repeat a year.

The children of the foreign workers have few advantages upon which to draw so as to succeed in the opportunities offered through school. They cannot depend upon homework help from parents who are not sufficiently educated in the German language; private lessons are too expensive; they may not even have a quiet place in which to study. The end result is that on the chief criterion by which success in German education is measured, that of cognitive achievement, the foreign workers' children are hard pressed to meet even the minimum standards. It is for reasons such as these that only .046 percent of all students in the Gymnasium are from guestworker homes.

When one surveys these difficulties faced by the immigrant children, as well as those not analyzed here (for example, curriculum, teacher expectations, or parental participation in the schools), the evidence is overwhelming that inequality of educational opportunity is the norm in German education. As the OECD (1972, p. 66) noted, it is a pervasive inequality that arises "not only from shortcomings in the *structure* of the educational system but also as a consequence of deficiencies in the *content* and *style* of schooling." Thus, the schools function in such a way as to systematically deny to many German and to foreign children alike tangible educational benefits.

## POSTSCRIPT

The present chapter has sketched in broad outlines the nature of the German educational system and the barriers, both universal and particular, which the children of the guestworkers face in their efforts to secure an education. However, it is not until the particular policies and programs of various Länder are examined in more detail that one is able to flesh out the pedagogical orientations developed specifically for this group of children. Within the general organizational structure of German education, there are distinctive approaches followed by each Land in the education of its latest group of immigrant children. Furthermore, it is at the level of the Land that some of the political and economic forces that predetermine the educational orientations are most evident.

The following two chapters will assess the educational programs for the guestworker children found in the Länder of Bavaria and Berlin. In choosing these two for more intensive scrutiny, the rationale is that one can find in them the clearest and most articulated pedagogical positions. Further, it is with the Bavarian and Berlin models that the sharpest disagreements over philosophies, policies, and programs emerge. While the Bavarian model is based on the assumption that the foreign workers come into and then go out of Germany on the basis of the rotation principle, the Berlin model strives for the full integration of the foreign children. If the former stresses the transiency and impermanence of the foreign communities within Germany, the latter is aimed at their assimilation and eventual absorption into German society.

In these two chapters, it should be immediately evident that the author espouses neither approach. In fact, they both seem ill conceived and erroneous in their assumptions and subsequent educational practices. Neither acknowledges the legitimacy of the emerging multicultural nature of German society. Both fail to respond to the fact that there are countless thousands of foreign worker families that are daily learning more of Germany and how to accommodate themselves to the country on a long-term basis, yet not discarding the cultural heritage and integrity that they have brought with them.

While Bavaria assumes the guestworkers and their families will never truly become German, the Berlin approach does not allow for the Turkish, or Greek, or Yugoslav side to be sustained and supported. The end result is that neither program nurtures the educational needs of children who are, in fact, growing up as Turkish-Germans, or Greek-Germans, or Yugoslav-Germans. Each program in its own way negates one side of the hyphen and thus works against what are in fact the beginnings of an ethnically pluralistic society. Unfortunately, the educational assumptions of both approaches reinforce incorrect perceptions of the social reality in which the children themselves live and grow.

# 9

# AN EDUCATIONAL ALTERNATIVE: THE BAVARIAN APPROACH

At first thought, the images of Bavaria are of alpine meadows, *Lederhosen*, Munich beer halls, and yodeling. To be sure, all these are part of Bavaria and are held dear by the people. But, needless to say, it is a much more complex and diverse region of Germany than is suggested by the popular image. It is an area with large concentrations of industrial activity including automotive production, chemical factories, and electronics. Further, it contains more than one quarter of all German citizens in the Federal Republic and nearly an equal percentage of all guestworkers and their families. In Munich, a city of 1.3 million persons, more than 200,000 are foreigners. One of every three babies born in that city is to foreign worker parents.

Bavarians bear the brunt of many sarcastic jokes made by other Germans. They are portrayed as the country folk, the people who have never quite joined the rest of the nation in forging a new country in the postwar period. They are frequently said to be simple, silly, but sincere. While such stereotypes are both selective and distortive, there does exist the half-truth behind them that Bavaria is a distinctive region within Gemany. Perhaps more than any other Land, it has nurtured social, cultural, and political institutions that have tended to set it apart. The end result is that the regional identity is quite strong. While persons in other parts of Germany are losing strong regional identification and simply defining themselves as German, in Bavaria the definition still has two distinct parts: the people are both German and Bavarian.

Central to this analysis is the fact that the one region of Germany where the collective "ingroup" definition and identity are seemingly strongest is also the region of Germany where the educational programs are most systematically aimed at sustaining an "outgroup." The criteria that determine who can be considered a Bavarian appear well established. Consequently, from the point of view of the schools as an instrument of socialization, there is little that can be done to make one a Bavarian if he/she is not one already.

## PERCEPTIONS AND POLICIES

Since 1973, Bavaria has implemented a model experiment in the education of the guestworker children (Harant 1976, p. 159). The term experiment may be somewhat misleading as there appears to be little if any empirical assessment of this effort. In fact, there are available no data comparing the success of this approach with any other or even showing that this plan is working well according to standards established by its own initiators. What has been termed an experiment has, in fact, been an exercise in administrative fiat whereby it was decided from within the Bavarian Ministry for Instruction and Culture that this approach would be used in Bavaria for the education of the foreign worker children. While publications of this ministry continue to tout the Bavarian "open model" as successful and worthy of emulation by the other Länder in Germany (Mahler 1976b, p. 19; Bavarian Ministry for Instruction and Culture 1976a, p. 1), there appears to be no evidence to support the claim (cf. Mahler 1976a; 1976b; Deutscher Caritasverband 1975).

Bavaria is basing its educational practice on economic and political considerations. The Bavarian view of the role of the foreign workers stresses their short-term presence and lack of commitment to German society. No empirical evidence has been found to substantiate the position that foreign workers are in Germany on a short-term basis, but that view is reiterated at every turn by advocates of the Bavarian approach (Mahler 1976b, p. 16; Bavarian Ministry for Instruction and Culture 1974, p. 20; 1975). As Mahler, who has served as one of the chief architects of this approach, has noted (1974, p. 16):

> The question is, however, whether these families and their children will stay in Bavaria until 1980 and later. . . . The responsible authorities of the Federal government and of the various states expect foreign workers to stay in the Federal Republic of Germany for only a short time. Thus the integration of foreign "fellow citizens" into the Federal Republic—a theme which has been proclaimed for years—has taken place within the most narrow bounds.

Although Bavaria continues to stress an educational program based upon the rotation principle of foreign labor in Germany, the evidence overwhelmingly discredits this view (Harant 1976, p. 165; Minzlaff 1976, p. 17). There are, first of all, the data on the growing number of family reunions in Germany, the decline in foreign workers leaving the country, the high number of births among the foreign worker communities, and the integration of foreign workers into the economy; but there is also the voice of policymakers at the federal level. As Bodenbender (1976, p. 13), a high official in the Federal Ministry for Labor and Social Affairs, has commented, "The Federal Republic of Germany rejects the principle of the rotation of foreign workers as the basis upon which our manpower needs are to be resolved."

An explanation for the Bavarian view must be couched in cautious terms. It appears that the rotation principle is the foundation for educational programs because Bavarian officials simply cannot bring themselves to legitimate the development of a multi-ethnic and multicultural Bavaria. The social identity entailed in being a Bavarian is so bound by history, tradition, and current cultural patterns that a rationale must be found for ensuring its preservation. Stressing the proposition that foreign workers will be shortly on their way out of Bavaria allows educators to develop programs to prepare the guestworker children for returning to a homeland many have never seen. It is Bavaria for the Bavarians as the schools strive to educate the thousands of foreign children born in Munich and elsewhere in Bavaria for a hypothetical school system located somewhere in rural Turkey or southern Yugoslavia.

## THE EDUCATIONAL PROGRAM

The Bavarian Ministry for Instruction and Culture has explicitly stated on several occasions that an educational approach that stresses the integration of foreign worker children into German society has generally failed. In 1974 this ministry stated (p. 20):

> In casting a retrospective glance, one can easily recognize that the heretofore existing arrangements concerning the education of the guestworker children were aimed at the philosophical and practical integration of these children into the German school system and also into German society. However, the fallacy in these arrangements has been that it was assumed that these children could integrate into the German schools with a minimum of difficulty. Those who had anticipated that the foreign children would be able to learn the German language in a rapid way have now had to admit that this could not be achieved.

From this view, the ministry concluded that a quite different approach to the education of the children had to be undertaken, namely, the "open model." This is a pedagogical program, states the ministry (1974, p. 20),

> . . . which proceeds from the actual educational needs of the children. In recognition of these needs, it is imperative that the only reason for their school education not to be considered their future integration into German society. Rather, various measures have to be initiated which enable foreign children to both integrate into the German school system (where German is the language of instruction) and also to return home and join the school system of their native country (where instruction would be given in the mother-tongue).

The foundation of the program is thus theoretically grounded in the view that the foreign worker children must be supported in an educational environment that encourages bilingualism. On this point the ministry is to be commended, for it is precisely such an environment that has been called for by many international organizations concerned with foreign workers and their children (cf. Council of Europe 1974a, p. 89; European Economic Community 1976, Article 3). The shortcoming, however, is that the Bavarian approach has twisted and subverted this orientation to rationalize the isolation and segregation of the foreign children. Under the guise of bilingualism, a system is maintained that is simultaneously supposed to prepare children for German classes in Munich and Turkish classes in rural Anatolia. But the end result, as a number of critics have noted, is close to functional illiteracy in both languages (Friberg and Hohmann 1976, pp. 11-25; Deutscher Caritasverband 1975; and Harant 1975, p. 164).

Officially, the following principles guide the development of the program (Bavarian Ministry for Instruction and Culture 1974, p. 20):

1) Foreign children who are already living in Germany and who wish to remain here with their families who are also intent on staying in Germany should be integrated into the German school system, provided that the parents so desire it and that the children have a sufficient command of the German language.

2) The interests of those parents and children who will be in the Federal Republic for only a short time must be considered as well. If they desire to maintain their ties to their native country and especially with the native school system, their children have the right to be educated in such a way that they will be able to continue their education in the home country.

3) Children who do not speak German sufficiently to function in German classes are to be taught in their mother tongue. To now, the importance of instruction in the mother tongue has been underestimated. It is unrealistic to assume that a child is not hampered in his learning when he is only in the first stages of grasping both the structure and meaning of the new language.

4) Children who have sufficiently mastered the German language shall be given the option to remain in the mother-tongue classes or switch to the German language classes, according to the wishes of their parents. This same option is to be given to foreign children who are presently in German language classes.

On the basis of these principles, the guestworker children are generally provided three alternative classroom situations.* First, in the standard German language classroom along with the German-speaking Bavarian children, are those immigrant children who have demonstrated sufficient skill in the German language to be able to receive their instruction in German. Approximately one-sixth (6,246 of 37,442) of all foreign worker children in Bavaria are in such classes. Foreign children are placed in these classes after their parents have so requested. These children are also given eight lessons per week in their mother tongue if there are at least 15 students with the same mother tongue in the school. If there are fewer, there is no mother-tongue instruction. The ministry has indicated in its material that these eight lessons are in lieu of other scheduled classes. However, Harant (1976, p. 161) challenges this contention and suggests that these courses constitute an "overload" of additional classroom work.

When criticisms are raised about other segregative components of the educational program for the foreign children, the Bavarian ministry points to these children in standard German classrooms as an indication of the willingness to give foreign workers and their children the option of either integrating into the society or maintaining closer homeland ties. The data released by the ministry, however, suggest that the absolute number of students in such classes declined between the 1975-76 and the 1976-77 academic years. (During this same period, the total number of foreign worker students in the state grew by more than 4,000.) Whereas in 1975-76, 6,502 students were distributed among 300 classrooms, in 1976-77 6,246 students were found in 326 different classes.

The second of the classroom situations devised for the guestworker children is the one seen as most unique to the Bavarian approach. Children who have not sufficiently mastered the German language to receive their instruction in German are grouped together in classes of at least 25 to receive all their school instruction in the mother tonge. Children whose parents desire only mother-tongue instruction would also be in these classes, regardless of the German language proficiency of the children.

In these classrooms the mother-tongue instruction is provided by teachers from the home country. During the 1976-77 academic year there were 403 foreign teachers working in the Bavarian public school system. (There were an additional 141 teachers in the private Greek school system.) In these classrooms where basic instruction is in the mother tongue, German is required to be taught as the first foreign language, and up to eight periods per week. The formal documents describing this alternative suggest that in those subjects where

---

*As might be anticipated, there are clear exceptions to this statement. The most self-evident example is that in Bavaria, 7,673 Greek students were during the 1976-77 academic year in private schools sponsored by the Greek General Consulate (Bavarian Ministry for Instruction and Culture 1977, pp. 2, 5).

language is not of prime importance—for example, music and crafts—German and mother-tongue classes can be combined. No data could be found to indicate how frequently such combining of classes does occur. The theoretical goal of these classes is to bring the foreign child to a level of proficiency whereby he/she can choose to continue in the mother-tongue classroom or move to a German language classroom. The mother-tongue classes are to provide a transition period for the child from reliance on the mother tongue to being able to participate in German language classes.

It is with these classes that the Bavarian ministry has issued its statements on the utility of mother-tongue instruction and the educational benefits to be derived thereby. Mahler (1976b, p. 16) has noted:

> There is yet one further reason why experts in educational policy and school officials have turned away from the demands to retrain all foreign children to the German language as soon and as exclusively as possible: they have come to realize that the foreign child cannot learn German and simultaneously improve his knowledge in those other aspects of the curriculum when the instruction is in German. To attempt to do so means a loss of valuable school time for the child. . . . Bavaria was the first to call for an educational procedure whereby the initial instruction of the child would be in the language in which he thinks, that is, his mother tongue. If the pupil has learned the subject matters by means of his mother tongue, and German has been taught sufficiently as a foreign language, it is not until then that one should suggest sending the child into a class where all subjects are taught in the German language.

Data from the state Ministry for Instruction and Culture indicate that this option of mother-tongue instruction has been rapidly expanding (1976b; 1977). Whereas in 1975-76 there were 8,623 students distributed among 255 classes, one academic year later there were 10,457 students in 318 classes. The same pattern of growth is also reflected in the number of foreign teachers working in such classroom situations. Whereas in 1975-76 there were 231 foreign teachers teaching in mother-tongue classrooms in the Bavarian public schools, the 1976-77 year found the number increased to 297. Thus in the same period, classes in which German was the primary language of instruction lost nearly 300 students, while classes taught primarily in the mother tongue gained almost 2,000.

The third classroom situation for the immigrant children is one that is put into effect when the numbers are too small to warrant mother-tongue classes. This third option has two alternatives. First, when there are too few students of any one mother tongue to build individual mother-tongue classes, students of different nationalities will be grouped into transition classes of at least 25 students per class. When there are still fewer foreign worker children in the schools, the policy is to initiate eight supplementary German lessons per week for the children. These lessons can be organized in any school where there are at least 12 students who would participate in them. These classes are to take the place of other classroom work. In circumstances where there are still fewer guestworker children in any one school, no provisions are made.*

## THE BAVARIAN APPROACH: A CRITIQUE

There are three different perspectives from which one can undertake an analysis of the current Bavarian approach to the education of the guestworker children: the philosophy of the program; the policies initiated to operationalize the basic assumptions about appropriate educational methods; and finally, the actual programs as they have been created and instituted in schools across the Land of Bavaria.

Philosophically, the cornerstone of the entire Bavarian approach rests on the assumption that the rotation model is an accurate reflection of the current relation of foreign workers to the German labor market. (To repeat, it is an economic condition that predetermines the educational response.) The fact that this assumption has been so strongly discredited is a point that has been reiterated several times, both in this and in previous chapters (cf. Chapters 3 and 5). The Bavarian Ministry for Instruction and Culture has cited in particular the relation of the Greek workers to Germany and the German economy as the basis for their assumption that the rotation model is appropriate. As Mahler (1976b, p. 17), a ministry official, has stated, "The programs we have developed are in accordance with the wishes of the sending countries, especially those of Greece and Yugoslavia. These governments as a matter of course, anticipate the return home of their foreign workers."† What is not stated, of course, is when such a

---

*In the data on the 1976-77 school year provided by the ministry, approximately 17,000 of the 33,200 guestworker children in the Bavarian public schools were tabulated as participating in one of the three options. No indication is provided with the remaining 16,200 as to how many were in schools with such small enrollments that no program existed or conversely, how many were in schools with programs but functioned well with German and sought no mother-tongue instruction.

†It is of interest to examine certain data on school attendance of children from the two countries, Greece and Yugoslavia. First, 56 percent of the Greek children residing in Bavaria are not even in the Bavarian public schools. Of the 7,673 Greek children, 4,283 are in the private national schools offered by the Greek consulate. Alternatively, only 11 percent of the foreign worker children in the public schools are of Greek origin. Second, the total number of Yugoslav children in the public schools during the 1976-77 school year was 4,817, or 13 percent of the total foreign student enrollment.

If one is willing to grant that the rotation principle does hold for the workers and their families from these two countries, and the author is not, one is confronted with the establishment of a set of policies based on at most 24 percent of the foreign worker children population in the schools. And this figure would have to hold true for every single Greek and Yugoslav child to be at the level of even 24 percent. (Parenthetically, one finds no citations in the ministry literature on the call for the rotation principle from the govern-

return is anticipated. The Bavarian model may have a legitimacy if, in fact, the rotation principle is in operation and the workers and their families will be back in the home country within a matter of only one or two more years. But, if that is not the case, and all the evidence since the ban on further immigration of foreign workers since 1973 would support this view, one must ask what the rationale is for preparing the children to return to school systems that the overwhelming majority will never enter.

Another way of phrasing this matter is to ask when the Bavarian approach reaches the point of diminishing returns with its continual emphasis on keeping open the options for a return to the homeland. At some point, this becomes an impracticability. Is it after two, three, or four years in a German school that one should acknowledge the child will most likely have German education for many years to come? Furthermore, what is the justification when compulsory education in the home country may be but five years? The Bavarian approach does not wish to address this matter. Instead, it emphasizes the marginality and continued nonintegration of the foreign workers and their families in Bavaria. Constant repetition of the theme that the foreign workers are in Bavaria on the basis of the rotation principle ensures the avoidance of serious efforts to prepare for the long-term presence of thousands of foreign children in the schools.

What must also be noted in this regard is that the emphasis upon rotation is a double-sided message. One the one hand, it can act as a reassurance to the Bavarian people that they need not be concerned with the situation of the foreign workers and their families, for they are but short-time residents who will shortly return to the home country. The rotation model provides a convenient justification for the lack of action on behalf of foreign workers.

The other side of this emphasis upon rotation is the message it gives to the foreign workers' community. Nowhere else in Germany are foreign workers and their families defined as being in the country on the basis of the rotation model. Only in Bavaria do the foreign communities continually hear that they are but migratory labor, impermanent in their stay in Germany, and soon to return to their home countries. It is contended here, and this point will be developed in more detail shortly, that it is this message that may well explain the willingness of foreign worker parents to place their children in the mother-tongue classes, even after their children are capable of functioning in German language classes. The large numbers of parents who choose to have their children in such classes is touted by the ministry as an indication of the success of their approach. What they may, in fact, have created is a self-fulfilling prophecy whereby the foreign workers' communities sense the Bavarian resistance to their presence and choose the mother-tongue classes as a hedge against the time of their rotation out of the country.

---

ment of Turkey, and it is Turkish children who comprise one-half of all foreign worker children in the Bavarian public schools—16,549 of a total of 33,159.)

In assessing the various policies that have been initiated to create an educational program for the guestworker children, there are several that clearly accentuate the views of the Bavarian approach. The first of these is that instruction is to be provided for the children in the mother tongue, a recommendation that continually finds support in policy literature on the instruction of foreign children. As one of the recommendations from the Standing Conference of European Ministers of Education, Council of Europe, (1974b, pp. 43-44) has stated:

> The Conference recommends that the Governments of the member states be invited to provide opportunities for migrants' children to learn, keep up and develop a good knowledge of their mother tongue and the culture of their country of origin so that they can both settle down well in the educational system of the host country and keep the door open for a return to their country of origin, while taking advantage, if they desire, of their bilingual situation.

In the Federal Republic of Germany, a similar recommendation has been made by the Conference of Ministers (1976a, pp. 3, 8):

> In manifold ways the various Länder have solved their task of enabling foreign children to cooperate successfully at German schools. They have also managed to reserve for them the possibility of a reintegration into their homeland schools. The aim of the schools within the Federal Republic is to enable foreign children to learn German and to succeed in passing their final examinations at German schools. Besides, they are to acquire proficiency in their mother tongue and to develop this proficiency.
>
> Foreign children who cannot follow the lessons in a German class because of their linguistic difficulties are to be enrolled in preparatory classes where the first language of instruction will be the mother tongue. These classes are to ease for the foreign students the transition and integration into German schools.

As suggested earlier, the Bavarian approach has instituted a series of policies that have modified in a significant way the recommendations listed above. The German Conference of Ministers of Culture and Education recommends that the schools enable the foreign children to develop a proficiency in their mother tongue, but the emphasis is on learning and passing school examinations in German. The Bavarian approach inverts this recommendation, placing primary emphasis upon maintaining skills in the mother tongue so as to enable the foreign children to return to the school system of the mother country. Further, especially for those children who receive all their school instruction only in their mother tongue, it becomes unlikely if not impossible that they will ever be able to learn German well enough to pass their final examinations at German schools. It is this approach that Bavaria recommends to the rest of Germany as the most appropriate for the education of the foreign worker children.

An additional aspect of this strong emphasis upon the instruction in the mother tongue deserves mention. The Bavarian policies are based on the assumption that the most difficult matter for the foreign children in their adjustment to Germany lies in the matter of language proficiency. One may grant that this is so, though no research evidence is provided by the ministry to substantiate the view. However, there does exist contrary evidence from a large-scale study in Canada (Ashworth 1975, pp. 84-94). The findings of this study of Canadian immigrant children from countries of the European South as well as from Asia suggest that the greatest challenge to the children is not language transition, but cultural adaptations. If the children are able to master the cultural norms and understand the new cultural and social system in which they are to function, the Canadian data suggest that language development comes much more quickly. The Bavarian approach posits the reverse of the Canadian findings. This is not necessarily to prove, on the basis of research findings, that Bavarian policies are going in the wrong direction, but to note that there are studies that indicate that a quite different model for assisting the adaptation of foreign children to a new language system has been found to be effective.

Furthermore, Harant (1976, p. 163) challenges the assumption inherent in the Bavarian policies that education is possible only in one language thought structure at a time. That is, the Bavarian model presupposes that the children come to the schools with a cognitive structure based on the language of the home country. What must be accomplished, then, for those who desire it, is to assist the child to develop cognitive processes based on the German language. Harant notes that this assumption of a unilingual thought structure is challenged by the experiences of many European countries where bilingual and even multilingual instruction of the children occurs with seemingly no deterrents to their learning. Rather than assuming that children are incapable of learning with multiple linguistic structures, he argues that such learning occurs for many children and adults alike throughout the world. It is a strength to be encouraged rather than dismissed on the basis of a questionable pedagogical principle.

A second policy area that is central to the Bavarian approach is related to the discretion of parents to choose either to have the instruction of their children in the mother-tongue classes or in German language classes. As has been noted, the number of students in the former is rising while the numbers in the latter are dropping. Bavarian officials cite these data on the growth of the mother-tongue classes as evidence of the interest of the parents in sustaining the linguistic and educational ties to the home country. As the ministry noted in a 1974 report (1974, p. 21), "Foreign pupils and their parents are eagerly making use of the mother tongue classes when they are offered. In fact, when such classes are instituted, the most difficult task is locating sufficient classrooms to meet the demand."

What is to be made of this support by parents for the mother-tongue classes? Is it, in fact, a reflection of the interest and aspiration of the parents to maintain an active and ongoing link for the children to the school systems in the various home countries? The Bavarian authorities say yes; if the parents wanted to stay for a long period in Germany, they would opt instead for the German language classes. That the mother-tongue classes are chosen is an indication, say the Bavarian officials, that the wants of the workers are being met.

There are several alternative explanations, however, for the interest that foreign parents do show in the mother-tongue classes. First, and one that would most closely parallel the early experiences of American immigrants, is to assume that these new immigrants to Germany do wish to remain, but not at the expense of having to shed their cultural identities. Just as the Irish, Italian, Japanese, Polish, and many other racial/ethnic groups that came to America sought to maintain cultural links to the home country by the establishment of parochial schools, mother-tongue newspapers, and social activities, so also perhaps the new immigrants into Germany are using the mother-tongue classes in the public schools in much the same manner. The fact that the schools are providing the lessons might mean that the communities of guestworkers have decided that is one activity that they themselves do not need to undertake. (For the Greek community, however, the desire for more autonomy and control over the schooling process has led to the formation of Greek national schools. As was noted, there are more than 4,000 Greek children attending these schools in Bavaria.)

A second explanation, and one alluded to earlier, is to suggest that the parents have opted for the mother-tongue lessons because they are unsure of their status in Bavaria and exactly how long they will be able to remain as guests. The continual emphasis by Bavarian officials that the workers are in the Land on the basis of a rotation model may well have the effect of creating uncertainty and a feeling of impermanence in the guestworker communities. If this is so, it is understandable that the parents wish their children to have an understanding of the mother tongue and be able to continue schooling in the home country on their return. In this light, the choice of the mother-tongue classes becomes a hedge for their children against the possibility of eventual rotation out of the country.

Yet a third explanation, and one posited by Harant (1976, p. 165), is that the social and cultural strains experienced by the parents with their coming to Germany have been so severe that they have begun to idealize the mother country. Thus, in the midst of their isolation, exploitation, marginality, and general insecurity, the parents come to believe that it would be better for the children to have the opportunity to return to the mother country where none of the ills that afflict them in Germany would be present. This projection of the social idealism of the sending country is then transferred to the children by way of making the choice for mother-tongue classes in the Bavarian schools.

Finally, one could posit that the guestworkers have a realistic assessment of the actual educational opportunities for their children in German schools: rather than put their children on a treadmill that would take the children nowhere, for the German educational system is so rigged against them that the options for success are nearly nil, better to give them the mother tongue and a stronger sense of the cultural identity of their mother country, even if they were born in Germany. In this light, opting for the mother-tongue classes is essentially an act of resignation on the part of the parents. They may realize how little chance their children will have to compete successfully in the German Gymnasium.* The choice of the mother-tongue classes becomes a protective act on the part of the parents to shield their children from the fierce competition, the near certain lack of success, and the cultural isolation they would experience in the German language school.

A third component of the policies established for the instruction of the guestworker children in Bavaria that is in need of scrutiny is that which has mandated the development of parallel curricular tracks for children in the mother-tongue classes. It has been the policy of the officials that the students in these classes are to be able to move along in their academic instruction in the mother tongue at a pace equivalent to that in the German language classes. By doing so, it is assumed that when the children have mastered sufficient German, they will be able to switch from the mother-tongue classes into the German language classes without a loss in grade standing. The basic assumption behind such a policy is that it is possible to provide instruction in the mother tongue, using materials from the home country, and enable the students to remain parallel to their German age-mates who are in German language classes using German materials. What in reality occurs is that the longer the guestworker children stay in the mother-tongue classes, the greater the discrepancies in the content of the two language tracks. The use of home-country curriculum materials that portray the historical, social, cultural, and economic life of the sending country does not prepare the children for having to deal with German life and society. To assume that taking no more than eight hours per week of German as a foreign language will prepare the student for moving into German language classes and functioning on a par in content and curriculum with German age-mates is questionable, to say the least. More likely, it is a pedagogical disaster.

---

*Data released by the Conference of Ministers of Education and Culture indicate that in the 1975-76 academic year there were a total of 196 Greek, 298 Italian, 91 Spanish, 218 Turkish, and 256 Portugese students in all Gymnasiums in the Land of Bavaria. These figures combined represented 0.004 percent of all Gymnasium students in the Land. (Conference of Ministers of Education and Culture 1976b, p. 31; Federal Ministry for Education and Science 1976, p. 32).

In examining the actual consequences of a policy such as this, it is clear that it works toward exactly the opposite end of the public pronouncements about its goals. Instead of facilitating the movement of the immigrant children into the German language classes, the longer the students stay with the mother-tongue instruction, the greater the probability that they will not be able to make the transfer.* In short, the mother-tongue approach serves to reinforce the segregation and isolation of the immigrant children from the Bavarian German-speaking children. It also goes far to ensure the educational failure of the immigrant children. Identical conclusions about the outcomes of this approach have been reached by the Deutscher Caritasverband (1975), the analyses by Harant (1976), Minzlaff (1975), and Friberg and Hohmann (1976). The Bavarian Ministry for Instruction and Culture, however, has most emphatically denied that the immigrant children are isolated and segregated as a result of these policies (1975).

## OPTIONS FOR FAILURE

Having examined both the philosophical background and particular policy approaches that have been taken by the Bavarian government regarding the instruction of the immigrant children, it is now possible to assess the three classroom options developed for the day-to-day education of the children.

The first option, that of placing the foreign children in standard classes where German is spoken and teaching them their own mother tongue for up to eight hours a week, is a feasible one for those students who come to the school with a sufficient knowledge of German to meet classroom demands. However, for those students who do not have that proficiency, this approach would appear inadequate. There are no provisions in it for the additional instruction in German that the children would need in order to come to some minimal level of proficiency. The children are instead taught their respective mother-country languages.

One consequence of this approach is that the foreign language students are frequently unable to successfully complete the requirements of the German schools. The time taken away from course work for learning the mother tongue and the lack of additional assistance for those who have difficulties learning

---

*The same outcome was found in a similar program initiated at one school in Frankfurt. As a result, the school inspector for foreign children in the city of Frankfurt has begun an effort to dismantle the program and return the foreign worker children to multilingual preparatory classes. (Cf. *Frankfurter Rundschau*, January 3, 1977, "Foreign Children in Frankfurt Too Long in Separate Classes.")

German mean that the opportunities for success are severely limited. While it is important for those children who want it to have mother-tongue instruction, it is also important to note that the time used for such instruction is time taken away from the class material on which examinations are based, and on which entrance into the stratified secondary level is determined. No marks are given in favor of the student who has had Turkish or Serbo-Croatian when at the end of the fourth grade the decisions are made on which students shall have access to the Gymnasium curriculum. The mother-tongue instruction, instead of being an integrated part of the education plan for the immigrant child, is set apart—an extra requirement that is not expected of German students and that takes away instruction time from the rest of the curriculum.

While the publications of the Bavarian ministry do not make the point, it is interesting to speculate whether the ministers believe that the eight hours per week of instruction in the mother tongue will be sufficient to enable the child to return to the home country and readily resume his education there. After all, if it is assumed that the rotation principle applies to all the foreign workers and their families, then the children in the German language classes can be anticipated to be leaving shortly as well. How sufficiently are they prepared for returning to Turkey, Greece, or Yugoslavia? The answer would have to be not at all. The outcome then works to the child's disadvantage. He receives insufficient educational preparation for either staying in Germany or going to the homeland of his parents. Grossmann had foreseen such consequences even before the Bavarian plan was put into operation (1972, p. 145):

> The controversial discussion about the extent to which foreign worker children are to be integrated as well as the extent to which they are to remain connected to their native countries results in programs where the children feel nowhere at home. They become illiterates in two languages. For after all, the educational programs frequently developed for foreign children are no more than simply adding together the German and the foreign programs.

It is with option two, that of all classroom instruction being carried on in the mother tongue with German offered as a foreign language, that the most unique component of the Bavarian approach is found. This option is based upon a belief that a linguistic handicap is the main deterrent to a successful education in the German language schools. To quote again from Mahler (1974b, p. 16) where the rationale is explicitly stated:

> Bavaria was the first to call for an educational procedure whereby the first instruction of the child should be in the language by which that child thinks, that is, his mother tongue. If the student has learned the subject matters by means of his mother tongue, and if German has been taught sufficiently as a foreign language, it is not

until then that one should suggest sending the child into a class where all subjects are taught in the German language.

This quote from Mahler suggests that there are two key assumptions that underlie the approach. If one or both of these were missing from the actual educational situation of the immigrant child, it would be reasonable to conclude that the approach would fail or at least seriously shortchange the educational opportunities and experiences of the child.

The first of the key ifs in Mahler's position is that the students will have learned the subject matter by means of the mother tongue. The tenuousness of such an assumption has already been noted. Not only do Mahler and the program he espouses have to presuppose that the curriculum materials developed in Belgrade or Ankara (and used in the mother-tongue classes in Germany) are parallel to those of the Federal Republic, but that the pace, depth, and scope of the immigrant children's instruction will match those of the instruction of their counterparts in the German schools. If these conditions are not met, the conclusion he draws as to the options for the movement of the foreign worker students into the German language classes appears unwarranted.

The second key assumption made by Mahler is that the immigrant children will receive sufficient instruction in German as a foreign language. Here again, the assumption is critical to the supposed eventual mobility of the immigrant child: if the German is not taught sufficiently, there will be little or no likelihood of the child's being able to move into the German language classes. No evidence appears in any of the literature, in fact, to support the notion that a potential eight hours' maximum instruction per week is sufficient to accomplish the task of bringing the child to a mastery of German to allow the crossover to German language classes. Further, no rationale or research has been cited that even suggests the basis for the present approach.*

It seems highly unlikely that the special circumstances required by Mahler's two assumptions do exist to any degree. It would be helpful if there were any research evidence whatsoever to substantiate that the conditions he presupposes do in fact exist. Are the curricular materials comparable between classes held in the mother tongue and the standard German classroom? Are the mother-tongue classes keeping pace in covering instructional material? Are the German-as-a-second-language classes succeeding? Answers to all these and the other questions surrounding this approach would have to be answered in the affirmative and with significant data, in order to continue to espouse the program with such certainty as is done by those involved with it. The total absence

---

*In a 19-page detailed exposition of the program, Mahler (1976a, pp. 132-50) provides not a single research citation in support of any of the contentions he makes.

of such data suggests that, in the end, data will be irrelevant to the program for it is being carried out for reasons that make research irrelevant.

The final and unstated implication of the quote from Mahler is that even if the child is brought to a mastery of the German language, and even if the mother-tongue instruction has kept pace with that received in the German language classroom, the child can continue indefinitely in the mother-tongue classroom. That is, the child could continue in the mother-tongue instruction throughout his educational career and not, it is implied, be handicapped in comparison with his German age-mates. *For if this is not so, then the option the program provides of staying with mother-tongue instruction is a systematic and pervasive tool of discrimination and injustice directed at the immigrant child.*

When the theoretical point has been reached of a nonhindered crossover from mother tongue to German, the Bavarian approach states the child does not have to go.* There is absolute silence in the literature from the ministry on what does happen or what one might anticipate happening in the long run to those students who do not exercise their crossover option. Nowhere does the ministry make clear just how far the student could go in the mother tongue and still stay on a par with his German peers. *If, in fact, an immigrant student could complete his education in the mother tongue and remain on a par, Bavaria would have accomplished a unique achievement—the creation of a totally separate but equal school system.*

Here the crux of the matter is reached. By establishing the system it has, Bavaria has created the means for perpetuating the isolation and segregation of its minority population. Under the guise of providing options, what is occurring instead is the systematic shortchanging of the immigrant children. Not wanting to hold the immigrant children to the standards or expectations held for the German children, the policies and programs will ensure that the former become no threat to the latter. Rather, the immigrant children are given their own schools and instruction in the mother tongue and are encouraged to stay where they are. The number of students in mother-tongue classes goes up. In the end, the immigrant children will be in their own schools, learning bits of German as if it were an exotic foreign language and not the language they must use every day outside the school. Their sense of dislocation and separation from German society will grow rather than diminish. Their contact with German peers will be

---

*It would be most interesting both from a research and a policy view to undertake a close-in ethnographic study of the manner in which parents make the decision on whether or not to push for the crossover of their children from mother-tongue instruction to German language instruction. When are the parents consulted by school officials? How are the options presented to them? What are the reasons that parents choose one option as opposed to the other? Do their reasons justify the rotation model? Answers to questions such as these would give important insights on how the foreign worker parents view Bavarian education and the opportunities (or lack thereof) for their own children.

virtually nil, and they will wonder where they belong. Critics of the Bavarian approach have argued that the program is producing a lost generation. It is an accurate assessment.*

## POSTSCRIPT

What for Bavaria is viewed as the necessary educational response to an undesirable social and cultural condition is for Berlin a welcomed opportunity to add new citizens to its community. If the Bavarian approach stresses isolation and the segregation of the children into mother-tongue classes from which they may never emerge during their school years, the Berlin system emphasizes German language acquisition and assimilation into the German schools as quickly as possible. While the present chapter has sketched one extreme in the development of an educational program for the children of the guestworkers, the following will present an effort at the opposite end of the continuum—the educational programs developed in Berlin for the guestworker children.

---

\*The third and final option, that of what is done where the critical mass of foreign worker students in German language schools is too small to provide mother-tongue instruction, requres little mention. The fact that it flies in the face of all the pedagogical principles underlying the rationale for option two has already been noted. At best, the notion of bringing immigrant children together, regardless of mother-tongue backgrounds, and giving additional German lessons is a makeshift response to an unfortunate situation. Interestingly, though it is only a stopgap measure, it is the closest any of the three options come to actually endorsing an assimilationist approach to the education of the immigrant children.

# 10

## AN EDUCATIONAL ALTERNATIVE: THE BERLIN APPROACH

The city of Berlin lies 110 miles inside the German Democratic Republic (East Germany). The postwar fate of this city has been comparable to that of the German nation: divided both physically and ideologically. Surrounded on all sides by East Germany, the Western sectors of Berlin have maintained during the more than 30 years since the end of the war their political, social, economic, and cultural ties to the Federal Republic of Germany. The portions of Berlin under the auspices of the Allies have been incorporated into the Federal Republic as one of the eleven Länder, though there continue to be certain prerogatives reserved to the Allies regarding political and military affairs. Berlin (West) is the largest city in the Federal Republic with approximately 2 million citizens.

The postwar history of Berlin has been constantly filled with high drama and international power plays. The Western sectors have time and again had to withstand the threats, harassments, and pressures placed on them first by the Soviet Union directly and now indirectly through its proxy, the East German government. The instigated riots in the immediate days after the end of the war, the blockade of all land and water traffic during the winter of 1948, the threats by Kruschev in 1959 that Soviet and East German troops would "liberate" the West Berlin citizens within six months, the building of the wall between the Eastern and Western sectors in 1961, and the ever present efforts even now to find ways of reducing the ties of West Berlin to the remainder of the Federal Republic, all give evidence of its continuing center-stage position in the drama of East-West relations. These latter intimidations include heavy road-usage taxes on the roads between West Berlin and West Germany; the claim by the Soviet Union that it has given up its control of East Berlin to the East German government (and thus the four-power agreement now applies only to the three Western sectors); the claim that there now exists the city of Berlin which is the capital of the German Democratic Republic and also the city of Westberlin which is under four-power supervision; the claim that the wall between the sectors of Berlin is not a division within the city, but constitutes national boundaries and thus can be legitimately defended by East German troops with all the rigor and hardware that they employ along other sectors of their frontier; the claim that Federal Republic of Germany passports are not legitimate for citizens of West Berlin; and protests that West Berlin citizens cannot join delegations from the Federal Republic to international meetings and assemblies.

For our present analysis, perhaps the key event of those listed above is the erection of the wall between the sectors of the city in 1961. Prior to the wall, more than 65,000 East Berliners commuted each day to work in the Western sectors, and the number of refugees escaping out of East Berlin into the Western sectors was running at a rate of more than 50,000 per month in the period just before the boundaries were sealed. What these figures suggest is that in the early years of the booming economic recovery and reconstruction of the city, Berlin did not lack the labor it needed to sustain such growth. But as the economy continued to expand and the supply of new labor shrank dramatically, Berlin was, along with the remainder of the Federal Republic, forced to look elsewhere—specifically, to the guestworkers.

Table 10.1 provides data on the numbers of officially registered guestworkers and dependents who came into Berlin (West) between 1960 and 1975. During this same period, the percentage of residents in Berlin who were foreign workers or dependents rose from less than 1 percent to slightly more than 10 percent. (As noted in the earlier chapter on housing, there is some ambiguity as to precise numbers and percentages of foreign workers in Berlin due to the large, and only roughly estimated, influx of illegal entrants.) In any event, approxi-

TABLE 10.1

Foreign Worker Population of West Berlin, by Nationality, 1960-75

| Year | Total Number | From Yugoslavia | From Turkey |
|---|---|---|---|
| 1960 | 21,449 | 472 | 217 |
| 1965 | 34,490 | 695 | 1,135 |
| 1970 | 91,339 | 17,799 | 24,554 |
| 1975 | 190,555 | 30,954 | 87,948 |

Source: H. Köhler, Daten zur Situation der Hauptschulen in Berlin (West) (Berlin: Max Planck Institut für Bildungsforschung, 1976), p. 82.

TABLE 10.2

Foreign Students in West Berlin,
by Type of School, 1968-76

|      |                 |                 | Secondary       |         |               |                    |         |
|------|-----------------|-----------------|-----------------|---------|---------------|--------------------|---------|
| Year | Total<br>Number | Elemen-<br>tary | Voca-<br>tional | General | Aca-<br>demic | Compre-<br>hensive | Special |
| 1968 | 2,840  | 1,556  | 146    | 76    | 472   | 555    | 35    |
|      | (1.4)  | (1.3)  | (0.8)  | (0.5) | (1.7) | (14.3) | (0.3) |
| 1969 | 3,915  | 2,474  | 241    | 92    | 475   | 590    | 43    |
|      | (1.9)  | (2.0)  | (1.3)  | (0.6) | (1.7) | (10.5) | (0.4) |
| 1970 | 6,345  | 4,421  | 601    | 118   | 518   | 630    | 57    |
|      | (2.9)  | (3.3)  | (3.2)  | (0.7) | (1.8) | (10.2) | (0.5) |
| 1971 | 10,701 | 7,741  | 1,275  | 205   | 778   | 547    | 155   |
|      | (4.7)  | (5.4)  | (6.7)  | (1.2) | (2.6) | (8.1)  | (1.3) |
| 1972 | 12,389 | 8,965  | 1,667  | 290   | 708   | 616    | 143   |
|      | (5.2)  | (6.1)  | (7.9)  | (1.5) | (2.1) | (7.8)  | (1.2) |
| 1973 | 16,310 | 11,388 | 2,674  | 502   | 720   | 703    | 323   |
|      | (6.6)  | (7.8)  | (11.6) | (2.4) | (2.0) | (7.4)  | (2.6) |
| 1974 | 17,603 | 12,283 | 2,934  | 605   | 746   | 739    | 296   |
|      | (6.9)  | (8.4)  | (12.4) | (2.7) | (1.9) | (5.6)  | (2.4) |
| 1975 | 20,001 | 13,751 | 3,177  | 706   | 1,177 | 839    | 361   |
|      | (7.7)  | (9.6)  | (14.2) | (3.1) | (2.9) | (4.5)  | (2.9) |
| 1976 | 19,241 | 13,064 | 3,254  | 735   | 830   | 983    | 375   |
|      | (7.9)  | (10.0) | (15.7) | (3.4) | (2.2) | (4.3)  | (3.2) |

Note: Figures in parentheses are percent of total school enrollment.

Source: Berlin Senator für Schulwesen, Das Schuljahr 1976/77 in Zahlen, 1976, p. 15.

---

mately one of every ten residents in Berlin is either a guestworker or a dependent thereof. Further, one of every three births in the city is at present to a guestworker family, and demographic trends indicate that by 1985 nearly one of every two births in the city will be to a guestworker family. From a different vantage, the number of Turkish workers and their families now makes Berlin the city with the third largest Turkish population in the world.

As could easily be anticipated, this rapid rise in the number of guestworkers and their families had an impact upon the schools. Table 10.2 provides the data on the period from 1968 through 1976, detailing both the numbers and percentages of foreign children in the various components of the Berlin school system.

Although this table provides an aggregate picture of the school population of foreign children in Berlin, a caution is in order. There is nothing close to a representational distribution of these children throughout the city. Rather, the guestworkers and their families are heavily concentrated in four districts of the city: Tiergarten, Kreuzberg, Schoneberg, and Wedding. The extreme concentrations of the workers and their families in these select housing markets has also had repercussions for the schools. The four districts together account for two-thirds of the nearly 20,000 foreign students in the elementary grades and 70 percent of the approximately 3,300 foreign students in the vocational secondary schools. When the guestworker children born during 1975 in these districts enter the elementary schools of Berlin in 1981, they will comprise approximately 87 percent of all first graders in Wedding and 85 percent of those beginning school in Kreuzberg (Jancke 1976a, p. 325). Various policies and programs have been established by the Berlin schools as they have responded to this new constituency.

## POLICIES AND PROGRAMS

Central to any discussion of the policies in Berlin for the children of the guestworkers is the position the school authorities have taken on the matter of rotation versus integration. On this point there is no ambiguity. The Berlin position is unreservedly aimed at the integration of the foreign worker children as quickly as is pedagogically possible into the German language classrooms. As one of the educational officials responsible for guestworker education has noted (Jancke, 1976a, p. 325),

> The pedagogical concept of the education for the foreign pupils depends upon the preceding political decision as to whether to follow the principle of rotation or the principle of integration. The Berlin Senate has been unequivocal in its charge to the school officials to follow the principle of integration.

Jancke offers two reasons for the rejection of the rotation principle. The first is that the foreign children are tending to stay in Germany for longer and longer periods, thus making their reintegration into the schools of their mother country exceedingly problematic, as compulsory education in those countries is generally no more than five years. The second part of the rationale for the rejection of the rotation principle is the more general proposition that it is simply not realistic to assume that the guestworkers who are remaining in Germany, bringing in their families to be reunited, and wanting their chilren to attend German schools, are going to return to their homelands any time soon. He cites 1972 data from the Federal Labor Office which showed that even prior to the immigration restrictions of 1973, a full third of all foreign workers who were in Germany with their families and had at least one child indicated in a survey that they intended to remain permanently in Germany. When there were three children in the family, the percentage wanting to remain jumped to 44 percent. In view of such aspirations of the workers to remain in Germany (along with the evidence of the years since that survey bearing out the fact that they are staying), there is no realistic alternative to bringing about the integration of the children into the German educational system.

In terms highly comparable to those used to support school integration efforts in the United States, Jancke argues that the integration of the foreign worker children into the German schools will have positive social effects that will ripple far beyond the confines of the classrooms. He notes (1976a, pp. 325-26):

> The creation of integrated educational settings in our schools, that is the teaching to foreign and German children in the same class with German as the language of instruction, has to be our main aim. This is so because instruction in German hastens the integration of the foreigners into German society. School integration is a necessary precondition to enable foreign students to receive the same education as German students, to be sufficiently trained to pass the examinations, and to have the possibilities for a professional education. The success of school integration will directly influence whether and how much the younger generation succeeds in securing the same civil rights as we Germans now have. Besides, the integration of the foreign pupils will sooner or later favorably decrease the present ghetto-like situations in the foreign worker housing areas.

In pursuit of this aim of the integration of the foreign worker students into the German language classes, the schools have been guided by a set of policies first enunciated by the Berlin Senate Office for Education in 1971 entitled "Regulations for the Instruction of Children of Foreign Workers and Juvenile Foreign Workers" ("*Ausführungsvorschriften über den Unterricht für Kinder ausländischer Arbeitnehmer und für jugendliche ausländische Arbeitnehmer*"). This policy statement provides the following directives, all with the aim of furthering the integration of the foreign worker children (Berlin Senator für Schulwesen 1971, p. 51):

The foreign worker pupil is to be placed in a standard German language classroom commensurate with his age and pedagogical development. During the early period of his attendance, he is excused from selected curricular material so as to receive intensive German language instruction. Such special instructions are to continue until the pupil is absolutely able to participate in the instruction and and activities of his class.

Where sufficient numbers of such elementary school pupils are available, special preparatory classes (*Vorbereitungsklassen*) will be established with no more than 20 students per class. It is the aim of these classes to serve as a transition period into the German language classes, with the time necessary for such a transition to be no more than 18 months.

For those foreign students in the secondary schools, two levels of special instruction are to be offered. For those who are newly arrived, beginners classes (*Anfangsgruppen*) will instruct in rudimentary German while the advanced classes (*fortgeschrittene Gruppen*) will be prepared for transition into the German language classrooms.

The percentage of foreign pupils in any standard German classroom shall not exceed 20 percent, as any number above this percentage hinders and forestalls successful integration.

For those areas where the percentage of foreign worker children is such that they cannot all be accommodated in standard German language classes and still maintain the 20 percent ceiling, special classes (*Besondere Ausländerklassen*) will be initiated where all instruction shall be in German and the curriculum shall be that of the standard German classroom. These classes are offered to insure that foreign students have access to the same curriculum and pedagogical instruction as are available to German students.

The consequence of such policies for the distribution of guestworker children in the Berlin schools is that while a sizable majority of the students are integrated into standard German language classrooms, there are many who are not (cf. Jancke 1976b). Of the 13,064 foreign worker students in the elementary grades during the 1976-77 academic year, 2,933 were in the transition classes and 1,577 were in the special German language classes where all their classmates were also foreign. At the secondary vocational school level, nearly 50 percent of the guestworker students were outside an integrated school setting (1,485 of the 3,254 foreign students were in either beginner, advanced or special classes). In the aggregate, 63.7 percent of all foreign worker students were in integrated school settings (cf. Berlin Senator für Schulwesen 1976, pp. 18, 22, 26).

If, in fact, the integration of the foreign worker children into the standard German language classrooms is of the utmost importance, nearly 2,000 more foreign students could participate in such classrooms, were the allowable percentage of foreign students raised above 20 percent. By retaining the figure of no more than one-fifth of a class being foreign students, the school authorities have created a large pool of foreign students with essentially nowhere to go. The response has been to improvise with segregated, all-foreign-student classes where German is the language of instruction.

Of additional interest here are the several policy options widely used in the United States to avoid exactly this outcome (cf. Rist 1976, 1978), but rejected by the school authorities in Berlin. If the authorities wished to maintain the 20 percent quota and still maximize the amount of school integration between the foreign worker students and the German students, they could have used either of two techniques: a pupil transportation program or the shifting of school boundaries. The former option, that of busing students to schools with a low number of foreign students, was rejected by the school officials on the basis of their assessment of such programs in England and the United States. As Jancke (1976a, p. 331) notes in this regard:

> The Berlin Senate does not believe in solving the problem with experiments like the so-called "busing programs" which have been and are still being carried out in England and the United States. The reports from these experiments show that the transportation of students for their daily class instruction to an area in other than that where the family lives does not even produce the illusion of integration [*Scheinintegration*]. New social relations among the students are not realized for they have no way to continue them in the private spheres of their home and neighborhood. The isolation of these groups from one another becomes even more obvious to them when it is only the bus which brings them together. Instead of the achievement of integration, what is achieved is a worsening of aggressive behavior as can be seen by situations in the United States and England.

Alternatively, the school authorities could also increase the number of foreign students in integrated classrooms by redesigning school district boundaries. By creating new attendance zones, it would be possible to decrease the concentrations of foreign students and provide for their dispersal into other school settings. This option has also been rejected by the school officials on the grounds that the overcrowded districts are in such close proximity to one another that redistricting would bring no relief. Further, those districts where there are few foreign students are at such distances from the areas where the foreign students are concentrated that they could not be reached without resorting to transportation programs.

The policy that has emerged, given the exclusion of either of the two listed above, has been to create the special classes, segregated and comprised solely of foreign students, while hoping at the same time that the problem of overconcentration of the foreign students will be resolved by noneducational processes. Jancke (1976a, p. 332) argues that housing policies will bring about residential dispersal of foreign workers and their families, thus alleviating the school overconcentrations. Housing policies will operate in two ways: first, by prohibiting the further in-migration of workers into designated areas of overconcentration, and second, by dispersing to other districts persons presently in these areas as the housing there is demolished and then only gradually rebuilt. It is evident that to rely on the gradual evolution of the housing situation of the foreign worker communities as the solution to the overconcentration of foreign worker children in the schools is to opt for very slow rates of social change. The result is that one can anticipate the presence of the special segregated schools well into the foreseeable future.

## INTEGRATION AND NATIONAL IDENTITY

In comparison to the Bavarian program under which the policies pursued by the school officials isolated the foreign students and denied them participation in German schools, Berlin officials have been accused of the other extreme— emphasizing integration to such a degree that what is sought is a Germanization of the foreign students (cf. Ferber and Müller 1977). The critics have traced this overemphasis on the creation of a German identity to the very beginnings of the school experience for the foreign children. Their studies of kindergarten classes in the Kreuzberg district have led them to conclude that the cultural integration motif was so strong that no recognition or legitimation of the national background of the students was tolerated.

School officials, however, categorically deny that they are seeking the Germanization of the foreign pupils. They claim that their intent is misunderstood and that surely there could be no comparison with earlier efforts at cultural integration which characterized, for example, the treatment of Polish-speaking coal miners and their families who immigrated into the Ruhr area in the early 1900s. Jancke (1976a, p. 329) states that the Berlin program is in total compliance with the December 1971 resolution passed by the German ministers of education which reaffirmed the right of foreign students to learn the language and culture of their mother country (cf. discussion of this resolution in Chapter 8). In this same resolution of the ministers, it was left to the discretion of each of the eleven Länder precisely how such cultural and linguistic preservation was to be implemented. In principle, all Länder affirmed that there should be voluntary supplementary instruction for the foreign children, which would emphasize the teaching of their mother tongue and the cultural knowledge and history of their native country. The implementation of this supplementary instruction, however, has been allowed to vary from Land to Land.

The option exercised by Berlin has been to entrust all such supplementary instruction to the consulates and embassies of the countries that have foreign workers in the city. Turkey, Yugoslavia, Greece, Spain, and Italy have all availed themselves of the opportunity to establish supplementary educational activities for the children from their respective countries. The school officials supply the facilities, the maintenance, and, when special circumstances merit it, the cost of faculty salaries. The countries that host the classes are responsible for the curriculum materials, the salaries of the staff, the provision of supplies, and so forth. The restrictions placed by the Berlin school officials on the provision of these classes are that the host countries pay for the expenses listed above, that they offer no more than five different lessons, and on no more than two days per week.

During the 1974-75 school year, the following numbers of foreign worker students participated in the supplementary classes: 2,200 of 11,380 Turkish students, 510 of 1,600 Yugoslav students, 101 of 220 Spanish students, and 89 of 550 Italian students. While no data could could be found that provided the numbers of Greek students in the supplementary classes, Jancke indicated during a January 1977 interview that the figure was nearly 100 percent. He commented that the Greek classes were so successful and so well attended that many of the Greek parents simply let their children skip German classes and attend only the afternoon Greek classes.

The result of this policy of allowing the consulates to provide the cultural and linguistic education of the homeland is that the Berlin schools themselves have had to make few if any modifications in their policies regarding the curriculum in the regular German language classes. This is not to ignore the nearly 180 foreign teachers hired by the school administration to teach the transition classes (cf. Rasch 1976), but only to note that once the children have left these classes, further information, instruction, or reinforcement of interest in the mother country is outside the purview of the public schools.

Changes in the policy of consulate-sponsored classes have been discussed, but actual modifications have been few and far between. What appear to have generated the most concern regarding the continuation of the consulate classes is that the teachers, curricula, and pedagogical approaches used in these classes are outside the authority of the Berlin school officials. Fears have been expressed that countries that have a different ideological view from that of the Federal Republic will send consulate teachers to promulgate that ideology (cf. Wilhelmi 1976). Jancke (1976a, p. 330) has responded to this general concern by stating that while there have been sporadic instances of ideological and nationalistic material in the classes, there are many more teachers in these same programs of whom such accusations could not be made and who are serving an important function for the children concerned.

## SCHOOL DROP-OUTS

While the orientation of the Berlin school program is toward the integration of the guestworker children into German schools and German life (Jancke 1976a, p. 332), the reality is that many guestworker students never stay in the schools long enough for such socialization to occur. Köhler's (1976) data on the school situation of the foreign worker children have presented the rates at which they are leaving school without completing their studies. While his analysis was limited to the vocational track of secondary school (Hauptschule), the data are nevertheless pertinent, because 68 percent of all immigrant students in the secondary grades are in the vocational track. Table 10.3 is his summary compilation of data from statistics supplied by the Berlin school system.

TABLE 10.3

Drop-outs among German and Foreign Pupils,
West Berlin Secondary Vocational Schools,
1974-75

| Status and Grade | Total | German | Foreign |
|---|---|---|---|
| 7th[a]  | 607     | 413     | 194     |
|         | (8.5)   | (6.5)   | (24.7)  |
| 8th[a]  | 996     | 781     | 215     |
|         | (13.9)  | (12.3)  | (27.2)  |
| 9th[a]  | 615     | 449     | 166     |
|         | (8.6)   | (7.0)   | (21.0)  |
| 9th[b]  | 2,184   | 2,055   | 129     |
|         | (30.5)  | (32.2)  | (16.3)  |
| 10th[b] | 2,215   | 2,135   | 80      |
|         | (30.9)  | (33.5)  | (10.1)  |
| 10th[c] | 546     | 541     | 5       |
|         | (7.6)   | (8.5)   | (0.6)   |
| Total   | 7,163   | 6,347   | 789     |
|         | (100.0) | (100.0) | (100.0) |

[a]Without certificate.
[b]With certificate.
[c]With certificate for postsecondary study.

Note: Numbers in parentheses represent percent of total students leaving school.

Source: H. Köhler, <u>Daten zur Situation der Hauptschulen in Berlin (West)</u> (Berlin: Max Planck Institut für Bildungsforschung, 1976), p. 92.

The critical finding in these data is that of the 798 guestworker students who were in the vocational track and who left school during the 1974-75 academic year, a full 70 percent (N = 575) left without a final certificate. Only 26 percent of the German students left in the same way. Since there were approximately 3,200 guestworker students throughout Berlin in the vocational secondary school track, it means that a fifth of all these students left school that year with no credentials. Assuming that a comparable percentage of guestworker students leave school each year without completing a certificate, then between 60 and 80 percent of all such students who first enter in this track leave with no certification. The magnitude of these percentages seems warranted, since the chief administrative officer of the Berlin schools has himself said publicly that 60 percent of the guestworker students leave before they have successfully completed their studies (Rasch 1976). (This figure of 60 percent was supplied, incidentally, in response to a newspaper article (Wilhelmi 1976) positing that a full 90 percent of all guestworker students left the Berlin schools without any certification or credentials.)

From these data, two important questions emerge: what are the long-term implications of such high rates of dropping out of school and what response is being made by the Berlin schools to this situation? The answer to the first can be given succinctly. Without secondary school certification, the foreign worker youths are relegated for the employment years to low status positions on the occupational ladder. The uncredentialed have the option of taking only those jobs ignored by others with stronger academic accomplishments. Uncertified, and with no hope of improving their positions, this generation of foreign worker youth is frequently referred to as the lost generation (cf. Deutscher Caritasverband 1975; Kinnigkeit 1977; and Wilhelmi 1976). What makes their situation critical is that lack of certification precludes mobility for the second generation (cf. Wilpert 1974, 1976). As has been noted several times earlier, the creation of barriers to social mobility among the youth of the second generation makes for, in the words of Bodenbender, a "social time bomb."

Berlin schools have reacted to this situation with both a short-term and a long-term programmatic response. The immediate effort has been to intensify instruction at the secondary level in the German language by providing additional beginning and more advanced classes. The beginning classes have 474 students with an additional 746 in the advanced classes, all within the vocational secondary track (cf. Berlin Senator für Schulwesen 1976, p. 22). But as the school officials themselves admit, such efforts are at best able to reduce only slightly the numbers of students leaving without certification (Rasch 1976). The officials are instead pinning their hopes on a long-term strategy: as more and more of the foreign worker children who come into the schools are Berlin-born and thus must begin their schooling in standard German language classes, they will gain the mastery of the language and thus be able to complete their studies successfully.

Though no school official would admit it, the inability of their programs to stem the numbers of school drop-outs means that there is, indeed, a lost generation among the youth in the guestworker communities. It may be a moot question whether the schools can do much at present to significantly reduce the numbers. Particularly for those students who came to Berlin after they had already begun (and perhaps finished) compulsory schooling in their home countries, the requirement of having to attend a German school has been given only minimal compliance. Further, the fact that employment has been available, menial as it may be, means that for the first time in the lives of many of these youths, they have the opportunity to earn a wage.

The view that the effectiveness of the schools is limited and that an improvement in the situation lies with the third generation is perhaps best expressed by Jancke (1976a, p. 331).

It is true, indeed, that there are still many fewer foreign than German pupils who succeed in attaining at least the standard certificate from the secondary vocational school. But do not let it be ignored that none of those foreign pupils who first began their formal schooling in Berlin in 1968 or any of the years thereafter have yet to have had the time to complete their studies. Many of these children come from families where the parents themselves had from zero to five years of schooling.

The break in cultures that the students experienced between the home country and Germany plus the time the more recent arrivals must spend in preparatory classes means the chances of successful completion of their course of study are greatly diminished. Those older students who suffer from shortcomings in the educational programs of their mother country, who now find themselves as "wanderers between two worlds" and who face the severe task of changing from an agricultural to industrial society cannot have their problems resolved by educational instruction, regardless of how well it is done and what it may be. This statement, however, is only valid for the older pupils who have had to accommodate themselves in an abrupt manner and have not had the benefit of a transition period.

But the problem is daily becoming less difficult due to the fact that the majority of those foreign students now in the elementary grades were born and brought up here in Germany. They are continually experiencing a bicultural environment. At home they will be speaking in the mother-tongue, but outside the home, they are exposed to the German language, to the German society, and to the German way of living.

Jancke's position, of course, is full of suppositions. Not only does he take an incremental view of social change with respect to the conditions of the guestworkers, but he also assumes that as such change is occurring, German society will be receptive to it. It is still an open question as to how the second and succeeding generations will be received. While the Berlin schools are seeking their educational integration, numerous economic, political, and cultural forces may negate all that the schools seek to achieve. Further, it appears to be a risky policy decision to assume the second generation is indeed lost, and that an upswing in the conditions of the guestworker communities will come only with the advent of the third generation. To wait for social improvements to come in the third generation is to choose a policy of inaction.

## THE BERLIN APPROACH: A CRITIQUE

As with the Bavarian approach to the education of the guestworker children, there are two levels on which to begin a critique of the Berlin approach: first, the philosophy of the program and second, the policies initiated to operationalize the basic assumptions of how guestworker education should proceed. Both levels allow us to assess their impact upon actual programs as they have been created and implemented in Berlin.

The integrationist approach that underlies the educational program in Berlin for the guestworker children is without doubt more realistic and humane than is the rotation principle of Bavaria. The integrationist perspective is more realistic because it acknowledges the fact that the guestworkers and their children are staying in the Federal Republic and that the children being born in these families are also likely to stay. It is more humane because it seeks to bring the workers and their families into the life of the society rather than to exclude them. That is, it is more humane to seek inclusion than segregation. There are, however, still fundamental propositions in the Berlin approach that need to be carefully assessed.

First is the proposition that the integrationist approach can successfully proceed, all the while ignoring and, in some instances, actively suppressing the cultural background of the guestworker children. Instead of building on the diversity and heterogeneity of cultures and experiences of the children, the schools are approaching the integrationist perspective solely from an assimilationist point of view (cf. Rist 1977, 1978). The schools are seeking integration based on benign neglect at best; at worst, on the idea of schools as a "cultural blast furnace" where the heritage of the students must be stripped away and replaced with that of the dominant culture. It is as though the only way integration can occur is for the children to give up what they are.

But such an approach need not necessarily undergird a program oriented toward the integration of the children into German schools and German society. It is possible that integration can proceed on the basis of affirmation of diversity and pluralism. However, as has been noted time and time again, Germany has yet to recognize or legitimate itself as a culturally pluralistic society. Until that recognition has come about, it is unrealistic to assume that the schools will do other than reflect the basic values and cultural perspectives of the larger society.

The results for the guestworker children are unfortunate. They must experience an education system that is caught in its own cultural assumptions and thus not able to see the social reality that is before it. By denying legitimacy to the cultural and linguistic background of the children, the schools are ignoring an important pedagogical tool with which to build the education of the children. As Willke (1975, p. 364) has noted: "Migrants' children should be assured of a good knowledge of their mother-tongue and indigenous culture, for the mother tongue is one of the foundations of their development and is likely to facilitate the learning of other languages."

Such an approach also legitimates and establishes linkages between the school and the home environment of the guestworker child. The pedagogical benefits of such a linkage have been noted by the American educational philosopher, John Dewey, as early as 1915. It was Dewey who clearly articulated the proposition that continuity is preferable to discontinuity, and that if the schools desire reinforcement by the families, there have to be viable linkages between the two (Dewey and Dewey 1915).

The Berlin approach seeks, on the other hand, to sever that tie between the home and the school and provide only German language, German curriculum, and German perspectives. In so doing, the schools are creating conditions for the failure of countless foreign worker children. While the German children have that continuity between home and school, and their families are able to reinforce it daily, the foreign worker students are left with no means of finding support, either inside or outside the school.

That there need to be linkages between the schools and the families of the foreign workers does not imply that the Berlin schools should establish full bicultural and bilingual maintenance programs. There is no intention here to advocate that the foreign students move through the schools with dual curricula and dual language instruction. To do so is neither feasible nor even necessarily desirable. Furthermore, the Berlin schools would not have the resources or staff to operationalize such a program. It is open to question whether the Berlin schools should actively seek to sustain the equal status of the mother-country culture with that of German culture (cf. Epstein 1977). The author's personal view is that they should not. However, it is both possible and desirable to move the curriculum and instruction in the schools in such a way that the backgrounds of the children need not be ignored and that the parents need not fear that the schools are actively trying to destroy their own values and set their children against them.*

It may well be this concern on the part of many foreign worker parents that moves them to send their children to the national classes sponsored by the various consulates and to keep them away from the German public schools. Such a move on the part of the parents should not then be construed as meaning that the parents are hostile to Germany or that they assume they and the children will be returning to the homeland, but rather that the parents do not believe that their children will benefit by the loss of their cultural heritage.

A second of the philosophical underpinnings of the Berlin approach toward guestworker education relates to earlier comments on the stance of the schools toward the preservation of ethnic attributes. Integration in the Berlin schools has so far been a one-way street. While it is reasonable and justifiable to

---

*It was precisely such an approach on the part of American schools with respect to the immigrants and their children that led to the formation of an extensive private and parochial school system (cf. Ravitch, 1973). Even now, one of every ten children in elementary and secondary schools in the United States is in private or parochial schools (National Center for Educational Statistics 1977, p. 74). It is also possible to go from nursery school through the completion of a Ph.D. degree in a church-related educational system.

assume that the new immigrants have to make adjustments in their move to Berlin, it does not seem justifiable that the Berlin schools can proceed with no adjustments on their part. That is, given that one-sixth of the school population in the city is now composed of foreign worker children and that with the current birth rates, one of every three children in the schools by the mid 1980s will be from this group, the schools can hardly refuse to take this constituency into account.

The schools have made accommodations to the foreign worker children, but only on the margins. The basic structure, philosophy, and methodology of the Berlin schools has remained intact and unchanged. The view that the schools can remain as they are amidst this dramatic change in their constituency must be traced to the historical legacy and current power of the institutional members. The essential structure of German education survived the Nazi period, survived the efforts at reform instigated by the Allies in the postwar period, survived the efforts at change from the protest movements of the 1960s, and is not now about to budge on account of foreign children. Accommodation, if any, will be on the terms of the schools, not the new community members.

The authority and power of the current institutional staff of the schools also ensures that change will not occur. These staff members, the vast majority of whom are tenured civil servants (*Beamte*), can successfully resist pressures on them to begin to understand Turkish ways or perhaps learn Serbo-Croatian in order to fulfill their occupational demands. If less than 400 foreign worker students find their way to join the more than 38,000 German students in the Berlin Gymnasium system, then so be it. The philosophical view is essentially one of the sanctity of the educational system. It is the individual who must make him/herself worthy of entrance.

To state this view from a different vantage, it is noteworthy that nowhere in the current discussions about the educational future of the foreign worker children does one come across the concept of affirmative action.* The schools are willing to acknowledge their complicity in the creation of lost generations, of

---

*A recent and articulate defense of the concept of affirmative action has come from the U.S. Commission on Civil Rights (1977). The commission notes (1977, p. 12):

> The justification for affirmative action to secure equal access to the job market lies in the need to overcome the effects of past discrimination by the employers, unions, colleges, and universities who are asked to undertake such action. It also rests in the practical need to assure that young people whose lives have been marred by discrimination in public education and other institutions are not forever barred from the opportunity to realize their potential and to become useful and productive citizens. The test of affirmative action programs is whether they are well calculated to achieve these objectives and whether or not they do so in a way that deals fairly with the rights and interests of all citizens.

a tracking system that relegates the foreign worker children to the lowest occupational categories, and of the total absence of legitimation of the cultural heritage of their homeland. Yet, having acknowledged this, the schools have indicated they are simply willing to wait and hope for improvements in the situation as yet another generation of students goes through the system. The schools do not see it as their role to take an active and interventionist role in promoting social justice and mobility among the children in the foreign worker communities. Given the comments made in Chapter 8, however, on the underlying rationale and ideology of German education, such a stance is easily anticipated.

Three school policies that emerge from the above-stated philosophical views on guestworker education are of importance. The first is foreign language instruction. Whereas all German children begin to learn a foreign language at the fourth- or fifth-grade level, the foreign worker children have been excused from this additional language instruction. During the class periods when German students are receiving instruction in English, French, or perhaps Latin, the foreign students receive additional German language lessons. At present, when these same students advance to the secondary grades, they are again excused from compulsory foreign language instruction, though it is open to them if they wish.

A second foreign language is required for an academic certificate at the end of secondary school. Thus students in these schools are receiving instruction in three languages: German and two foreign languages. This means that by the time the foreign worker students complete the academic track of secondary school (which, incidentally, extremely few ever do), they are likely to have had exposure to four languages, the three of the school and their mother tongue. Rasch (1976) has suggested that one of the two non-German foreign language requirements be suspended for the guestworker students if they can demonstrate proficiency in their mother tongue. This suggestion stands as the sole instance of possible legitimation of mother-tongue proficiency for the foreign worker students.

School officials have recently proposed to make foreign language instruction compulsory for all guestworker children who begin their schooling in an integrated classroom (cf. Rasch 1976). The rationale is that by the time the immigrant children are at the age and grade level when foreign language instruction is to begin, they will have sufficient experience and competence with German to be on a linguistic par with their German peers. It is also proposed that foreign language instruction be included as a mandatory component in the special classes in the overcrowded areas of the city where entire classrooms are composed of guestworker children. Heretofore, at the time when the German students were beginning foreign language instruction the guestworker students in these special classes were provided with additional German language instruction, though they were already in a German language classroom.

The current foreign language requirements of the Berlin schools demonstrate one of the classic propositions of social policy analysis: the resolution of one issue by the formulation of a policy may create a new set of problems that have implications as severe as the original condition. The situation for the foreign language instruction of the guestworker children is such an instance. It is a sensitive and appropriate move on the part of the school officials to be concerned with not overwhelming the foreign worker children with language instruction. If all the school language requirements for these children were followed explicitly, the majority of their school hours would be consumed in the study of languages.

But the bind in having created these exceptions for the foreign worker students is that the students are thereby being denied the opportunity of pursuing any form of postsecondary education. It is a basic requirement of the German school system that if students do wish to undertake postsecondary studies, they must have received the appropriate certification from the secondary school, and that certification is awarded only when the requirement of two foreign languages has been met.

While it can be argued that such restrictions on the educational options of the foreign worker students are essentially irrelevant, since the drop-out rate among these students is approximately two of every three, it is nevertheless of concern. To institutionalize a pattern of discrimination that denies to the foreign students certain educational options available to German students sets a poor precedent. Furthermore, it is but one more example of the inflexibility of the schools in evolving criteria for assessing competency and successful completion of studies that are not in the classical pattern of nineteenth-century German education. To exclude such a sizable percentage of the student population from any possibility of further study not only relegates those students to lower status positions, it unfairly promotes the entrance and advantages of German students. The German students essentially are able to compete only among themselves for the positions in postsecondary education, as public policies ensure that literally thousands of their age-mates who come from foreign worker families are excluded.

A second of the policy decisions undergirding the program in Berlin that bears scrutiny is one which assumes that a certain critical mass of foreign students inhibits the integration of these same students into the German schools. At one level, of course, this is a correct proposition in that the greater the numbers of foreign students and the fewer the native German students, the fewer the opportunities for interaction with and knowledge of German society. The extreme example is that a class composed solely of foreign students would of course be a hindrance to integration.

But what does need examination is the assumption, unsupported by empirical evidence so far as could be ascertained, that 20 percent was the highest level for foreign student numbers in a classroom before "dis-integrating" forces began to work.* The setting of this figure appears to be a purely arbitrary de-

---

*It is interesting to compare the Berlin figure of 20 percent as the watershed

cision.* The Berlin school officials are to be commended for their concern that the numbers not grow to such a magnitude that the classes become essentially de facto segregated classes (Kinnigkeit 1977, p. 3). Yet the rationale has not been clearly articulated for this particular percentage. Further, what would be the consequence for the more than 2,000 guestworker children now isolated in segregated special classes with only other guestworker children, if the percentage allowed in integrated classrooms were to be raised to 25, 30, or even 40 percent? What appears lacking is the exploration of how various levels might influence the composition of schools and the degree to which the isolation of 2,000 or so students in the segregated classes might be reduced.

The lack of flexibility on this matter across grade levels, across varying forms of schools, and across the different districts of the city all adds up to the creation of a segregated school experience for a sizable number of foreign worker children (Wilhelmi 1976). It becomes even less justifiable to maintain this percentage if the 2,000 foreign worker students in the segregated special classes are indeed following the same curriculum, and in German, as are their German peers. Either these schools are on a par with the integrated schools and there would be no difficulty in moving these students into the integrated classrooms, or they are not. If not, then the end result of this approach of sustaining special classes so as to keep integration at a minimum level is no different from that of the Bavarian rationale of creating model classes. Both approaches, having begun with vastly differing rationales, thus end up at the same place, that is, essentially segregated and unequal education.

It is incumbent upon the Berlin school authorities to spell out a clear rationale for the preservation of the 20 percent quota, and to indicate what would be the impact upon the integration of the 2,000 now segregated students if the quotas were lifted. If the special schools have been successful, there is no justification of maintaining the exclusion of these students from the integrated classrooms. To perpetuate the special schools in their present form is simply to preserve segregated education, a form of public discrimination that should not be tolerated.

---

mark for effective integration with what the research in the United States has suggested. Pettigrew (1974) has suggested a minimum of 20 to 25 percent minority student enrollment in order that these students not feel the isolation and loneliness that would come with fewer of their own group. St. John (1975) suggests anywhere between 15 and 40 percent while Jencks and Brown (1975) found academic benefits accruing to minority group students so long as they were more than 10 percent and less than 75 percent of the total.

*While the choosing of 20 percent may in itself be arbitrary, the decision of the Berlin school officials was not without a precedent. The Standing Conference of Ministers of Education and Culture (KMK) stated in their March 8, 1976 paper on guestworker education that "so far as it is possible, the number of guestworker children in standard German classes should not surpass one-fifth." (Cf. Chapter 8 for a more detailed analysis of the recommendations contained in the 1976 position paper.)

A third critical area of interest with regard to the social policies of the Berlin schools has to do with the stance the schools have taken on early childhood education. There exist in Berlin no special programs for the preschool guestworker children. This program omission is of particular importance in that it calls into question a key assumption held by the school authorities on the ability of the foreign worker children to function from the beginning of their school careers with German as the language of instruction. Jancke and Rasch have publicly expressed their opinion that those guestworker children who have been born in Berlin will have had sufficient exposure to German by the time they are ready to begin school that they can successfully function in German language classrooms.

As the quote from Jancke cited earlier in this chapter would indicate, it is the view of the school officials that the guestworker children are being raised in a bicultural setting—the home reinforcing the culture of the mother country and the larger society reinforcing German culture. The schools are assuming that the secondary socialization of the children by the larger society (in contrast to the primary socialization of the family) is sufficient to permit them to function in German language classes. This proposition is open to serious question. No evidence has been found to sustain the view that the language acquisition of the children has been such as to make them ready for German language instruction.* Furthermore, if one examines in detail the housing patterns of the guestworkers, it is evident that they live in rather concentrated communities. During the early years of their lives, the children are thus more likely to function only in their ethnic community and consequently only in their mother tongue—and doubly so if the parents themselves speak to the children in the mother tongue. The child who enters a classroom on the first day of school where all instruction is in German has been programmed to fail. To be in German society, but not of it, does not seem to be a sufficient basis upon which to assume the children are equipped to perform in German classes.

The reason for stressing this particular point is that the preschool program could fill a vital need as a transition period for the children from the language and milieu of the home to the language and expectations of the German classroom (see, for example, Arbeitsgruppe Tagesmütter 1977, pp. 188-202). As it is

---

*The absence of data in this instance may simply be due to the author's inability to locate it. However, it should be noted that in the Berlin schools, there is a paucity of research on such questions. The schools collect extensive data on enrollments, attendance, costs, pupil-teacher ratios, and the like, but in those areas where policy matters of a pedagogical nature are being decided, it appears decisions are made at best on the basis of informed guessing rather than systematic evaluation. The author could not find evidence that indicated that the school officials had data on the actual language proficiency of the foreign worker children when they first entered school. The fact that the Berlin schools have begun, since 1976, to sponsor a professorship on guestworker education at the technical university may be a step to remedy this situation.

now, the preschool program functions in the same manner as do the schools: German is the language of instruction and no alternatives or modifications are allowed.

To create such a preschool program would also be beneficial in providing contacts and means of sharing information with the parents. As it is, no evidence has been found to suggest that the schools have developed a means for communicating with the parents of children in German language classes. The assumption is apparently that the medium of communication will be German and if the parents are not able to so communicate, then it will be up to the children to provide the bridge for communication between the home and the school, a tenuous link at best when the children themselves are in the process of learning German. Perhaps this critique is no more than to say that it is not possible to consider the integration of children within the narrow confines of the schools without also considering the social and cultural milieux in which these children live out the other portions of their lives (see, for example, Council of Europe 1977, pp. 37-46). What is of concern is that the Berlin schools are functioning as if such a dichotomy is indeed possible.

An examination of the current statistics on the attendance patterns of both German and guestworker preschool children shows that approximately 90 percent of all German children are in preschool programs while the comparable figure for the guestworker children is 30 percent (Jancke 1976b, p. 97). While neither preschool nor kindergarten is compulsory in Berlin, it would be of interest to speculate on the impact a program more attuned to the needs of the guestworker children might have on their later school careers. If the children had the opportunity to interact with adults speaking to them in German, to work with German language curriculum materials, to learn correct pronunciation, and to gain at least a minimal facility in the language, this would be an important contribution. As it is, the schools assume these pedagogical and language skills have been gained through a process of osmosis.

## ON THE WILL TO INTEGRATE

To summarize the philosophical and policy approaches of the Berlin school officials toward the education of the guestworker children is to suggest that school integration can occur with little guidance or forethought. The syllogism is essentially based on the assumption that children born in Berlin can function in Berlin schools. Therefore, since increasing numbers of guestworker children are born in Berlin, they can successfully function in the schools. As has been emphasized, this logic is open to serious question, especially as school officials have presented no data to substantiate these contentions.

Furthermore, the schools are working from a very narrow perception of what can constitute integration. By limiting the percentage in any classroom to no more than 20 percent guestworker children, the schools assume that a larger number would diminish the potential for interaction and integration into German society. This, too, is open to question, especially since the consequence of this policy is that more than 2,000 children are being segregated in special classes so as to preserve the 20 percent level in other classes. The maintenance of these classes is a far worse option than integrating these children into regular German classrooms. These special classes should be abolished as quickly as possible. One wonders if school officials are more concerned with the integration of the guestworker children or the preservation of German student hegemony. In Berlin, where the percentages of elementary school pupils who are guestworker children range from 3 percent in one district to nearly 40 percent in another, no German child under the present policy is in a classroom where the German majority is less than 80 percent.

To achieve a viable integrated educational program for the guestworker children, the Berlin schools must actively pursue those means which promote contact and interaction among guestworker and German children. Further, the schools need to support those programs which allow children to bridge the gap between the culture of the home and that of the schools. Most specifically, the schools should facilitate language transition programs, rather than simply assume that being in Germany is sufficient to learn German.

An effective integration program in Berlin, one that will not only carry the children through the schools, but into those aspects of German society and culture that they desire to explore, must be a program that does not force children to hide and deny their past. To legitimate the cultural heritages of the guestworker children is also to acknowledge the legitimacy of their present bicultural identity. The schools have instead thought integration was a one-way process of assimilating the guestworker children into the German language and forms of education. *What the schools have sought is not social and cultural integration, but rather accommodation and acquiescence.*

To have it otherwise, the schools will have to change their relationship to the guestworker communities. They will have to reach out actively into these communities and convince the parents that the schools are indeed sensitive to the backgrounds and experiences of the children. They will also have to make it explicit that they reject the role of being exclusively a Germanizing agent and will not seek to strip the students of their ethnic and cultural backgrounds (as if they really could). The schools will also have to think about new programs and new ways of providing instruction and learning experiences for the guestworker children. Of special concern should be initiating early childhood education, providing afterschool assistance, working with parents and perhaps providing them language instruction as well, and revamping the content of curricular materials to reflect the diversities of history and geography present in the guestworker communities.

That the Berlin schools have publicly committed themselves to a program fostering the integration of guestworker children into the schools is admirable and surely preferable to assuming that the children should be educated for eventual schooling in Turkey or Yugoslavia. If the Berlin pronouncements are to be more than mere public relations, however, the schools are going to have to go an extra mile, to change in structure as well as in content, for there is no way one can realistically foresee the integration of guestworker children into the schools as long as present arrangements persist. It is unjust for the schools to espouse equal educational opportunity while perpetuating policies and programs that promote segregation and failure. In a very real way, the future of Berlin itself will depend not on their words but on their deeds.

# POSTSCRIPT:
# THE PROSPECTS FOR PLURALISM

The policies governing guestworkers' lives in Germany exist in a state of confusion and contradiction. The continual slippage between pronouncements of a concern for foreign workers' integration and well being and realities of policies that tend to produce opposite outcomes can only reflect the deeper ambivalence of the Federal Republic toward the foreign workers.

The cumulative impact of these and other regulations makes the guestworker's life full of difficulty and stress. The difficulties are plentiful: the lack of residential mobility; the lack of opportunities to live among friends and relatives; never knowing how long one will be tolerated, not being welcomed and treated as a "guest," having to cope with a set of employment regulations that restrict personal mobility as well as deny opportunities for employment to spouse and children, and finally, confronting the stark realization that real financial barriers are placed in the way of the basic human right to be reunited with spouse and children. The outcomes engendered by these policies belie much that is said and done by the government under the theme of the integration of foreign workers into German society. The policies and practices currently in force can more realistically be said to both create and sustain the guestworkers' institutional marginality.

Succinctly, it has been the basic thesis of this book that Germany has become a multicultural society with an evergrowing number of persons who claim social and cultural identity traits from their mother country as well as from Germany, their country of immigration. What has emerged are people who carry a hyphenated identity. The ramification of this pluralism is to be found not only in the psychosocial identity of individuals, but in the patterns of social organization within the broader society. Individuals as well as institutions have had to respond to the new immigrants. The economic centrality as well as the sheer numbers of guestworkers has not allowed them to become invisible.

That one finds economic integration coinciding with social marginality among the foreign workers is entirely predictable if one accepts the rationale reiterated time and again that the workers and their families are not immigrants, but rather "guests." It is as if the more this stance is enunciated, the more it can be trusted to be true. Reality, however, has its way of intruding. The overwhelming evidence suggests that guestworkers are immigrants, that their children are growing up in Germany with all the classical manifestations of being second generation, and that Germany is now becoming mother country to those who a scant decade or two ago were toiling the fields of rural Turkey or Yugoslavia.

It is, of course, within the realm of the possible that Germany may at some time decide that the social costs of the guestworkers exceed their economic benefits and thus decide to expel them; this, however, is not likely. The social, economic, political, and international ramification of such an upheaval are immense. The scope of such a massive disruption of German society makes implausible any such move.

It appears then that the direction for the future of the guestworkers in Germany is set. They will stay, but they will stay on or near the bottom for at least the next generation. The imponderable is whether farsighted and humane social policies will be instigated within the Federal Republic so as to open up avenues of mobility and status to the new immigrants; if so, it is possible that Germany can evolve into a society that both sustains its democratic foundation and legitimates its own diversity. If, on the other hand, it is assumed that the new immigrants can be kept indefinitely outside the means for mobility and used as a labor force to service and sustain the good life for Germans, the social fabric as well as the democratic process are in jeopardy.

# REFERENCES

Abadan-Unat, N., K. Rusen, R. Penninx, H. Van Renselaar, L. Van Velzen, and L. Yenisey. 1976. *Migration and Development*. Ankara: Ajans-Turk Press.

Aker, A. 1975. "A Study of Turkish Labour Migration to Germany." In *International Conference on Migrant Workers*, ed. A. Kudat and Y. Özkan. Berlin: Wissenshaftszentrum.

Allefresde, M. 1972. *Finnish Emigration to Sweden and its Consequences*. Paris: OECD, MO(72)8.

Akpinar, Ü., A. Lopez-Blasco, and J. Vink. 1977. *Pädagogische Arbeit mit ausländischen Kinder und Jugendlichen*. Munich: Juventa.

Andic, F.M. 1970. "The Development Impact of the EEC on the French and Dutch Caribbean." *Journal of Common Market Studies* 8, no. 2.

Arbeitsgruppe Tagesmütter. 1977. *Das Modellprojekt Tagesmütter*. Munich: Juventa.

Ashworth, M. 1975. "Results and Issues from a National Survey of ESL Programs." In *Education of Immigrant Students*, ed. A. Wolfgang, pp. 84–94. Toronto: Ontario Institute for Studies in Education.

Bavarian Ministry for Instruction and Culture. 1974. "Die Brücken zur Heimat nicht abbrechen–Das Offene Modell Bayerns." *Schul Report*, no. 2.

———. 1975. "Das Kultusministerium weist Angriffe auf das bayerische Modell zur schulischen Betreuung der Kinder ausländischer Arbeitnehmer züruck." *Pressereferat*.

———. 1976a. "Ein neues Angebot: Besonder Förderung ausländischer Schüler an bayerischen Gymnasium." *Pressereferat*.

———. 1976b. *Unterricht für Kinder ausländischer Arbeitnehmer*. Munich: Bavarian Ministry for Instruction and Culture.

———. 1977. *Unterricht für Kinder ausländischer Arbeitnehmer*. Munich: Bavarian Ministry for Instruction and Culture.

Berlin Senator für Schulwesen. 1971. *Ausführungsvorschriften über den Unterricht für Kinder ausländischer Arbeitnehmer und für jugendliche ausländische Arbeitnehmer*. Berlin: Senator für Schulwesen.

———. 1976. *Das Schuljahr 1976/1977 in Zahlen*. Berlin: Senator für Schulwesen.

*Bildzeitung*. 1966. "Gastarbeiter Fleissiger als Deutsche Arbeiter? " March 31, 1966, p. A-3.

Blitz, R.C. 1976. "A Benefit-Cost Analysis of Foreign Workers in West Germany, 1957–1973." Nashville, Tenn.: Vanderbilt University, unpublished manuscript.

Bodenbender, W. 1976. "Zwischenbilanz der Ausländerpolitik," Paper presented to the Conference on *Bildungsprobleme und Zukunftserwartungen der Kinder Türkischer Gastarbeiter*. Munich: Südosteuropa-Gesellschaft.

Böhning, W.R. 1972. *The Migration of Workers in the United Kingdom and the European Community*. London: Oxford University Press.

———. 1975a. "Some Thoughts on Emigration from the Mediterranean Basin." *International Labour Review* 3 (3): 251–77.

———. 1975b. "Return Migrants' Contribution to the Developmental Process— The Issues Involved." In *International Conference on Migrant Workers*, ed. A. Kudat and Y. Özkan. Berlin: Wissenschaftszentrum.

Bonhedji, A. 1974. "Return and Resettlement of Migrant Workers in Their Home Countries." *IILS Bulletin* no. 12.

Borrie, W.D. 1970. *The Growth and Control of World Population*. London: Weidenfeld and Nicolson.

Borris, M. 1974. *Ausländische Arbeiter in einer Großstadt*. Frankfurt: Europäische Verlagsanstalt.

Braun, R. 1970. *Sozio-kulturelle Probleme der Eingliederung Italienscher Arbeitskräfte in der Schweiz*. Zürich: Erlenbach.

Brinckmann, P. 1977. "20 Projects to Determine How Best to Teach Foreign Children." *Die Welt*, April 29, 1977, p. 17.

Brockmeyer, R., and G. Oelmann. 1976. "Stress in der Schule." *Neue Unterrichts Praxis* 9 (6): 333–47.

Bund-Länder Kommission für Bildungsplanung. 1973. *Bildungsgesamtplan*. Stuttgart: Ernst Klett.

Castles, S., and G. Kosack. 1973. *Immigrant Workers and Class Structure in Western Europe*. New York: Oxford University Press.

Cerase, F.P. 1974. "Migration and Social Change: Expectations and Reality." *International Migration Review* 8 (2): 245-62.

Conference of Ministers of Culture and Education, Federal Republic of Germany. 1964. *Instruction of Foreign Children and Youth*. Bonn: KMK.

———. *Foreign Students in the Federal Republic of Germany*. Bonn: KMK.

———. 1976a. *Unterricht für Kinder ausländischer Arbeitnehmer*. Bonn: KMK.

———. 1976b. *Neufassung der Empfehlung "Unterricht für Kinder ausländischer Arbeitnehmer."* Bonn: KMK, mimeographed.

Council of Europe. 1974a. *Ad Hoc Conference on the Education of Migrants*. Strasbourg: Council of Europe Documentation Centre for Education in Europe.

———. 1974b. *Record of the Proceedings of the Ad Hoc Conference on the Education of Migrants*. Strasbourg: Council of Europe Documentation Centre for Education in Europe.

———. 1975. "Action Taken by the Council of Europe in Connection with the Return of Migrant Workers to Their Home Country." Strasbourg: Council of Europe.

Daniele, L. 1971. "Labour Scarcities and Labour Redundancies in Europe by 1980: An Experimental Study." Florence, Italy: University of Florence, unpublished.

Deutscher Caritasverband. 1975. *Die verlorene Generation?* Frieberg: Deutscher Caritasverband.

Dewey, J., and E. Dewey. 1915. *Schools of Tomorrow*. New York: E. P. Dutton.

Diakonisches Werk der Evangelischen Kirche in Deutschland. 1976. *Die 2. Generation*. Stuttgart: Diakonisches Werk der Evangelischen Kirche in Deutschland.

Diamant, M. 1970. "Bemerkungen zur sozialen und rechtlichen Lage der ausländischen Arbeitnehmer." *Ausländergesetz '65, Alternativentwurf '70*. Bonn: Neue Gesellschaft.

Didzoleit, W. 1977. "A New Success Story: How Turkish Migrant Workers have Set Up Their Own Companies." *Frankfurter Rundschau*, April 9, 1977.

*Die Bonner*. 1976. "EG und Türkei erzielen Weltgehende Übereinstimmung." December 22, p. 2.

Die Zeit. 1976. "Plight of Foreign Workers Aggravated by New Legislation." April 9.

Diricks, Y., and A. Kudat. 1975a. *Ghettos: Individual or Systemic Choice.* Berlin: Wissenschaftszentrum.

———. 1975b. "Instability of Migrant Workers' Housing." International Labor Migration Project. Berlin: Wissenschaftszentrum.

Epstein, N. 1977. *Language, Ethnicity and the Schools.* Washington, D.C.: George Washington University Institute for Educational Leadership.

Ettinger, S.J. 1965. "The Association of Greece and Turkey with the European Economic Community." *Public and International Affairs* 3 (1): 130-61.

European Economic Community. 1961. *Athens Treaty for Associate Membership.* Brussels: EEC.

———. 1963. *Ankara Treaty for Associate Membership.* Brussels: EEC.

———. 1976. "Revised Draft Directive on the Education of Migrant Workers' Children." Brussels: EEC, mimeographed.

Federal Labor Office, Federal Republic of Germany. 1973. *Repräsentativuntersuchung '72.* Nürnberg: Federal Labor Office.

———. 1976. *Federal Labor Statistics.* Nürnberg: Federal Labor Office.

———. 1977. *Federal Labor Statistics.* Nürnberg: Federal Labor Office.

Federal Ministry for Education and Science, Federal Republic of Germany. 1970. *Bildungsbericht '70.* Bonn: Bundestag Publication Vi/925.

———. 1976. *Grund- und Strukturdaten.* Bonn: BMBW.

Federal Ministry for Labor and Social Affairs, Federal Republic of Germany. 1976. "Continuous Reporting System on Migration: A Report to the Organization for Economic Cooperation and Development." Bonn.

———. n.d. "Information Brochure for Foreign Workers." Bonn.

Federal Republic of Germany. 1949. *Grundgesetz d. Bundesrepublik Deutschland.* Bonn: Bundestag Publication.

———. 1965. *Ausländergesetz.* Bonn: Bundestag Publication.

———. 1975. "Status Report of the Federal Government on the Guest Workers in the Federal Republic of Germany." Bonn: Bundestag Publication.

Ferber, B., and H. Mueller. 1977. "Probleme einer gemeinsamen Erziehung deutscher und ausländischer Vorschulkinder—Ergeibnisse und Interpretation einer Befragung in Kreuzberger Kindertagesstatten." Bonn: *Arbeitsgemeinschaft der Katholischen Studenten – und Hochschulgemeinden.*

Francis, E.K. 1976. *Interethnic Relations*. Amsterdam: Elsevier.

*Frankfurter Rundschau.* 1975. "Eine verlorene Generation ausländischer Kinder?" October 4, p. 2.

Franz, F. 1972. "Die Rechtsstellung der ausländischen Arbeitnehmer in der Bundesrepublik Deutschland." In *Gastarbeiter, Analysen und Berichte*, ed. E. Klee. Frankfurt: Europäische Verlag.

Freiburghaus, D. 1975. "Die Bedeutung der rechtlichen Struktur des Wohnungsmarktes für die Wohnungsversorgung der ausländischen Arbeitskräfte." Berlin: Wissenschaftszentrum.

Friberg, D., and M. Hohmann. 1976. "Die Schulsituation ausländischer Kinder: Schulpflicht und Schulrecht." In *Unterricht mit ausländischen Kindern*, ed. M. Hohmann, pp. 11–25. Düsseldorf: Schwann.

Frijda, N.H. 1961. *Characteristics of Overseas Migrants*. The Hague: Government Printing Office.

Galtung, J. 1971. "A Structural Theory of Imperialism." *Journal of Peace Research* 8 (2): 81–117.

Gaserow, V. 1976. "Konflikte in Berlins 'verbotenen Bezirken' verschärft." *Frankfurter Rundschau*, April 1.

Geiselberger, S. 1972. *Schwartzbuch: Ausländische Arbeiter*. Frankfurt: Fischer Taschenbuch Verlag.

German Federation of Labor. 1973. "Reform des Ausländerrechtes." Bonn: Vom Bundesvorstand des Deutschen Gewerkschaftsbundes.

Getler, M. 1976a. "With Cold War Crises Over, West Berlin Seeks New Identity." Washington *Post*, March 8, A 14.

———. 1976b. "When Guests Become Burdens." Washington *Post*, May 9, C 3.

Giersch, E. 1971. *Kontroverse Fragen der Wirtschaftspolitik*. Munich: Piper.

Gordon, E. 1971. "Toward Defining Equality of Educational Opportunity." In *On Equality of Educational Opportunity*, ed. F. Mosteller and D.P. Moynihan, pp. 3-10. New York: Random House.

Goshko, J. 1975. "A Troubled Labor System." Washington *Post*, July 31, p. 1.

Grossmann, W. 1972. "Situation der Kinder ausländischer Arbeiter." In *Ausländische Arbeitnehmer*, ed. S. Geiselberger, pp. 139-48. Frankfurt: Schwarybuch.

Harant, S. 1976. "Schulprobleme von Gastarbeiterkinder." In *Gastarbeiter*, ed. H. Reimann and H. Reimann, pp. 149-68. Munich: William Goldmann.

Haworth, D. 1977. "EEC: The Question on Both Sides is How Deep A Commitment?" *International Herald Tribune*, May 23, pp. S1, S5.

Hemmer, H.O., and G. Leminsky. 1974. "Berichte aus der Praxis." *Gewerkschaftliche Monatshefte* 1, no. 3.

Hoffman-Nowotny, H.J. 1970. *Migration: Ein Beitrag zu einer soziologischen Erklarung*. Stuttgart: Enke.

———. 1973. *Soziologie des Fremdarbeiterprobleme*. Stuttgart: Enke.

———. 1976. "European Migrations after the Second World War." Paper presented to the Conference on Migration, New Harmony, Indiana, April 14.

Homze, E.L. 1967. *Foreign Labor in Nazi Germany*. Princeton: Princeton University Press.

Horowitz, I.L. 1972. *Three Worlds of Development* 2nd ed. New York: Oxford University Press.

Husén, T. 1976. "Problems of Securing Equal Access to Higher Education: The Dilemma Between Equality and Excellence." *Higher Education* 5, pp. 407-22.

International Catholic Migration Commission. 1975. "Muslim Migrant Workers." *Migration News* 24 (1): 35-38.

Jancke, E. 1976a. "Zur Schulsituation der Kinder ausländischer Arbeitnehmer in Berlin." *Neue Unterrichts Praxis* 9 (6): 324-33

———. 1976b. "Zur Schulischen Situation der Kinder ausländischer Arbeitnehmer in Berlin." *Forum* 3 (4): 94-99.

Jencks, C.S., and M. Brown. 1975. "The Effects of Desegregation on Student Achievement: Some New Evidence from the Equality of Educational Opportunity Survey." *Sociology of Education* 48 (4): 126-40.

Kayser, B. 1971. *Manpower Movements and Labour Markets*. Paris: OECD.

Kindleberger, C.P. 1967. *Europe's Postwar Growth; The Role of Labor Supply*. Cambridge, Mass.: Harvard University Press.

Kinnigkeit, W. 1977. "Kreuzbergs Zweisprachige Analphabeten." *Süddeutsche Zeitung*, April 19, p. 3.

Kleindorfer, P.R., and A. Kudat. 1974. "Economic and Managerial Aspects of Foreign Labor in West Germany." *Preprint Series*. Berlin: International Institute of Management.

Knebel, E., and M. Kempe. 1975. "Lenkungsinstrumente auf dem Wohnungsmarkt für Ausländer als Mittel zur Integration—Darstellung und Kritik." Berlin: Wissenschaftszentrum.

Köhler, H. 1976. *Daten zur Situation der Hauptschulen in Berlin (West)*. Berlin: Max Planck Institut für Bildungsforschung.

Kudat, A., and A. Gitmez. 1975. *Emigration Effects on the Turkish Countryside*. Berlin: Wissenschaftszentrum.

Kudat, A., and Y. Özkan. 1976. *Internal and External Migration Effects on the Experience of Foreign Workers in Europe*. Berlin: Wissenschaftszentrum.

Kudat, A., and M.R. Sertel. 1974. "Toward a Simple Understanding of Saving Behavior Away From Home and Homeward Remittances." Berlin: Wissenschaftszentrum.

Kudat, A., and B. Stevens. 1974. "Price Discrimination in the West Berlin Housing Market." Berlin: Wissenschaftszentrum.

Kudat, A., C. Wilpert, and F. Özae. 1974. "International Labor Migration: A Description of Preliminary Findings." Berlin: Wissenschaftszentrum.

Littmann, U. 1976. *An Introduction to the Confusion of German Education*. Bonn: Deutscher Akademischer Austauschdienst.

Lohrmann, R. 1975. "Ausländische Arbeiter und Einwanderungspolitik." In *International Conference on Migrant Workers*, ed. A. Kudat and Y. Özkan. Berlin: Wissenschaftszentrum.

Lutz, V. 1961. "Some Structural Aspects of the Southern Problem: The Complementarity of Emigration and Industrialization." *Banca Nazionale del Lavoro Quarterly Review* 14.

Mahler, G. 1974. "Das bayerische Schulmodell in der Diskussion." *Die Inner Mission*, pp. 473-81.

———. 1976a. *Zweitsprache Deutsch*. Donauwörth: Auer.

———. 1976b. "Das bayerische Modell—Vorbild einer Ländereinheitlichen Regelung." *Schul Report* No. 4, pp. 16-19.

Marshall, A. 1974. "International Migration, Labour Market and Theory of Economic Growth." Seminar on Demographic Research in Relation to International Migration. Buenos Aires: University of Buenos Aires, mimeographed.

Mehrländer, U. 1975. "Wohnverhältnisse ausländischer Arbeitnehmer in der Bundesrepublik Deutschland." Berlin: Wissenschaftszentrum.

Mendez, J.I., and O.C. Moro. 1976. "The Relation Between Migration Policy and Economic Development." Geneva: Intergovernmental Committee for European Migration, mimeographed.

Minzlaff, G. 1976. "Weg in die Isolation? Zur Schulsituation von Kinder ausländischer Arbeitnehmer." *Forum Europa* 1 (1): 15-19.

Mühlens, B. 1976. "Wohnsituation ausländischer Arbeitnehmer," *Forum Europa* 1 (1): 21-25.

Müller, H. 1975. *Auslandische Arbeiter in unserer Gesellschaft*. Munich: Kösel.

Müller-Meiningen, E. 1977. "More Liberal Attitude Urged Towards Immigrant Workers." *Süddeutsche Zeitung*, March 30, p. 7.

Myrdal, G. 1963. *Economic Theory and Underdeveloped Regions*. London: Duckworth.

Nally, M. 1976. "Dangerous Plight of Europe's Migrant Workers." *The Observer*, April 28, p. 35.

National Center for Educational Statistics/DHEW. 1977. *The Condition of Education, 1977. Vol. 3*. Washington, D.C.: U.S. Government Printing Office.

Nikolinakos, M. 1975a. "The Concept of the 'European South' and the North-South Problem in Europe." Berlin: Wissenschaftszentrum.

———. 1975b. "The New Dimensions in the Employment of Foreign Workers." Berlin: Wissenschaftszentrum.

———. 1976. "Die Internationalisierung des Arbeitsmarktes innerhalb der Europäischen Gemeinschaft." Berlin: Wissenschaftszentrum.

Organization for Economic Cooperation and Development. 1972. *Reviews of National Policies for Education: Germany*. Paris: OECD.

———. 1974. *OECD and International Migration*. Paris: OECD.

———. 1975a. *OECD and International Migration*. Paris: OECD.

———. 1975b. *SOPEMI Continuous Reporting System on Migration*. Paris: OECD.

———. 1976a. *SOPEMI Continuous Reporting System on Migration*. Paris: OECD.

———. 1976b. *OECD Economic Outlook: A Growth Scenario to 1980*. Paris: OECD.

Özkan, Y. 1974. "The Legal Status of Foreign Workers in the Federal Republic of Germany with Special Focus on Turkish Laborers." *International Labor Migration Reprint Series*. Berlin: Wissenschaftszentrum.

Paine, S. 1974. *Exporting Workers: The Turkish Case*. London: Cambridge University Press.

Pekin, H. 1975. "Placement Assistance to Returning Migrants and Other Types of Assistance Including Reception and Accommodation." *Adaptation and Integration of Permanent Immigrants*. Geneva: Intergovernmental Committee for European Migration.

Pettigrew, T. 1974. "A Sociological View of the Post-*Milliken* Era." U.S. Commission on Civil Rights *Hearings on the Implications for Metropolitan School Desegregation*, Washington, D.C., November 9.

Pfahlmann, H. 1968. *Fremdarbeiter und Kriegsgefangene in der Deutschen Kriegswirtschaft, 1939-1945*. Darmstadt: Wehr and Wissen.

Power, J. 1975. "New Policies for Migrant Labor in Europe." Paper presented at the Conference on European Migration, Aspin Institute, Berlin.

*Quick*. 1976. "So können Sie ihrem Kind helfen," *Quick* 24, December 28, pp. 28-29.

Rasch, W. 1976. "Ausländische Schüler in Berlin." *Frankfurter Rundschau*, April 11, p. 13.

Ravitch, D. 1973. *The Great School Wars: New York City, 1805-1973*. New York: Basic Books.

Reimann, H. 1976. "Die Wohnsituation der Gastarbeiter." In *Gastarbeiter*, ed. H. Reimann and H. Reimann. Munich: Goldmann.

Richter, H. 1970. *Probleme der Anwerbung und Betreuung der Ausländischen Arbeiter aus der Sicht der deutschen Gewerkschaften*. Düsseldorf: Deutsche Gewerkschaft Bund.

Rist, R.C. 1972. *The Quest for Autonomy: A Socio-Historical Study of Black Revolt in Detroit*. Los Angeles, Calif.: Afro-American Studies Center, University of California at Los Angeles.

———. 1976. "School Integration: Ideology, Methodology, and National Policy." *School Review* 84 (3): 417-30.

———. 1977. "Imperatives of Integration." *Society* 14 (4): 32-34.

———. 1978. *The Invisible Children: School Integration in American Society*. Cambridge, Mass.: Harvard University Press.

Robinsohn, S., and J. Kuhlmann. 1967. "Two Decades of Non-reform in West German Education." *Comparative Education Review* 11 (3): 88-102.

Rochcau, G. 1975. "Migrants' Rights." *ICMC Migration News* 24 (3): 3-10.

Rojhan, D. 1976. "Die Rechtsstellung des Gastarbeiters in der BRD." In *Gastarbeiter*, ed. H. Reimann and H. Reimann. Munich: Goldmann.

Rose, A. 1969. *Migrants in Europe*. Minneapolis: University of Minnesota Press.

Ronzani, A. 1975. "Der Gastarbeiter zwischen zwei Gesellschaften." In *International Conference on Migrant Workers*, ed. A. Kudat and Y. Özkan. Berlin: Wissenschaftszentrum.

St. John, N. 1975. *School Desegregation: Outcomes for Children*. New York: Wiley-Interscience.

Schiller, G. 1970. *Europäische Arbeitskraftmobilität und Wirtschaftliche Entwicklung der Mittelmeerländer*. Darmstadt: Bläschke.

———. 1975. "Channelling Migration: A Review of Policy." *International Labor Review* 3 (4).

Schiller, G., and C. Diefenbach. 1975. "Technischer Wandel und Ausländerbeschäftigung." In *International Conference on Migrant Workers*, ed. A. Kudat and Y. Özkan. Berlin: Wissenschaftszentrum.

Schrader, A., B.W. Nikles, and H.M. Griese. 1976. *Die Zweite Generation.* Kronberg: Athenäum.

Stark, T. 1974. "Family Migration as a Human Right." *ICMC Migration News* 23 (1): 9-16.

Stevens, B., and A. Kudat. 1975. "Simulation of a Housing Model for West Berlin." Berlin: Wissenschaftszentrum.

Stirn, H., ed. 1964. *Ausländische Arbeiter im Betrieb.* Cologne: Frechen.

Strange, S. 1973. "Die aufenthaltsrechtliche Stellung der Fremden in der Bundresrepublik Deutschland unter besonderer Berücksichtigung von Ehe und Familie." University of Frankfurt, unpublished paper.

String, J. 1975. "Probleme der Beschäftigung Ausländischer Arbeitnehmer in der Bundesrepublik Deutschland." In *Minoritäten in Ballungsräumen*, ed. M. Eisenstadt and W. Kaltefleiter. Eichholz: Eichholz Verlag.

Thomas, B. 1961. *International Migration and Economic Development.* Geneva: UNESCO.

———. 1973. *Migration and Economic Growth.* 2nd ed. Cambridge: Cambridge University Press.

Timur, A. 1975. "The Housing Situation of the Foreign Workers in West Berlin." Berlin: Wissenschaftszentrum.

Tomuschat, C. 1974. "Die politischen Rechte der Gastarbeiter." In *Gastarbeiter in Gesellschaft und Recht*, ed. T. Ansay. Munich: Beck.

U.S. Commission on Civil Rights. 1977. *Statement on Affirmative Action.* Washington, D.C.: U.S. Government Printing Office.

U.S. Department of State. 1976. *1975 Annual Labor Report, Federal Republic of Germany.* Bonn: U.S. Department of State.

———. 1977. *Annual Labor Report, 1976, Federal Republic of Germany.* Bonn: U.S. Department of State.

Van Velzen, L. 1974. *International Labour Migration and Development Processes in Yugoslavia and Turkey.* The Hague: REMPLOD.

Varlier, O., and S. Ilkin. 1975. "The Role of International Migration within the Turkish Planning Perspective." In *International Conference on Migrant Workers*, ed. A. Kudat and Y. Özkan. Berlin: Wissenschaftszentrum.

Warnock, M. 1975. "The Concept of Equality in Education." *Oxford Review in Education* 1 (1): 3-8.

*Welt der Arbeit*. 1976. "Grundrechte mit Entscheidungsspielraum." *Welt der Arbeit*, May, p. 28.

Wilhelmi, J. 1976. "Analphabeten in zwei Sprachen," *Frankfurter Rundschau*, April 10, p. 10.

Willke, I. 1975. "Schooling of Immigrant Children in West-Germany, Sweden, England." *International Review of Education* 21 (3): 357-82.

Wilpert, C. 1974. "The Socialization of the Children of Migrant Labourers." Paper presented to the International Conference on Migrant Workers. Berlin: Wissenschaftszentrum.

———. "Zukunftserwartungen der Kinder Türkischer Arbeitnehmer." Paper presented to conference on *Bildungsprobleme und Zukunftserwartungen der Kinder Türkischer Gastarbeiter*. Munich: Südosteuropa-Gesellschaft.

Wolf, M. 1976. "The Education and Cultural Development of Migrants." Paper prepared for the Committee on Culture and Education, Parliamentary Assembly, Council of Europe. Strasbourg: Council of Europe.

Worth, L. 1928. *The Ghetto*. Chicago: University of Chicago Press.

Yannopoulos, G.N. 1975. "Migrant Labor and Economic Growth: The Post War Experience of the EEC Countries." In *International Conference on Migrant Workers*, ed. A. Kudat and Y. Özkan. Berlin: Wissenschaftszentrum.

# INDEX

Abadan-Unat, N., 40, 48, 89, 91, 95, 100, 105
Akpinar, Ü., 203
Allefresde, M., 41
Arbeitsgruppe Tagesmütter, 241
Ashworth, M., 215

Bavarian Ministry for Instruction and Culture, 207-8, 209, 210, 211, 215, 218
Belgium
  Country of immigration, 6
Berlin (West)
  Economic status of guestworkers, 49-52
  Education (see, Federal Republic of Germany)
  Guestworkers (see, Federal Republic of Germany)
  Housing (see, Federal Republic of Germany)
Berlin (West) Senator für Schulwesen, 227-28, 233
*Bildzeitung*, 126
Blitz, R.C., 36
Bodenbender, W., 41, 74, 111, 112-13, 115, 117, 118, 120, 192, 202, 207
Böhning, W., 37, 39, 41, 44, 51
Bonhedji, A., 46
Borrie, W.D., 5
Borris, M., 142, 163, 164, 166, 167-68
Braun, R., 73
Brinkmann, P., 190
Brockmeyer, R., 185
*Bund-Länder Kommission für Bildungsplanung*, 181
Castles, S., 5, 57, 58, 59, 120, 121, 124, 126-30
Cerase, F. P., 48
Conference of Ministers of Culture and Education, Federal Republic of Germany, 188, 193, 214
Council of Europe, 47, 188, 189, 191-92, 209, 214, 242

Daniele, L., 117
Deutscher Caritasverband, 207, 209, 218, 233
Dewey, E., 235-36
Dewey, J., 235-36
*Diakonisches Werk der Evangelischen Kirche in Deutschland*, 120
Diamant, M., 62
Didzoleit, W., 129
*Die Bonner*, 101
Diefenbach, 53
*Die Zeit*, 79
Diricks, Y., 150, 155, 159, 169, 173, 174

Epstein, N., 236
European Economic Community (EEC), 6, 13, 16-17, 98-104, 209
  Migration policies, 22-27, 28, 31, 34
  Relation to European South, 13-14, 16-17
European North
  Consequences of immigration, 28-30, 53-55
  Countries, 7
  Economic development, 18, 28, 81
  Immigration halt of 1973, 31-32, 41, 52-56
  Relation to European South, 28-29, 32, 34, 54-55
  Unemployment of guestworkers, 33
European South
  Consequences of emigration, 30-31, 37-40, 112
  Countries, 12-13, 54-55
  Economic development, 16, 17, 18, 28, 38, 40-41, 49, 51, 56
  Labor force employment, 38-42

Migration, 7, 12-14, 18, 31-32
Relations to European North, 25-26, 32, 41-42, 49, 54-55, 56
Remittances, 42-48, 56, 82, 113

Federal Labor Office, Federal Republic of Germany, 49, 118
Federal Ministry for Education and Science, Federal Republic of Germany, 181, 182-83, 186, 201, 203
Federal Ministry for Labor and Social Affairs, Federal Republic of Germany, 75, 78, 85
Federal Republic of Germany
  Balance of trade, 24
  Country of immigration, 7, 57, 71-73
  Economic expansion, 109-10, 119-20
  Gains through guestworker immigration, 35-37, 111-12
Guestworkers
  Admission to congested areas, 78-82, 138, 153, 174
  Alien Act (1965, 1975), 135-41, 144-45, 146, 148
  Economic integration, 71, 113-14, 119-20, 126-27, 133
  Economic status, 49, 117-18, 119-21, 187, 194
  Education
    Bavaria: Mother-tongue instruction, 210-11, 213-21; National classes, 194; "Open Model" program, 207, 208-12; Preparatory classes, 202, 210-11; Principle of rotation, 204, 207-8, 212-14; Segregation of guestworker children, 202, 209, 218, 221
    Bilingual/bicultural, 193, 236, 241
    Berlin (West):Affirmation action, 237-38; Early childhood education, 241-42;'school dropouts, 231-34; German language instruction, 238-39, 241-42; Mother-tongue instruction, 230-31, 235; Options for integration, 228-30, 242-43; Policies, 227-30; Principle of integration, 204, 226, 227, 230, 234-35, 242-44; Promotion of national identity, 230-31, 236-38; Segregation of guestworker children, 229-30, 239-40, 243; Student population, 225-26, 228
    Employment of foreign teachers, 192, 202
  Equality of opportunity, 196-204
  Finances, 185-87
  Reform, 180, 182, 200-1
  Employment opportunities, 116-20
  Encouragement of repatriation, 82-84
  Family allowance payments, 84-88
  Family reunions, 77, 81-82, 115, 117, 151, 163
  Housing
    Berlin (West), 80, 155-58, 160-61, 168-75, 229
    Concentration, 115-16, 169-70, 171, 173-74
    Discrimination, 150, 158, 159, 170, 171, 174-75
    Frankfurt, 161-69
    Federal policies, 150-55
    Ruhr region, 35
  Hyphenated identities, 57, 193, 205, 243
  Illegal entrants, 62, 78
  Labor policies, 112-14, 117, 136-37
  Legal rights, 133-34
  Political rights, 129, 141-48
  Population, 4, 35, 52, 56, 61-66, 72, 89, 110, 113, 115, 224-25
  Residence/work permits, 75-77, 113, 136-38
  Residential mobility, 80, 166-67, 169-70
  Second generation youth, 53, 116, 120, 139-40, 187, 193, 233-35
  Social conditions, 114-17, 121, 124
  Trade unions, 120-32

Immigration halt, 1973, 63–66, 74, 77–78, 113
Labor recruitment policies, 61–65, 77, 111–14
Recruitment ban, 1973 (*see*, Immigration halt, 1973)
Unemployment, 24, 33, 71, 118–20
Ferber, B., 230
Filbringer, H., 84
France
 Country of immigration, 7
 Guestworker population, 30, 32, 33, 35
 Relation to European South, 13
Francis, E.K., 3
*Frankfurter Rundschau*, 196
Franz, F., 76
Friberg, D., 209, 218
Frieburghaus, D., 153, 154
Frijda, N. H., 18

Galtung, J., 17
Geiselberger, S., 128
German Democratic Republic, 5, 7
 Loss through emigration, 35–36, 61, 224
German Federation of Labor, 127
Getler, M., 118, 156
Giersch, E., 110
Gitmez, A., 105
Gordon, E., 197
Goshko, J., 75
Great Britain, 7
Griese, H. M., 53
Grossmann, W., 219
Guestworkers
 Assimilation versus pluralism, 105, 235–37
 Contributions to host society, 35–36, 111–12
 Economic integration, 34, 53–56, 71
 Economic underclass, 35, 49, 55, 56
 Integration versus segregation, 53, 55, 74, 80–81, 88, 133
 Return to homeland, 47, 82–84
 Socio-political marginality, 34
 Unemployment, 33

Harant, S., 197, 207, 209, 210, 215, 216–17, 218
Hemmer, H. O., 170–71
Hoffmann-Nowotny, H. J., 3, 16, 35, 73, 75, 117
Hohmann, M., 209, 218
Homze, E.L., 59
Horowitz, I. L., 48
Husén, T., 200

Ilkin, S., 17
Illegal immigrants, 14, 62, 78, 90
Industrial reserve army, 18, 34, 53, 55, 117
International Catholic Migration Commission, 95
Italy
 Labor migration, 6, 13–14, 25, 32, 56, 58, 61, 116, 162

Jancke, E., 191, 226–27, 228, 229, 230, 231, 233, 242

Kayser, B., 39
Kempe, M., 156
Kindleberger, C. P., 35
Kinnigkeit, W., 233, 240
Kleindorfer, P. R., 110, 128
Knebel, E., 156
Köhler, H., 196, 231
Kosack, G., 5, 57, 58, 59, 120, 121, 124, 126–27, 129, 130
Kudat, A., 33, 34, 49, 51, 71, 73, 98, 105, 110, 119, 128, 129, 150, 155, 159, 169, 173, 174
Kuhlmann, J., 180

Leminsky, G., 170–71
Littmann, U., 181, 183
Lohrman, R., 32
López-Blasco, A., 203
Lutz, V., 16

Mahler, G., 190, 207, 211, 212, 219, 220
Marshall, A., 46
Mehrländer, U., 159–60

Mendez, J. I., 39, 46, 49
Migration
  European, 3, 6–12
  European Economic Community, 22–27
  Manpower, 3, 6, 7, 19, 20–22
  North-South patterns, 52–56
  Post-World War II, 4–6
  Theoretical perspectives, 14–19
Minzlaff, G., 207, 218
Moro, O.C., 39, 46, 49
Mühlens, B., 153
Müller, H., 188, 230
Müller-Meininger, E., 114
Myrdal, G., 17, 18

Nally, M., 110
Netherlands
  Country of immigration, 7
  Migration policies, 26–27
Nikles, B. W., 53
Nikolinakos, M., 12, 13, 14, 17, 19, 30, 44, 55, 110, 117, 130–31

Oelmann, G., 185
Organization for Economic Cooperation and Development (OECD), 19, 20–22, 26, 28, 29–30, 32, 34, 35, 46, 47, 49, 52, 54, 56, 63, 179, 181, 184, 186, 196, 197, 198, 199, 200, 204
  Manpower policies, 19–22
  Migration policies, 22–24, 25–26
Özkan, Y., 34, 49, 51, 71, 98, 105, 110, 119, 128, 137, 138–39, 141, 144, 146

Paine, S., 42
Pekin, H., 47
Pfahlmann, H., 60
Power, J., 35

*Quick*, 185

Rasch, W., 230, 232, 233, 238
Reimann, H., 153
Remittances by guestworkers to mother country, 42–47

Richter, H., 125
Rist, R.C., 120, 228, 235
Robinsohn, S., 180
Rojhan, D., 142, 144, 145
Ronzani, A., 18
Rose, A., 16, 60, 150–51
Rotation principle, 16, 190, 207–8, 212–13, 226

Schiller, G., 17, 35, 46
Schrader, A., 53, 116
Second generation immigrant youth, 27, 53
Sertel, M.R., 33
Stark, T., 81
Stevens, B., 169
Stirn, H., 59
Stingl, J., 190
Strange, S., 138
Sweden
  Country of immigration, 7
  Guestworker population, 30
  Migration policies, 25, 75
Switzerland
  Country of immigration, 7
  Guestworker population, 52
  Migration policies, 25

Thomas, B., 16
Timur, A., 160
Tomuschat, C., 143, 148
Treaty of Rome, 6, 22, 31, 138
Turkey
  Development, 17, 95, 98, 103, 104–6
  Economic status of Turkish guestworkers, 49
  Labor emigration policies, 90–93
  Member of European South, 12
  Relation to European Economic Community (EEC), 28, 98–104
  Worker emigration, 31–32, 41, 90–93, 95, 113, 116, 162, 168, 224

United Kingdom
  White Paper on European Economic Community, 25
United States Department of State, 72

Van Velzen, L., 89
Varlier, O., 17
Vink, J., 203

Warnock, M., 200
*Welt der Arbeit*, 136
Wilhemi, J., 231, 233, 240
Willke, I., 191, 202, 235
Wilpert, C., 233
Wolf, M., 192

Worth, L., 163

Yannopoulos, G. N., 25
Yugoslavia
  Labor emigration, 28, 93, 162, 224
  Member of European South, 12
  Return of workers, 32

Zubrzycki, J., 73

# ABOUT THE AUTHOR

RAY C. RIST is a visiting professor in the College of Human Ecology at Cornell University. He has also served as the Senior American Fulbright Fellow in the Federal Republic of Germany and as Associate Director of the National Institute of Education, Washington, D.C.

Rist received his Ph.D. in sociology from Washington University, St. Louis. *The Invisible Children* and *The Urban School: A Factory for Failure* are among the six books he has authored or edited. He has written more than 60 articles in such areas as social policy, education, social deviance, qualitative research methods, and the sociology of knowledge. His current research efforts focus on study of social policies in Western Europe and of educational policies in the United States.